Praise for

Schizophrenic in Japan
An American Ex-Pat's Guide to Japanese and American Society/ Politics & Humor

"American ambassadors are enforcers of the imperial will, rather than negotiators of peace and friendship. Thank goodness those of us who love freedom have our own ambassador to Japan, Mike Rogers. With great humor and knowledge, as well as a good heart, Mike in Tokyo helps us understand a little about that great nation, and US relations with it. He deserves the anarchists' Nobel."—Lew Rockwell, LewRockwell.com

"Mike Rogers is a one-man United Nations. With a wickedly astute sense of humor he successfully cross-pollinates two seemingly divergent worlds with daring insight and aplomb. He's a fearless David in a land of Goliaths; his perfectly aimed slings and arrows hit the bulls-eye every time."—Pamela DesBarres, "I'm With The Band," "Rock Bottom," and "Let's Spend the Night Together"

"Social commentary seldom surprises experienced readers. Once we figure out the writer's allegiance to some faction, we can predict what the writer is going to say. Not so with this writer.

"Mike Rogers pledges allegiance to himself, to his family, and to the truth; his view of the truth is unique to who he is, and what he has done with his life. Mike Rogers is a poet, a painter, a musician, a writer, a husband, a father, and an entrepreneur. In addition, he is grounded in two cultures; West meets East in this man.

"This is also true of his humor. Like his Western namesake, Will Rogers, and his Eastern mentors, Mike Rogers sees amusement in the commonplace events of life and politics. It takes a special talent to poke fun at the crimes of state, and their perpetrators, yet he does it.

"You will have fun reading this book, and enjoy these essays over and over, as I have. In the end, if we anarchists are destined to hit the barricades, we will do so laughing, thanks to Mike Rogers."—Robert Klassen, author of "Atlantis, A Novel about Economic Government"

"Unlike most books on Understanding Japan, this one is written by a real, live American-Japanese disc jockey. This means: (1) you will be able to understand him; (2) you have a reasonable shot at understanding a little bit more about Japan. Trust me: any book called Understanding Japan is as likely to deliver as one called Understanding Women.-Gary North, author of "Mises on Money." Visit http://www.freebooks.com.

Schizophrenic in Japan

Schizophrenic in Japan

✦

An American Ex-Pat's Guide to Japanese and American Society/Politics & Humor

Mike (in Tokyo) Rogers

iUniverse, Inc.

New York Lincoln Shanghai

Schizophrenic in Japan
An American Ex-Pat's Guide to Japanese and American Society/Politics & Humor

iUniverse books may be ordered through booksellers or by contacting:

iUniverse
2021 Pine Lake Road, Suite 100
Lincoln, NE 68512
www.iuniverse.com
1-800-Authors (1-800-288-4677)

ISBN-13: 978-0-595-34662-2 (pbk)
ISBN-13: 978-0-595-79406-5 (ebk)
ISBN-10: 0-595-34662-6 (pbk)
ISBN-10: 0-595-79406-8 (ebk)

Printed in the United States of America

Edited by
Anthony Gregory
Manuel Miles
Robert Klassen
Elizabeth Gyllensvard

Cover Art by Hydrotokyo.com

Author's Note
The events, stories, and recollections in this book are not fiction. However, I do write
them from my point-of-view (of course) and I do accept that I am often called a cynic.
Perhaps I am quite a cynical person, but with the way the world is now, I like to think
that being a cynic is the only way to keep a sense of humor.

This book is dedicated to my mother,

who gave me this wonderful life;

To my children:

Wray, Wendy, Sheena, and Julie;

And to my wife, Yuka, who saved my life.

Oh yeah, and to my dad, too. He's cool!

Everyday is an adventure.

Contents

Special Thanks

There are so many people I need to thank that I don't even know where to begin, but thanks to everyone with whom I've worked, fought and laughed, and to those who took care of me.

Also thanks to:
Alfred Miller, Lew Rockwell, Eric Garris, Robert Wolff, Anthony Gregory, Manuel Miles, Gary North, Pamela DesBarres, Robert Klassen, Elizabeth Gyllensvard, Paul Craig Roberts, Ted Rall, Tim Foley, Ron E. Fast, Hirokazu Toshi, Youichi Endo, Bob Wallace, Shigeo Numata, Ikumi Hiroki, Masako Ohtake, George Williams, Atsushi Iinuma, Ryohei Matsunaga, Carole Hisasue, Scott Horton, Phester Swollen, Tom Chartier, Ray Charles Hearn, Sakura, Scott Herren, Alec Empire, Taro Furukawa, Mike Tarna, Ira Hata, Anna Hata, Ali Morizumi, Dr. Watanabe, Matsuzawa Hospital, Peter MacKenzie, Arya Sabahi, Ken Nishikawa, Kenya, Hyland, Mr. Hayashi (E.A.U.), Bob and Bonnie Neilson, Jeff Hughart, Johnny Condom, Rip Chord, Page Porazzo, Keith Cahoon, Aki Morishita, Adam Engel, Dave Rogers, Bob Rogers, Seth Fisher, Yuji Wada, George W. Bush, and the entire American and Japanese society and body-politic for making this book possible.

Foreword

Imagine the most impenetrably beautiful, surreal place in the world. That is Japan. Here is my tribute to the country in which I have lived and worked, married, and fathered children. This book is a gathering of more than 21 years of joy and wonder. I don't believe it is possible to fully detail the idiosyncrasies of Japanese society. As an expatriate American of 49 years of age, I have come to the conclusion that I could live in Japan for over 100 years and still not understand everything. Reading accounts of Japan, as written by American scholars, I have more than a few times thought, *That's wrong.* Why? Well, I don't think it is possible to write about Japan unless you can speak and understand the native tongue. Not only is the language of the people the key to their soul, but also it is the song of their past and future. Without knowing the language, one could have, at best, a superficial view of Japan. Even then, the view the Japanese wish one to have is superficial. This is because what is said and done is often "theater"—a kind of protective coloring to charmingly deceive foreigners. There are about 10,000 foreigners living in Japan at the moment; most of them are "bugged." The underlying glory of Japan is derived from its ability to passively resist outsiders.

In 1955 my Japanese mother came to the United States from Japan, and there she remained for the next 40 years. As a result, she never lost her Japanese accent when speaking English. I shall never lose my American accent when I'm speaking Japanese. That's just the way it is. I am no longer even concerned with this part of my Japanese language studies.

What is more exciting to me is that in Japan today, among the younger generation—born in the late 1980s—there are some who are completely steeped in both western and Japanese cultures and speak both English and Japanese fluently, effortlessly—without a tell-tale accent. I write about one of them in this book. I have yet to meet anyone from my generation, or even people 15 years younger than myself, about whom the same could be said.

What does the West look like to the modern Japanese? How do the Japanese perceive America? And how can Americans and Westerners understand Japan? In this short book, I have attempted to answer those questions.

When I was living in the United States, my mother, who was born and raised in Japan, would go outside our suburban Californian home daily and wash off the sidewalks and the driveway. Mother insisted that we remove our shoes at the front door of our house. My father couldn't understand why my mother went through this washing ritual everyday. No one else in America does this——except the Japanese. Although I was used to the way in which my mother performed her chores, I did think it was strange.

Then in 1979, I came to Japan, as an adult. On January 10 at 5:30 in the morning, I arrived at Tokyo's massive *Shinjuku* train station. I heard a splash of water, the metal clink of a bucket, the familiar whoosh-whoosh of a brush on pavement. One of the train station employees was washing the platform. The act of washing the platform was performed unselfconsciously, with skill and with dignity. Mother! Of course!

Later on, I asked a Japanese friend why the stationmaster washed the platform. I mean, it was just going to get dirty, right? The answer made sense to me and was so very Japanese:

"We wash the sidewalks and concrete areas to keep the dust down."

For over 20-some years I had watched my mother wash off the sidewalks at home, and it never dawned on me why she did that. Now I knew: all Japanese do that everyday. Every morning, in every city, town, or in front of anyone's home, you will see someone with a hose or a bucket of water, washing the street or sidewalks. It's because they want to keep the dust down. Why do they want to keep the dust down? Because they don't want people bringing dust into their homes. It makes perfect sense now.

Now, I wonder why my father got mad at my mother for washing the sidewalks. His irritation did not phase her. She had been born and raised in a culture where keeping dust out of the house is considered *atari mae* (obvious). That was an easy lesson.

However, it took me more than 20 years to understand the meaning of the spoken word. I don't mean that I couldn't understand what people were saying. I could. But understanding what the Japanese say and what they mean is a fine art. I remember my Japanese language instructor telling me in about 1985, "To understand a Japanese, do not listen to their words; listen to their heart."

English speakers can become frustrated because, after talking to a Japanese and arriving at what they thought was an understanding or agreement, the English speaker is chagrined to learn that they didn't have an understanding at all. Many times I have had the unpleasant experience of being the bearer of that sort of bad news.

Typically, the English speaker throws a fit. "But we were speaking English!"

I have to explain that the misunderstanding is cultural, and that, even though the Japanese was speaking English, they were still steeped in their own culture. I would ask the English speaker, "Do you really expect that a 40-year-old Japanese man—even though he can speak English—can throw away 40 years of conditioning just because he spoke with you for 30 minutes or 1 hour?"

To understand the Japanese, not only must you listen to their words, but also you must listen to their hearts. It is for this reason that I find that Japan and the Japanese are very romantic.

Over the past 20 years, I have gone through cycles when I hated and loved this place. Today, I'd have to say that I love Japan. It's not that Japan has changed; it's because Japan has changed me. I have learned not to take things too seriously. I try to enjoy every day as it comes. Each day is an adventure—offering opportunity if you just take it easy and keep your eyes and ears open. In essence: live for the moment.

I very much enjoyed writing this book. Please read it with your mind and with your heart.

Mike (in Tokyo) Rogers

Introduction

The Japanese are world renowned, not only for respect of tradition and ceremony, but also for courteous behavior and polite speech. Japanese people eschew interrupting one another during conversational exchange, whether speaking in their native tongue or in English. Such qualities make the Japanese great listeners. From a western perspective, I wonder if this makes the Japanese great conversationalists as well.

One of the most critical features of the Japanese language is the concept of *ma*. *Ma* means space, interval or term. The Japanese use the concept of *ma* as a space in conversation to acknowledge that they are listening to and thinking about what is being said. Westerners may find frustrating the use of *ma*, or dead air, as a conversational tool. In the West we have been taught that conversation must continue without silent spaces. Not so in Japan. In Japan, a master conversationalist will know how to use a pregnant silence to convey a message. Therein lies the reason why, after 21 years, I am sometimes bewildered when a Japanese grows silent while talking to me. Is the Japanese using *ma* in conversation? Or is he silent because he does not know what to say to me, a dumb foreigner?

To overcome the western fear of *ma*, I have undertaken to write this book. Silence requires confidence and self-knowledge.

One of the great benefits of living outside the United States is that I have come to know my country better. I have been able to observe the actions of my own people from a different, perhaps more objective, point of view. The first section of this book examines how 21 years of residence in Japan has influenced my view of the United States.

The Japanese experience in World War II can be compared to the American experience in the Middle East today. The second section will deal with war, viewed from the Japanese perspective.

The third section describes life in modern Japan. Is Japan more modern than the Japanese? In the battle between modernity and tradition, which triumphs: innovation, or the sponge-like absorbency of a very old culture?

In these few pages, let me share with you that which I have learned from the most beautiful and wise people on this earth.

The Name Without a Country

I am an expatriate. I am an American living in Japan. I think, speak, and dream in English and Japanese. My waking and sleeping moments are set in America and in Japan. Like all expatriates, I am a hybrid—neither one nationality nor the other; I am defined by both. I see America through the lens of Japanese culture. I live in Japan as a guest. My passport should read "Citizen of Limbo."

So, let me guide you through Japan, my home since 1984. Let me also tell you why I do not plan to return to the United States. That's what marks an expatriate; he doesn't go home. He is an ex-patriot.

The most famous expatriate in American literature is Philip Nolan. He was *The Man Without a Country* in the 1863 story by Edward Everett Hale, which was originally published anonymously in a Northern magazine during the American Civil War. It is the story of a true patriot who was cast away by the United States and left as a man who would die without ever hearing his country's name again.

Of course I cannot claim to even come near such an ignoble, yet glorious fate, but I can understand this story, after all these years of living outside the United States. I use the term "the United States," because I believe that "America" no longer exists. It hasn't existed since 1861, when the government that was elected by the people launched an illegal war of aggression against those very same people it was elected to protect, killing over 600,000 Americans. Americans killing Americans. Brothers killing brothers. Families killing their own kin. And for what? America? The freedom of individual Americans? So you or I could be free to do and live as we wish and desire? No. The Civil War was not launched for the betterment of America. It was launched so that the federal government could protect its supreme position. The Civil War was launched *only* for the benefit of the federal government.

The day the American Civil War started—some may even argue the day the United States invaded Mexico—was the day America began to disappear. It continues to fade into memory to this very day under the weight of the Leviathan known as the federal government.

1

Philip Nolan's story is a parable. Reading it over and over again, especially when I am in Japan, makes me wonder whether Nolan actually left America, or whether America left him?

I wonder how many Americans could truly understand this story these days? Sadly, I reckon that not many could.

Surely I cannot be the only one, but I have always thought that even more than a place on a map, America was an idea. "America" is not just the name of a country; it is a concept. A concept whereby the people control the government, and not the other way around. I am afraid that my countrymen, even my own family, do not realize how much freedom and control over their daily lives they have lost. America was once a country that stood for individual rights and freedom; today the United States is an empire. It is an empire that is growing more hideous and monstrous by the day, yet its people seem to fail to recognize or care about the horror it has become.

I suppose it's easier to see the problem when you are on the outside looking in, rather than vice versa. You cannot see your own face unless you look into a mirror, and it seems that few Americans wish to do so nowadays. I would like to, if I may, give you folks a glimpse of what your country has become from the eyes of one of your own—from the eyes and ears of what I see as to how the United States is perceived from one of your best allies: Japan.

It is indeed a worrisome view. America is no longer respected, but feared—feared like an out-of-control drunk at a bar just looking for a fight. Japan is your friend, but Japan can only stand by and watch as you continually pick on others and hurt the ones you need most, all the while destroying yourself. Like an abusive spouse who batters his partner, you will only set yourself up for immense sorrow when someday even your friends say, "Enough is enough."

From living in Japan, I have seen the horrors of an empire up close. I have spoken to many bombing victims and war veterans; I have seen the atomic bombing site in Hiroshima. I know the thinking of the average person on the street. They are the ones who suffered the grotesque terror brought upon them by an empire—a government—that the people could not control. And through these people's experiences, one can see the very near future of the United States. It is an ugly picture—a picture of war, death, and destruction. The most pitiful part of it all is that Americans are allowing their own government to set them and their children up for a nightmarish future. History is repeating itself, right under your noses.

When I first came to Japan, over twenty years ago, I had always "known" somewhere in my heart that I would return to the land of my birth—the land that I loved: "America."

Even though my mother was Japanese, I was an American. I had always felt that being "American" was a special thing.

I had always had in my heart a "spot" to which I would return, if nothing else but to die and be buried in the country of my birth.

But now I doubt that I ever will. Maybe I can't. Not because I don't want to, though.

My mother—born in Kyushu, Japan, (God rest her soul) in spite of living in America for over thirty five years—wished to be buried in the country of her birth when she died.

She got her wish.

My mother and father in the late-1970s

I have never met a person who didn't love his or her own country the most. This is something that I think few Americans realize: everyone loves their own country. And the ones who love it the most are the ones willing to fight for it.

My life now seems like it was all some sort of cosmic plan, or predetermined destiny for me to come to Japan.

I remember that when I was a young boy, I was always fascinated by my mother's country. I actually tried to understand the Japanese language when I was little by using some sort of mathematical equation that I had devised, which made profound sense at the time.

I showed my mathematical English-to-Japanese-to-English calculations to my mother, and she just laughed.

I guess so. Now I know that there are ideas and concepts that are unique to a specific country or culture. It doesn't matter if that culture is "American," "Anglican," or "alien." There are some things that are unique and, in turn, in common to all peoples of all countries: All people love their place of birth.

This is where I now realize that the idea *I am American, therefore I am special* is unique to Americans and is completely wrong.

When I was a small boy, my mother told me stories about Japan. She sang me Japanese children's songs before bedtime. I loved that. I don't remember her doing the same for my brothers. Maybe she did.

When she died, I was here in Japan. I had learned the language and was the "conduit" for my Japanese relatives and my American family. There was no one else who spoke both languages except my mom, my cousin, and me.

I brought my American family to southern Japan. I met my Japanese family and introduced them all. I felt it was extremely unfortunate to have to introduce them all for the first time at such a sad occasion, but introduce them all I did.

We all rode in a car and drove to a beautiful ocean-side beach. The scene was breathtaking. And there we washed my mother's ashes into the straits between the Sea of Japan and the Pacific Ocean.

I sat on a hill and watched my American family hug and cry immeasurable tears. I also observed my Japanese relatives standing above me staunchly, seemingly emotionless, as this scene unfolded.

Undoubtedly, I felt, Americans and Japanese have a different way to show overflowing emotions.

I supposed my American family was somewhat angry at me because they might have expected me to react to this situation the same way as they did—with open, uncontainable sobbing. They probably expected me to cry with them and hug them in return.

But I did not. I reacted, I suppose, as a Japanese would.

I watched the "funeral" and felt somewhere in my heart that *I knew this was going to happen…I knew this was going to happen, even when I was a child.*

That was more than a decade ago.

Now, my Japanese wife's family has accepted me completely. They have even held a solemn religious ceremony for me and put my name on the "headstone" on their family burial place. They have even found it in their hearts to accept my mother's urn and my father's—the day he passes away.

Japan is a very old country. To be accepted as one of the country's own is quite unusual for an outsider—never mind a foreigner—to be taken into a family, especially in death. There are family members buried in their burial spot who have been there for over 250 years.

I am so pleased that they have decided for me where I will go after I die. I am pleased, but I also cried, because these last few years "America" and "Americans" seem to have either disappeared or changed so drastically that I had wondered where I wanted to be buried.

I cannot consider a country that rejects liberty, rejects freedom of speech, wages wars of aggression, kills innocent children, and has a government that profits from death, as well as a populace that refuses to educate themselves on history and the truth about current events, as my home anymore.

Is it that America has changed? Or have my eyes just been opened?

Now I wonder if what is happening in America, and in my life, really is some kind of "destiny."

I love Japan. The America I love, or should I say loved, is gone.

I didn't run away from America. America disappeared while I was gone.

How I would love to hear its name once again, as it was intended to mean, before I die.

Impressions of a Quiet City

The city lies on ancient flatlands in a basin between two drowsy rivers that lead to the ocean. It's not a very big place at all. One could get from one side to the other in just a few minutes.

As I arrived by car from the airport, I noticed a high ridge of mountains behind me, and to my right and left. It was in a "bowl" shape that had one side split open leading to the city and, just beyond that, the ocean.

The mountains were lush and covered in green. Upon the top of them were no buildings or houses, but sprinkled around, here and there, stood some ancient Buddhist shrines.

This is a very old part of a very old country. Much of the history of this age-old place started here. It is a place steeped in history and culture.

Persisting from the distant past, the souls of the people who died here seem present. So many times over the last 1,000 years, this place violently changed hands. It was the birthplace of many famous samurai; it is also their resting place.

Of course, along with the warring, there has always been the prayer. This was also a sacred and holy place that had attracted monks and priests to visit, live, and worship. It still does. The holy people are the only ones who would choose to live on these mountains; I'm quite sure it has always been this way.

The entire area has a mystical aura about it. Even the mountains, covered in mist, call out some long forgotten phrase—like the singing of sirens from days long gone.

In the flatlands, between and around the two rivers, live the inhabitants in the center of the city. This is a sleepy fishing town. It is famous for a wide variety of seafood due to its location on the Seto Inland Sea.

The Seto Inland Sea is one of the calmest bodies of ocean in the world. Miya-jima Buddhist Shrine, which was constructed in the year 808, is here. The shrine is built in a very curious place, as it sits right on top of the ocean bed. It must have been quite an achievement to build. At high tide, the ocean runs through the temple; at low tide you can see how the entire structure sits on the ocean floor.

This is an amazing piece of architecture in a spiritual place; the shrine itself is the size of a football field. How could people from 1,200 years ago have had the technology to build such a thing? The switch between high and low tides is only 6 hours, but due to the natural calmness of the ocean here, the shrine is never washed away by storms.

This tranquility of the Inland Sea seems to seep into the very fabric of this city and into the lives of the people who live here.

Today, it is a peaceful place that somehow reckons with its vicious past.

The people living here do not seem to be in a rush. Things are slower here; the pace not so frantic as it is in the bigger cities. The fact that this place still exists today shows its inhabitants that in life, nothing is so important—nothing is so crucial that one should fret and strain while losing sight of what is truly important.

And that important thing is one's family and the serenity of that family.

After all, the only certain thing in life is death and that there may not be a tomorrow, so people should enjoy today what God has given them and make the best of it.

I think this best sums up my impression of this quiet city.

I looked around and I contemplated what had happened here. It made me wonder: how could anyone be so cruel to ever, even for a moment, consider dropping an atomic bomb?

What About Those Indians?

"…it was calculated that some 30,000 to 45,000 Indians (men, women and children) died at the hands of whites in formal wars between 1775–1890."—Russell Thornton, *American Indian Holocaust and Survival*

Are you ready for some shocking news? Every letter I received from Americans concerning "Impressions of a Quiet City" were in consensus. Americans freely admit that the US government has committed war crimes and continues to do so until this day. Not a one deviated from this. Not a single person tried to argue that the atomic bombings were not a war crime. Extraordinary!

This was a stunning revelation, coming directly by e-mail written to me from every single individual who took the time to write. I am astounded, and I am pleased. But I am also perplexed. While everyone voluntarily agreed that the atomic bombing of Japan was a heinous war crime that in turn amounted to genocide, I don't ever remember bringing up that point in my article at all.

My entire point was to ask, "How could anyone ever consider dropping an atomic bomb?" I didn't care whether we were talking about Hiroshima and Nagasaki or Houston and New York. I, for one, cannot conceive of ever even thinking about committing such a monstrous crime. But I guess Americans can. I guess Americans do.

I do not agree with this kind of thinking at all. I believe that two wrongs don't make a right. But who am I to argue with so many people living in America? I am just a self-exiled ex-pat who has my own opinion. What do I know?

It seems like it used to be, long ago, that most Americans tried to rectify their guilt about Hiroshima and Nagasaki by saying, "Yes, but Japan attacked America first."

This idea seems to have fallen out of favor with the average person, as this argument is legally untenable and not true. Pearl Harbor was a legitimate military target, whereas Hiroshima and Nagasaki were civilian cities. Everyone agrees on this point.

Even if I agreed with this cowardly, childish argument on face, I'm still not convinced that it "justifies" a war crime. I suppose if Japan had openly told

America, "Yes. We are going to attack you at Pearl Harbor on December 7, 1941, sometime in the early morning. Please be ready for us." then people wouldn't use this weak "Pearl Harbor argument". There are still a very few Americans who want to claim that this was a war crime, therefore somehow resolving the US government from its war-crime of deliberately killing civilians.

Wrong. American pilots flying bombing missions for China against Japanese troops in the famed "Flying Tigers" *as early as 1937* was an act of war. America's oil embargo against Japan *in 1940* was an act of war. American troops firing on Japanese troops in Manchuria*in 1939* was an act of war. (By the way, what *were* American troops doing in China as early as 1927?) The bombing of Pearl Harbor in 1941 was an act of war.

The atomic bombings were a war crime.

But let's say Pearl Harbor was a war crime. Then the people who use this rationale admit that the atomic bombing was a war crime, but it can be justified by Japan's "war crime."

No. Wrong again.

Everyone knows that surprise is a critical part of war, so this argument seems to have gone by the wayside.

The argument today that most people used to attempt to "justify" a blatant American war crime was, "What about Nanking?" Yes. Exactly! What about Nanking? This can be used to illustrate my entire point.

The Imperial Japanese army, by many accounts, killed between 30,000 and 600,000 Chinese, depending on whose account you read. Definite war crime. I agree. All people are correct in considering Nanking a war crime. Absolutely.

So, in following this line of reasoning, America expects me to believe that committing a war crime justifies your enemy committing a war crime? I'm sorry. I don't agree.

This opinion, taken to its logical conclusion, could say, "If a nuclear weapon is ever detonated in an American city, killing millions of innocents, Americans (and people the world over) can just shrug their shoulders and say, "Yeah, but America killed all those Iraqis, or Afghanis, or Vietnamese, etc., first." Or "Yeah, but America supports the Israeli slaughter of Palestinians." Or even "America wiped out all those Indians…"

It is a sad day when Americans justify war crimes by using this "law of the jungle" type of nonsense.

It is a sad day when Americans who think that they are defending the atomic bombings as "tit-for-tat" are actually admitting war crimes; they merely fail to realize the implications of their own argument. But then again, I reckon that it's pretty hard to argue with the ugly truth.

It will even be a sadder day if a nuclear device ever *is* exploded in an American city and the culprits use the exact same logic to justify it as the average American uses it to justify the atomic bombings:

"They attacked us first" a la September 11, 2001. Or "What about Nanking?" Yes. What about Nanking?

"What about those Iraqis, Afghanis, and Palestinians?" I can hear people say. Are there that many Americans who have become so gutless and pathetic that they have to whine like little children? Can't some people just say it without making lame excuses? Isn't there anyone left in America who can stand up and have the courage, pride, and self-respect required to say it straight out? "I'm sorry. We made a mistake. Never again." Or, in the near future, will "they" take the same cravenly despicable attitude and say, "What about those Indians?"

America! Have No Regrets: Love It or Leave It

"Regret for the things we did can be tempered by time; it is regret for the things we did not do that is inconsolable."—Sidney J. Harris

There comes a time in everyone's life when they must make a judgement about where they stand. Be it in their job, their personal relationship with someone else, or even better, in an inner search towards personal and spiritual growth. There comes a time when we must all "weigh" our present position against our expectations and our dreams and wishes for ourselves and our future.

This is not a one-time process, either. I think that wise people will go through this process many times in their lives, for there is nothing to live for in this world except to strive to live without regret. I think that this period of introspection may be called many things in today's society: angry youth, a mid-life crisis, depression, even, in some cases, suicidal. For many people living in today's United States, I suspect that time is here.

Many people have written to me, telling me that my predictions for a Bush defeat in the 2004 elections should force me to make an apology. I will not make an apology. I was still right. What I basically wrote was, "(In a fair election in America) George W. Bush will be re-soundly defeated in a landslide."

I was 100 percent right. There is no need for me to "eat crow," as they say. Sure, it might be a bit of a redundancy to say "In a fair election in America," because America is supposed to be the Land of the Free—a country where fair play is the rule. Is it my fault that Americans have allowed their country to become so corrupted today that to cheat and steal have become fair play? Is it my fault that Americans have become so jaded that they *expect* their own government to be corrupt? I don't think so. But you live there; I don't. The only thing that I may apologize for is that I wrote, "No amount of cheating could possibly make a Bush victory." Okay. I got that part wrong. I'll admit that much. I'm sorry. But is it my fault that you folks will allow yourselves to be cheated? Is it my fault if you willingly allow yourselves to be robbed? What am I, a policeman? No, I am not.

If you were at a gambling table at some casino and someone threw the dice, would you allow them to turn one of the dice over after they had stopped tumbling? No you wouldn't, would you?

But then again, if you were at a gambling table and this happened to you, what could you do about it? You could complain, but if everyone at the table told you to shut up; if the dealer called the cheating legal; if the security cameras were conveniently turned off; what could you do about it? Probably not a lot.

I know what I would do. I would try to convince everyone that there is cheating going on. But if they don't want to listen or stand up for fair play, what would I do? I'd leave and never gamble at that place again.

In the late 1970s, I was a university student. I have always been able to get along with foreigners; it didn't matter to me where they came from.

There was a guy named Sabahi from Iran. Sabahi was one of my best friends. The football jocks and other meatheads picked on this guy constantly. They hated him because of the Iran Hostage Crisis. One day, in the dormitory cafeteria, the jocks came and sat by us and started hitting Sabahi. I think people back in those days thought I was a psycho (they still do), and I said to them in my best Clint Eastwood imitation, "Look, figure it out, you guys. This Iranian guy is here because his family hates the current government of Iran, okay? They are in the United States because they ran away from Ayatollah Khomeini. Now why don't you just leave him alone?"

The jocks had a look of shear terror on their faces. It was probably the very first time they had even heard my voice. Like I said, I think people feared me as some sort of maniac. Even though these guys were twice my size, they never bothered Sabahi again. I was pretty pleased with myself.

Just before my 30th birthday, many of my friends were telling me just how terrible their 30th was. Some told me that they were happy all day and then, just all of a sudden, they started crying. I feared this experience and waited for it to happen to me. But it never did. And I figured out why, too. When we are young, say 17 or 18, we all have dreams. Some of us want to be famous, some rich, some rich and famous. Some of us want to swim with dolphins or become rock stars. Some of us want to change the world; we all have these kinds of dreams in our youth. But then we go to college. We study, and we have it drilled into our heads from high school that you can't do this or you can't do that; you have to work as an accountant or in an office. You must conform.

In college we choose a field of study. Some of us choose a useless field that we never wind up using. Some stick with their dreams and study to become their dream. While in college, we meet a girl or a guy whom we like. We are conditioned to believe that the American Dream is to get married, buy a house, have children, and get in debt up to our ears. Then reality strikes! You really have no freedom; you pay taxes and then you die.

I know that the reason many people are so sad and melancholy on their 30th birthday is because they've come to realize that the dream they held at 18 is gone, and it is never going to come back.

That's why when I turned 30, I wasn't sad. I was happy. I was ecstatic! I had always wanted to be rich and famous, and I was still chasing my dream. I was on TV and the radio, and I was still living "on the edge," so to speak.

And, at almost 50, I'm still happy. You know why? I'm not rich. I'm not famous, but I am still chasing my dream. I still have the heart of a kid, and I am not going to ever give it up. I can see where I've already made it past the hard part; and that hard part is to "just stick with it." So you have to make up your mind. Are you going to chase your dream, or are you going to allow outside "pressures" to guide you along a set path?

The 2004 US presidential election was a farce; the United States is not a democracy; there is no more "America." The mass media will never report this information. I know it. You *must* know it. What are you going to do about it?

When a toy becomes rusty and broken, are you going to try to fix it, or will you throw it away? Rusty parts may be replaced, but when the entire toy is rusted through and through, there is no way to repair it. The US government became rusty and broken a long time ago. What are you going to do about it? I don't believe there is any way to fix this toy. I suppose it must be destroyed.

A return to "America" would require a revolution—an overthrow of the United States government. This is your right—no, it is your duty as a citizen of the United States of America—to do as is written in the Constitution of the United States of America. But it is a huge task; it would take a Herculean effort on everyone's part to throw the current government into the rubbish bin, and I cannot see my brothers and sisters moving in that direction today. The direction the United States is moving today is away from freedom and towards more state control. It is a direction towards socialism. To disregard what I have written here is to live in stark denial.

That the "People of the South" seemed to be heavily in favor of George W. Bush in the 2004 election should not come as a surprise to any of us. Why? Well, when the people who did love freedom wanted it; they stood up for it. After that, the federal government waged an illegal war on them. The South lost; that was in 1864. The American Civil War was *not* about slavery. It was about States' rights and taxation. States have the right, under the Constitution, to secede from the

Union. Why did the federal government wage war on free people who were try-ing to exercise their rights?

Now what makes you think that the victors of this war against liberty would want the children of the South to be educated enough to know what had hap-pened to their forefathers? They wouldn't, would they?

And, finally, as my friend Anthony Gregory points out, "America was not sup-posed to be a democracy (America is a republic)...It's time for Democrats to stop believing in democracy."

I'd agree. The only thing I might add is that you should stop believing in America, for the real "America" no longer exists; it hasn't since 1861. What are you going to do about it?

I figure you have two choices only. Working within the system doesn't work, because the system is broken, so you will have to create a revolution. Without a revolution, you would have to leave.

I know what I would do. I know what I did; I left. And you know what? It gets easier to leave every day; it becomes clearer by the day, that for me, I made the right choice. It's not my fault that others willfully allow themselves to be cheated and robbed of their freedom without doing something about it.

America! Where have you gone?

The United States? Good-bye. America was great while it lasted. I might return when "America" does, or when your people really do dedicate their love for you and are ready to fight for liberty again. Until then, I have no regrets.

The Little Japanese Girl Who is Far Smarter Than George W. Bush

Well, we already know that attacking Iraq was a huge mistake, even a war crime. We all know George W. Bush doesn't read, has a limited knowledge of history, geography, economics, etc. We also know that he has no desire to learn about these things; he even admits it himself.

George is the epitome of the stupid *Ugly American*. He is an excellent example of typical hardheaded "American ethnocentric thinking."

I reckon that Americans think they are the smartest people in the world. Sometimes we are not too willing to accept the fact that we have no knowledge or common sense in areas that are so blatantly obvious to people in other countries. Once they are pointed out to us, we feel, well...stupid.

Case in point: me.

Here I have been living in Japan for all this time, and I didn't know what I am about to tell you until the day before yesterday.

Let me ask you a question. Who is the most famous Japanese person in the world? Baseball player Hideki Matsui or Ichiro? No way. They are only known in America and Japan. Famous movie director Akira Kurosawa? Perhaps. But did you know that he is not so famous here in Japan? Seiji Ozawa? Who? How about Emperor Hirohito? Hideki Tojo? Nope. They are past history. By far, the most famous Japanese person in the world today is named *Oshin*.

Now I know what you are thinking. "Who is Oshin"? Well, of course from living here, I had heard the name many times, but I never really paid too much attention. *Oshin* is the main character in a very famous TV drama that is, far and away, the most successful TV drama ever made in this country.

The reason why I never really paid much attention to *Oshin* is because *Oshin* is a "tear-jerker" TV drama about a young girl who goes through some very serious hard times in her life, only to finally overcome all and gain happiness.

Oshin goes something like this: The story starts before 1920. Japan was a desperately poor country. Oshin is a very young girl, growing up in an extremely poor and starving family. By second grade in elementary school, due to her parents failing health, she had to quit school to take various jobs to help feed her family.

After being kicked, beaten, and abused by various employers, she gets a job at a rice store. That too, is extremely backbreaking work, as she is forced to do manual labor by husking rice and scrubbing floors, but she never complains and every penny she gets—and sometimes a cup full of rice that she has filled by picking up grains off the dirty floor—she takes home to give to her family.

She grows older and has a simple dream of becoming a hair stylist. One day she meets a dashing, handsome, but humble man, and they fall in love. They marry and everything looks great.

They have a child. And Oshin, with the help of her loving husband, opens a hair-styling salon. She is happy.

Then tragedy strikes! The Great Kanto Earthquake of 1923 hits Tokyo. 120,000 people die in one day. Oshin's house and shop are burned to the ground, along with all of her possessions and what little money they had. Oshin, her husband, and child are lucky to have escaped with the shirts on their backs. Hungry, with no money or shelter, they have no choice but to return to her husband's hometown in the country to live.

At about this point in the story is where the script follows a very familiar pattern to Westerners: At Oshin's husband's home, her mother-in-law is extremely cruel to Oshin. Oshin must work the rice fields and do all the housework chores, while the mother-in-law's daughter sits around the home all day, doing nothing except combing her hair and making outlandish demands of Oshin.

Kind of reminiscent of "Cinderella," isn't it?

Well, after a while, Oshin cannot take any more abuse, and she runs away with her child in tow. She returns to Tokyo. In the meantime, her husband is heartbroken. He leaves his family forever and spends the next several years of his life searching for Oshin and their child.

Oshin works hard in Tokyo. Through all the suffering she has endured, and all the pain, she has learned well. She has become a very smart woman. She starts her own business, selling fish by delivery in Tokyo. It's a smash success. Then she parlays that success and her experience into opening the very first supermarket in Japan.

The supermarket takes the country by storm. Oshin's secret was to sell "ready-made, already cooked" food to housewives to make their daily chores just a bit easier.

She becomes wealthy, but something is missing in her life—It is her love. Her child sometimes asks about Daddy, but Oshin always avoids the subject. Oshin cries at night, praying for thanks and hoping that at least her husband is safe, healthy, and has perhaps found someone new to take care of him—someone better than her. She sometimes wonders if she had just withstood a bit more…If she had just been a touch stronger, could things have turned out differently? She lives with guilt.

She still loves him so. She wishes things were different, but they are not. If her life has taught her anything, it's that Oshin knows that she must always follow her heart and do what's right.

Her life is good, but her heart has a hole in it—a hole from a lost love.

And then, one day, there is a knock on the door. She opens it—and it's him! After all these years of desperate searching, he has found her at last!

Well, anyway, that's basically the story. I have to get back to the point of this; otherwise, I'll get all teary eyed.

The point of all this is this: sometimes I am amazed at what people think and do. Before I came to Japan, I was amazed at the Japanese. Now, after having been here so long, I am often amazed at the stupid things Americans do. What I mean to say is that, People are often wise or foolish in the most curious of ways.

Sorry, folks, but I know that the average American thinks that Americans are smarter than everyone else, but I have a point here where the Japanese just blow Americans away in the common-sense area. There is no competition.

Think about *Oshin*. Think about that story and that kind of suffering. I don't think Americans can relate to that. Of course the Japanese can.

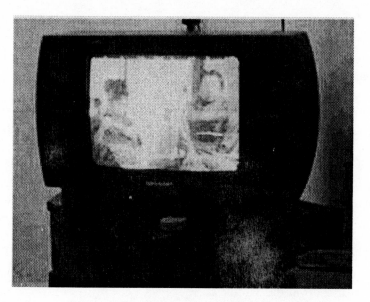

Oshin on TV in Iraq (note the Arabic sub-titles)

And, get this: *Oshin* has been broadcast in most Middle Eastern countries for at least the last 12 years. Iran? Sure. According to the Nikkei Shimbun News *Oshin* scores a remarkable 82 percent viewer rating. Iraq? Of course; 76.7 percent; Thailand? 81.6 percent; China? (I thought most Chinese people hate Japanese because of the war!) Yeah, well, maybe so, but they love *Oshin*! 75.9 percent viewer rating in China. Poland? 70 percent. And the list goes on.

Gee, I wonder if the people in the Middle East can relate to this kind of starvation, suffering, and pain? Of course they can.

Which brings me to the next part of this puzzle. The Japanese military has ordered all troops in Iraq to grow beards and moustaches. Weird, eh? Well, no—smart. Besides understanding the ways of society in the Middle East, Oshin's husband has a moustache. Don't believe me? Check this out: Japanese army opts for new form of camouflage: (http://www.iol.co.za/index.php?sf=2813 &click_id=2813&art_id=qw1075886642437B236&set_id=6)

Just about every Japanese soldier in Iraq that I've seen on TV has a moustache.

So now when Iraqi people see Japanese soldiers with beards and moustaches, they all yell, "Oshin! Oshin! Oshin!"

Traditionally, Japan has always had good relations with countries like Iraq and Iran. The Japanese may often seem quizzical and enigmatic to Americans (me too, sometimes), but this is just so ingenious, so brilliant in its simplicity, that it just blows my mind.

And here we have all our US soldiers over there, looking like they just stepped out of Miami Vice or Darth Vader's death star.

The Japanese also know that the big sport in the Mid-East is soccer. The Japanese soldiers are not handing out 35-cent chocolates, like the American soldiers; they are handing out $35 soccer balls. Don't believe me again? Check here: Japanese troops go to Iraq with soccer balls: (http://www.expressindia. com/fullstory.php?newsid=27481)

Think about it. Isn't the purpose of giving these "gifts" to the children a sort of method to create goodwill? And isn't that goodwill a sort of "protection"?

The American soldiers are handing out junk chocolate that might give a child 3 seconds of happiness. The Japanese are handing out high quality soccer balls that will bring wonderful memories to last a lifetime. Those soccer balls must seem like treasures from heaven to those poor children. Soccer is, by the way, the most popular sport in the Middle East.

And isn't having friendly relations with the children and their parents very important to your personal safety? Iraq is a war zone. These "presents" are a sort of "life insurance" for our soldiers, aren't they?

If you were in a war zone, would you buy the 35-cent life insurance policy, or the $35 life insurance policy?

The US government will waste hundreds and hundreds of billions of dollars on new high-tech junk, but be incredibly foolish and cheapskate in the most absurd of ways.

Our soldiers are handing out cheap junk—food, while the Japanese are giving out gold.

This is a case in point where the Americans must seem incredibly stupid and inept, but you can't really blame our foot soldiers for this too much. The federally run education system in America is a disaster, and people are not getting nearly the education they need. For example, Japanese students study calculus one and two by the 8th grade and already have 6 years of English by that time. Americans students? Do they even teach foreign languages any more?

No wonder most American soldiers don't have a clue when they go overseas. After all, they come from a very ethnocentric country. How would they know about another culture? They certainly didn't learn about it in school. Even if American soldiers did know, they couldn't afford soccer balls; they have a hard enough time having to pay for their own equipment, like body armor, that should be provided by the US government for free.

It reminds me of that Clint Eastwood movie, *Heartbreak Ridge*. After some military exercises, a high-ranking officer looks at Clint and says, "Sergeant? What's your assessment of this situation?" Eastwood answers, "It's a cluster-fuck, sir!" And it sure is.

Now, you tell me, who has more common sense? The Japanese or the Americans?

Who do you think the Iraqi children like more—Darth Vader or Oshin?

(As of the date of this writing, not a single Japanese soldier has been killed or wounded in Iraq).

When In Rome,
Who Cares What the
Romans Do?

My previous article, "The Little Japanese Girl Who Was Far Smarter Than George W. Bush," brought me the most e-mail I have ever received from an article I had written. I cannot say that all responses were reassuring. While the vast majority were from intelligent people with open minds who have no problem dealing with new information, there were more than a few responses that only served to make me think that the point of that particular article was right on the mark. Most Americans are incredibly hardheaded and ethnocentric; the educational system in America is failing; and the US government wastes even more money than most people could ever imagine. And far too many Americans couldn't care less.

As usual, I got the knee-jerk response of being called "Anti-American," as well as several benighted responses accusing me of being disrespectful to the military. I had thought it was quite obvious from reading the article that I was criticizing the lack of Social Studies given in American schools and the actions (or lack thereof) of the US government—not the poor foot soldier.

Forgive me for stating a cruel truth. I do not wish to insult a loved one of yours, but it doesn't matter what country you are in; generally speaking, *well-educated people do not accept employment where part of the job is getting shot at.*

I suppose that since many people failed to grasp that particular point, it just serves as further evidence that the American educational system is in startling decline, and the average American's reading comprehension level is dismal, at best.

I even got one e-mail from a self-proclaimed "pacifist" that included a veiled death threat towards me.

Another reader tried to convince me that, "Giving chocolate to starving children is better than giving a soccer ball. Why? Because the memory of receiving chocolate will last a lifetime. A soccer ball will soon be lost and forgotten." I am not making this up. But I'm sure in a rich and decadent society like Iraq, children will be children, and are always losing their toys like American kids are.

It is obvious that this particular reader failed to grasp what I had written, but for the sake of this painfully illogical argument, let me give you a quote, word for word, from a gentleman who lived through the German occupation in World War II:

> *Mike, I keep thinking of your last essay, about the "little Japanese girl" and the moustaches, the gifts of balls. So true. And I am discovering again, that Americans don't understand that story!*
>
> *My own memories of American soldiers at the end of WWII are the same. I was in Holland, as you know (now you're supposed to say the Netherlands; Holland is a province of the Netherlands). It seems the end of the war came so suddenly that there were no Allied troops to come to us. So we, the Resistance, were given arm-bands, and told we were in charge. The Germans were locked up in their own barracks, but were allowed to keep their arms because otherwise the people would have stoned them (to death) probably. Then, maybe a week later, Canadian troops came from Italy. They looked as soldiers are supposed to look: worn out, gray, dusty. Very quiet. They were "men."*
>
> *After another week, there was some change in command, or whatever, and the Canadians left, and American troops came. They were all "boys," we thought. Clean, fresh. They set up camp in city parks. The first tent that went up was the PX.*
>
> *They handed out chocolate bars to the kids—disaster! We were starved, had not had any food for six months, chocolate was much too rich. Children actually died.*
>
> *The first American civilians I met were people from Hollywood! Nice people, I'm sure, but they did not have a clue. I remember showing them around Amsterdam (which looked awful, of course; 10 percent of the population had been Jewish, whole neighborhoods were deserted). We were sitting at some cafe by a canal. I offered the man one of my cigarettes. At that time (for several years after, actually) everything was rationed, to be fair, so that rich people would not get more than the poor. I remember cigarettes were 10 per week. So it was very magnanimous of me to offer one to him. At the time I would pick up butts from the street to make new cigarettes...He took one puff, said "How can you smoke this stuff?" and threw it in the canal. I still feel the horror of that moment. He said, "Why don't you buy Lucky Strikes?"*
>
> *"Because I cannot buy them here, of course," I said.*

This was written by a European. He was on "our" side fighting the Nazis, and even he said, "Americans don't have a clue."

Do you feel insulted by this? Why? This is the recollection of what actually happened by a person who was there. Perhaps, instead of feeling insulted, Americans should take it as a lesson. No?

I'm sure that many people think that giving chocolates to starving children could not possibly have any harmful effects. Once again, I can't really blame you. Just one more bit of proof that the educational system in America is in dire straits and that Americans are not getting the common sense education that they should.

Ask any doctor, dietician, or even any parent who has had a child with any kind of serious illness, like say, cancer, "Is giving chocolate to a sick child okay?" They'll all tell you, "Of course not!" Chocolate is one of the "forbidden foods" to give to sick children. Giving chocolate to sick children is very dangerous. And that is no exaggeration.

I know. Several years ago, when my 1 1/2-year-old daughter was diagnosed with Rhabdomysarcoma cancer, the first thing the doctor told me was: "Absolutely no chocolate!" I already knew that! (My daughter has since recovered; thank you.)

Some other people wrote to me and told me, "Americans don't need to care what Iraqis think!" Yeah? Well, not only is that idiotic because Iraq is, well, Iraq—that's really brave of you to say. You are not over there getting shot at.

My article was not an indictment of the actions of the US foot soldier. (That can be written about by someone who is far more informed on that subject than I am). My article was an indictment of American society, the "cultural superiority complex" held by far too many Americans, and the pathetic, inept command of the US soldiers in Iraq. Iraq is an Islamic society. If we were truly interested in capturing the "hearts and minds" of the locals, then I suppose it would make common sense to show some respect, and at the very least to make it appear that the US foot soldier was attempting to accommodate local customs.

US soldiers "winning hearts and minds" in Iraq

"Nah! We're Americans! We don't need to do that! We're number one!"

Once again, really brave of you to say that, when you are not the one over there getting shot at.

If I were you and I had a father, brother, sister, son, or daughter over in that fiasco going on in Iraq, I'd write them a letter right now, telling them to "grow a beard; try not to stand out; and please show some humility." It just might save their lives.

Several years ago, a friend of mine moved to Japan. He is a typical bull-headed, stubborn "Ugly American."

When he first arrived here, I picked him up at the airport with my Japanese father-in-law. My father-in-law was the president of a very big company at that time. In Japan, you show respect to elders, whether you know them or not, and in Japan, elders expect younger people to give some respect. Is this "good" or "bad"? Neither; it's the "way it is."

My friend came out of airport customs with a toothpick dangling out of his mouth. This is a definite no-no in Japan. (Perhaps you've seen a Japanese person using a toothpick before? They always cover their mouth with one hand while using a toothpick).

I was embarrassed. Before he saw my father-in-law, I asked him to take the toothpick out of his mouth, as the only people who walk around with toothpicks dangling out of their mouths are Yakuza boss-types or idiots looking to start a fight.

Nope. He wouldn't do it.

"Who cares about a toothpick?" he griped.

"This is Japan. You don't do that here!" I pleaded. No good. He was a typical know-it-all American. He didn't care about the ways of other people in another country.

Of course, my father-in-law disliked him from the start. He said he didn't like my friend's attitude; neither did I, actually. Needless to say, while there were many foreigners earning $70,000 a year (and much more) at that time here in Japan, working a tough schedule of 30 hours a week, my friend kept getting fired, over and over, from different companies.

He never learned the language, in spite of being here for several years. It goes without saying that he is no longer in Japan.

In his defense, though, I will admit it takes a lot of effort, an open mind, and patience to adjust to the ways of another society, but thinking you are a hotshot American is not a good way to do it. Probably in Iraq, thinking you are a hotshot American is a good way to *get* shot at and killed.

Let me ask you a question: If someone came from a foreign land to America and didn't try to at least minimally accommodate themselves to local ways and customs, wouldn't you say, "This is America. This is the way we do things here. If you don't like it, go home." I know the vast majority of Americans would.

Now, what makes some of you hotshot cowboys think you can do as you please in another country?

I am the son of a US marine. I have had family die in World War II, and Vietnam. I like to think when I tell my own countrymen that they are doing something foolish, my countrymen are at least intelligent enough to have an open mind and contemplate the subject. However, being born and raised in America and knowing how Americans think, and understanding how they were educated—sadly, I reckon I expect too much to ask them to have a little more humility and common sense.

After all, America is number one—for now—just like Rome used to be.

Baghdad Buffet

Well, mea culpa! Mea culpa! Mea culpa, Caffe Latte, and a Caramel Mocha for my friend here.

After having pointed out the crass cynicism and error of my ways, I must sincerely apologize and ask for your kind forgiveness. I have to admit that I have been repeatedly and overly bashing of our good President Bush. And for that I am deeply sorry; it will never happen again.

I was often underhanded in my planning to single-handedly make the president look like a buffoon. It was a sickness, really. I couldn't help myself. I lived for it; I saw it in my dreams at night. I couldn't stop thinking about it. When it came to bashing President Bush, I ate, drank, slept, even *shat* Bush. It was an obsession, 24-7. But I've gotten better now. I really have.

Yes, I know I've been mean—sometimes downright nasty, and I take full responsibility for that. All I can do is kneel down at the altar of your forgiveness with a dagger held to my heart until you pardon me for my mischievous ways. From now on, I'm going to be on the straight and narrow. You'll see.

I will use my God-given creativity not as a tool for mockery, but as a golden stream for a positive message. And let me start right here, right now.

As you all know, Iraq is free—and getting freer by the day. They will even enjoy more freedom after the elections. Let me be the first to congratulate President Bush and the Iraqi people for a job well done. President Bush said the Iraqi elections would bring peace. Thank God. But I've also heard some rumors that there are still some "dead-enders" trying to ruin the party—that even though Iraq is enjoying greater freedoms and stability, there are still those who hate freedom! Here is where I'd like to submit my idea for real freedom for Iraq and for the benefit of our good President Bush.

Let us show the world that when America says that the Iraqis will be free, we mean *free!* Freedom is not just another word for nothing left to lose. After all this hassle and trouble America has gone through to make these Iraqis free, I think it is our duty as Americans to make sure that the Iraqis are the freest people on the entire face of the planet! Let's make *everything* in Iraq free, not just the people or freedom of religion or political thought. Let's make the water, air, land, education, electricity, oil, cars, houses, jobs, everything—free! Let's make them so damned free that they can't stand themselves. Let's eliminate starvation and skinny Iraqi children by making the food of Iraq free too! Free money! Let's make sure that they are so free that their children grow into the world's fattest and freest people. I don't mean fat-free people, either. I mean fat *and* free! No dieting for Iraqis! Hell, we'll *make* them fat!

Wasn't it that famous American cooking lady, Aunt Jemima—or was it Betty Crocker—who said, "The way to a man's heart is through his stomach"? Well, we all know it's true. I have come up with a really super way to get it through these terrorists' thick skulls that when it comes to freedom, we Americans mean business.

I wonder whether, until now, we haven't been going about it the wrong way in bringing freedom to Iraq and the terrorists into the fold? Perhaps by slogging it out with them in places like Fallujah, Baghdad, Mosul (insert your favorite Iraqi city name here), we shouldn't have been trying a different tactic? I think we should have. That's why today I'd like to give President Bush my plan for bringing together these terrorist forces and showing them that we really are their friends. And I want to volunteer my plan for free! My plan is so simple, yet so brilliant, I wonder why no one has thought of it up until now.

"Mike, this all sounds great, but how do we bring the terrorists to the table, so to speak?" Well, therein lies the genius of my plan. We don't bring them to the *table*; we bring the table to *them*! That's right. I propose that instead of spending hundreds of billions of dollars on bombs and stuff, we spend the money on "meatier" projects—something the Iraqis will want to take part in and can be proud of. Let's give Iraq its own 7th wonder of the world! Yep, the Chinese have their Great Wall, the Egyptians have their spincters, the Braves have their Atlantis; let's give the Iraqis the Great Buffet! The longest and greatest free buffet in the entire world! It will be open for 24 hours a day, seven days a week, and be completely free to all Iraqis.

The buffet will begin in Mosul, with trays and cutlery: napkins, forks, spoons, butter knives, things like that. A little bit further down the way towards Baghdad will be the serving and bread plates. After that, we can have the breads and salads. Still a tad further down will be the various vegetable dishes, and still further down will be the meat dishes: beef, lamb, mutton, camel, what have you. We follow up that with the seafood and crab legs. Who doesn't like Alaskan King Crab and baked swordfish? On the other side of Baghdad, towards Basra, will be the International Cuisine: lasagne, enchiladas, and sushi. A little further down are the desserts, cakes, coffee, tea and refreshments. I think we can probably work out something with Wolfgang Puck's or Starbucks to help handle this section, thereby saving the US tax—payer some money.

Now, how about the freedom-of-religion part that Ann Coulter so often talks about? (She's right, you know.) Well, we need to convert all these people to Christianity, but how? Well, everybody who is anybody has heard about the Baghdad Airport Highway, right? It's now called "RPG Alley." (RPG means "rocket propelled grenade.") Well, since the place already has name recognition value, let's not waste some prime real estate by changing the name. Let's be smart about this and use our Madison Avenue marketing skills and keep the name "RPG Alley," but we'll *change the meaning* to "Roast Pork and Gravy Alley." Is that a great idea, or what? We can even have Ann as the hostess who greets the arriving Iraqis who want to load up on split-hoofed delicacies.

"Hello. Welcome to RPG Alley. How many in your party? Your name, please? Will that be smoking or non-smoking? Would you like a table with a view of flaming airlines, or the oasis?"

"Which is better?"

"Well, burning airlines give you so much more."

Yeah, laugh now, smart guys, but if you really thought about it for a moment, you'd realize that my plan has just as much of a chance of success, if not more, than anything the White House or the Pentagon has come up with so far. Sure, there are some architectural and construction issues to be dealt with, so what's the problem? We are the United States of America! If we can rebuild the Twin Towers after Saddam and Osama crashed their planes into it, then I think it should be child's play to build a buffet the length of California. It's not like there's any rainy season to get in the way of construction plans.

Sure, we'll have to figure out a way to enclose the Buffet Mall and keep the sneeze screens from blowing off during sandstorms, but I think that will be the *least* of our worries.

The problem we'll have is getting those Iraqi terrorists to *like* us, and like I said, the way to a man's heart is through his stomach. So let's start constructing this buffet today.

Damned I'll be if those Iraqi children won't be the freest and fattest kids in the world after all this trouble we've gone through. And if they don't line up at the cafeteria and load up on the carbohydrates and drink Cokes; if they don't want to eat for free, and become fat just like us Americans, then that's proof that they don't like the freedoms that we enjoy. What'll we do then? Well, we'll shoot their asses. That'll teach them that we mean freedom when we say freedom. That'll teach them to look a gift horse in the mouth. Hell, we'll teach them to be free! We'll make them fat. We'll teach their grandmothers to suck eggs!

(Apologies to David Rees and Brian Eno.)

Say It Loud: "I'm Communist and I'm Proud"

Let's put the cards on the table, shall we? Regardless of what you want to call it, America is on the verge of a total and complete Communist take-over—And judging from the mail I receive and what I read and see on TV, the average American doesn't even know it or seem to care.

I'm sure Anthony Gregory's recent article, "The President Speaks, the Crowd Goes Wild," (http://www.lewrockwell.com/gregory/gregory30.html) rattled some cages by stating that George W. Bush's 2004 "Republican" platform is "National Socialism," as opposed to the "Democratic," platform which is nothing less than straight-out Socialism.

Let's not get tied up into semantics here. As Dr. John Coleman puts it in his book, *One World Order*, "Socialism has nowhere to progress but Communism."

Just about everyone agrees that there is not much difference between the Republicans and the Democrats. I gather the insinuation from the many people I talk to is that there is no longer a Democratic party; the Democrats have become like the Republicans—a Republican-lite. I think this is completely false. If anything, the Republican party—the supposed party of small government of the United States—has ceased to exist.

The Democrats have taken over. How else would you explain the biggest spending administration in the history of the United States under a so-called "Republican president"?

Consider George W. Bush's remarks during his acceptance speech concerning Medicare, enrolling children in a socialized medical scheme, creating more affordable homes, and on and on.

In America, this is called democracy. It's called democracy because it is an easier sell to the average American. But what exactly is this democracy?

It is, and always has been, sold to you as a way to "level the playing field." Whether that field is in your business or in your child's education or any number of other areas, it sounds really good: share the wealth; there's plenty for everyone; a chicken in every pot.

But when you get right down to it, sharing the wealth is in no uncertain terms Communism. Think about it. What else could you possibly call it? What else could you call penalizing people with money to pay for people who don't have it? And you've got it, America, and it didn't come from Russia, either. It came straight to you from Washington D.C. and the Communist party of the United States of America—or as Americans would say, Democrats or Republicans have brought it to you and are laying it right in your lap—and you are eating it up.

When are you folks going to wake up? The Communist government of the United States has been tearing away at your civil rights consistently for decades, yet most Americans are under the illusion that they live in the freest country in the world. Laughable!

You are either 100 percent dedicated to freedom, or you are not. There is no in between. When you start making rules that marginalize the habits and rights of people, then you are exhibiting Communist tendencies.

Personally, I have an aversion to guns. This happened to me as a boy when I went hunting with my father and I blasted a pheasant. I guess when I was a kid I was a pretty good shot, but shooting that bird made me feel guilty. Hey! I was just a little boy, all right? But that's just my own psychological hang-up. Everyone has a heart and everyone has a brain. Regardless of whether I want to own a gun or not, I certainly do not want the government to make any laws or restrictions on who can and cannot have one, if they so choose.

I am for freedom. I am not for limited freedom. When you start putting limits on freedom, then it is the road to Communism. For me to want any sort of rules made by the government on behavior by people who do not interfere with others, that would be completely hypocritical. Not only hypocritical; it would be a form of Communism. There are no two ways about it. You are either for freedom or you are not.

Let me break it down to a very simple and easy-to-understand example: public smoking. Let's say you are a guy who has worked all your life for someone else. You've somehow managed to make enough money to become your own boss, in spite of the socialist system that surrounds you. Congratulations. You deserve a pat on the back. You've suffered, fought, and succeeded.

Now you decide that you'd like to be your own boss. You would like to take it easy and enjoy the fruits of your labor. So, you open up a local pub in the image of what you think local pubs should be like—a place to enjoy a drink, a smoke, and perhaps good conversation. You are proud of your establishment, and life looks good. Business is going well.

Then one day, the Communists who run the US government decide to tell you how to run your business. There's a mountain of rules and regulations, half of which are never enforced—until "they" decide it's time to give you a hard time. But the one that is enforced—the one that hurts your business the most—is the "No Public Smoking Law."

Everyone knows that drinkers often like to smoke. This is your place. You are the boss here. Who the hell do these people think they are, telling you who you can and cannot serve to? If you want your place to allow smoking, that is your *right* as the owner of that business. If you don't want to allow smoking, then that is your right also. If you want to play Satanic rock music or country and western, then that is your right, as owner of that establishment, to decide. If you think what I have written here is wrong, then take a good look in the mirror and you will see a real Communist. As Fred Reed would point out, "If they don't like the smoke, or the music, or the food, or my ugly mug, that thing in front with the hinges on it is available. A 'door,' we call it."

The part that astounds me the most about all this is how "educated" Americans—people who claim that they are for "Capitalism" and "Freedom"—fail to recognize this situation for what it really is: a Communist takeover of America.

Everyone with half a brain knows that the government can't do anything right. Everyone knows that anything the government tries to do will be over-budget, past deadline, and screwed up. Not only that, but the government will have to rip it all up in a few years and do it all over again. You don't think so? How about, say, the freeway you drive on everyday? So why in the world do Americans want their government to control more and more of their lives? I know why—because most Americans are Communists; they just don't call it that.

The Social Welfare State that America has become (and it's getting worse) is the biggest example of American Communism I can think of. Why should you have money taken away from your family and children because some other family cannot afford to take care of their own? Yes, this sounds very cold, but speaking as a former "Leftist," I have come to know that this is the way it is. And why should you have to pay for some people who are homeless and "out of their luck"? I don't think I should. I don't think you should, either.

Several years ago I was discussing this question about the homeless with a Leftist friend of mine. I made the statement, "Each and every one of us is the master of our own destiny."

My friend replied, "Yes. But what percentage of that person being homeless is society's fault?"

I retorted, "So what you are saying is that the homeless guy who is now sleeping under the trains tracks over there, his being homeless is partially your fault?"

He replied, "It's not my fault!"

"Well, it most certainly isn't my fault either. So if you and I are not 'part of society,' then whose fault is it? Just who is 'society'?"

The fact of the matter is that the best we can possibly hope for is that the government gets off of our backs and makes an atmosphere where people can be and do their best, which means minimal or no government. That's it. That is what freedom means. To do otherwise is to head down the road to Communism.

Even if the government did set up a system whereby all the homeless people could be housed and fed, it wouldn't work. Why? It's very simple. Think about why those people are homeless. They are homeless (and they all have different reasons), but it basically all boils down to the fact that their homelessness is due to not wanting to be a part of society and the responsibilities that go with it.

Like I said, even if the government set up a system to take care of these people, it wouldn't work. Since such a system would involve paperwork and a bureaucracy—this is, after all, the government we are talking about here—there would have to be some kind of organizational process that would keep track of these homeless people. How many meals have they had? Have they been showing up every night? Do they have medical care, etc.?

But remember that some of these homeless people are so derelict, or just plain "mad," that they would not show up at the government office to even sign up for such a program. It just wouldn't work. They are homeless because they don't want to deal with society and having to do things like sign their names, give out personal information or history to someone they don't even know, etc.

In Osaka, Japan, they had a very severe "problem" with the homeless. In about 1996, when the Socialists (read "Communists") were in power here, the government decided to build a huge tent to house and feed anywhere between 6,000 to 8,000 homeless people. It was claimed as a "Victory for democracy and a great way for a great society to share the wealth." Well, guess what? It was a disaster. Less than 80 homeless people even showed up to this grand scheme in the first week. Today, the tent is being used as an open-air site for rock concerts. Score "one" for millions of dollars of our tax money well spent.

Now why didn't the homeless show up? Who wouldn't want free food and a warm place to sleep? The homeless, that's who. I gather, from volunteering with the homeless for almost ten years in Iidabashi in Tokyo, thank you, that they want to be homeless, because being "homeless" means being free.

Now that the Communists are running America—be they called Republican or Democrat—they want you to spend your money so that not only will you have to support the poor people in your own neighborhoods in your own nation, they want you to support the poor people all over the world.

As George W. Bush also said in his acceptance speech, "In our world, and here at home, we will extend the frontiers of freedom." He went on to say, "We will help new leaders to train their armies and move toward elections, and get on the path of stability and democracy as quickly as possible."

Wonderful! And the Communists want to use your tax dollars and your children's blood to spread this "democracy" and freedom.

Freedom for whom? For you in America? I think you know the answer to this question by now. Go ahead, average America, say it loud: "I'm Communist and I'm proud!"

Kumiai

I have a kick in the teeth for those of you who think Japan is a government-run "nanny-state." At this point in time, it's the United States that is becoming the epitome of a Socialist Dream State.

In Japan we get to watch the world news—and no, it's not like the so-called world news you have in America. We have *real* world news. Every morning I can watch 20-minute news programs from Spain, France, Germany, Russia, the United Kingdom (BBC), China, South Korea, Thailand, ABC, and CNN. Of course, we have Japanese news, and we also have a 24-hour BBC and CNN channel.

Sorry, America, but you don't get the world news. You may have programs called "World News," but they are world news in title only. Americans are completely held in the dark about what's really going on and how the world perceives the United States.

Americans have become "busy-bodies." Many are always interfering with other's private affairs. Whether it is the subject of prayer in school, homosexual marriage, abortion, or any other number of a plethora of "problems," it seems to me that just too many Americans want to stick their noses in other people's business.

I'll admit it right now: I am an anarchist. All government is bad (whether it's federal or state, democratic or communist), and I think what other people want to do with their lives is none of my business. It's none of yours, either. And it most certainly is not the business of the central government.

A while back, a friend from the States asked me about the "homosexual marriage controversy" you had in America. He asked me what the Japanese thought about it, as if the entire world revolved around America and this nail-biting crisis. Sometimes I watch CNN, but I usually turn it off quickly because of the nonsense they consider news. So I knew that all of America was going through some sort of mid-life crisis due to this homosexual marriage question. How idiotic!

In Japan, it is a non-issue. Japanese people generally mind their own business and couldn't care less what other people want to do. You folks in the States should wise up and figure that out, too. Or are Americans so rich and pleased with their lives that they have nothing better to do than to sit around, filing their nails, and worrying about other people whom they don't even know?

I believe that so many Americans think that the Japanese do not enjoy as many "freedoms" as Americans do because you've all been fed this "America is the freest country in the world" line for so long that you do not question it.

I've said it before, and I'll say it again: I don't think the USA can compare to Japan when it comes to freedom. Sure, Japan has its problems; everywhere does, but I do not fear for my safety, or my family's safety, at night. I do not fear the police here. And I certainly do not live in fear of "terrorism" in Japan. Can most of you living in America honestly say you do not fear any of the above three? (Uh, don't look now, but if you didn't have some fear, then why do so many Americans carry a weapon?)

There also seems to be some idea that the Japanese do not think for themselves or organize themselves to do anything without the government's permission. I've heard this a lot, but I don't think that is so. In many ways, Japanese people are more motivated to "do things by themselves" than Americans are, and they have some very beneficial things to teach Western society. I'll give you a good example of it, but first, let me give you an observation about Japan.

There are vending machines standing on the streets everywhere here. I very rarely see one broken. I have never heard of one being stolen. People keep beautiful Bonsai trees out in front of their homes. Some of these trees are over 100 years old and are quite valuable. No kids run around at night, kicking them over. No one steals them. Kids don't spray paint graffiti on walls here like they do in America. Why?

Many professional sociologists claim Japan has a stronger family unit than the West, and that this is the reason for a more stable society. This is true, I think. But there is one more thing Japan has that America does not have; it's called *Kumiai. Kumiai* means "group." And the Japanese have *Kumiai* everywhere. This "group" is not what you think it is. This Kumiai can be anywhere from 3 to 4 people or 30 to 40,000 people. I suppose the closest thing in America would be the P.T.A., but I'm not so sure.

The *Kumiai* are a group of people who live in a neighborhood or in an apartment complex—or who work for the same company. They have absolutely nothing to do with the government or management, and they do not require any taxes.

One day, in 1984, when I first moved to Japan, I saw many of my neighbors out cleaning the drainage ditches in the neighborhood. I asked my wife what these people were doing. She answered, "It's the *Kumiai*. You should go and help them."

So out I went and shoveled mud and dirt out from the ditches, along with 12 or so of the neighbors. They were young and old, probably the oldest being in her late 60s. (I grabbed her shovel from her and did the shoveling.)

After an hour of so, the ditches were cleaned and everyone bowed profusely and thanked each other. I was puzzled. I asked my wife why the people did this. I said, "Don't the people pay taxes to the government to have the ditches cleaned?"

My wife wasn't sure exactly how it worked, but she explained that the *Kumiai* does this in an effort to lower their taxes. It's a way for all the folks in the neighborhood to meet and work together and grow mutual understanding and communication. They also had meetings every once in a while to discuss neighborhood problems and how they should deal with them. The *Kumiai* was a group, but perhaps the better definition of *Kumiai* might be "community."

I look back on that day as a lesson in politics. Had the central government come in to clean the ditches, they would have brought in a dozen men, a few trucks, and a tractor with a shovel. That would have taken all day and cost a lot of tax money. But the local people got together and they took care of it themselves. It was the community that took care of the problems. It was up to me, as an individual, to decide whether or not I wanted to be a part of that community, which I did, because I felt it to be beneficial in case I ever needed help from one of the neighbors.

I think this is another big reason why kids don't vandalize the neighborhoods here and just raise hell for no particular reason. Why? Because Mom and her friends would just have to clean it up anyway.

There are many kinds of *Kumiai*. Japan is an ancient country, and probably this *Kumiai* custom is a left over from many years gone by. It is one of the big reasons for safe streets at night and peaceful neighborhoods. It is one of the big reasons I think Japan offers a very free society—definitely freedom from crime or fear.

Americans are giving up their neighborhood identity and turning authority over to a faceless central office somewhere downtown. I remember living in Los Angeles and not even knowing my own neighbors. Tokyo is slowly becoming this way, but to this day most of Japan is not. People know their neighbors and greet one another when they meet.

America needs more of this kind of *Kumiai* type of thinking, and I don't mean programs like Neighborhood Watch or TIPS.

How about a little neighborly cooperation? Or, are Americans too individual-
istic for that?

Japanese Freedom v. American Freedom: Redux

In "*Kumiai*" I pointed out that today's Japan is a freer society than today's America. Now I'd like to clear the air, so to speak, and tell you a little more about Japan's government and society, as well as its freedoms, versus those of America.

For this comparison I will combine several angry e-mails I received about *Kumiai* and go through them one by one. The remarks from readers will be in quotes. My responses will follow. I'll let you be the judge: which country is freer—Japan or the United States?

Let's start with the most common comments.

"You forgot to mention that Japan has one of the most oppressive, crushing governments in the world."

This shows that this person is either confused and "talking through his hat," or doesn't know geography and politics, or else it is proof once again that the American education system is a dismal failure. But I three-peat myself.

Where do people get these ridiculous ideas? Japan has a parliamentary system modeled after the British and a Constitution modeled after the US Constitution. Japan also has a Bill of Rights in that Constitution which is much like the American Bill of Rights.

"Why is Japan's legal system so repressive? And aren't prisoners tortured into [making] confessions?"

Torturing of prisoners in Japan occurred under the constitutional rules of 1908 and was allowed until the constitutional changes and reforms of 1946 and 1948. While the current system of Japanese prisons is structured for strict obedience and the following of prison rules, torture is forbidden, and I have never heard of a prisoner being raped in a Japanese prison.

As of 2004, there are 2.1 million Americans in prison and fewer than 60,000 incarcerated in Japan. 718 out of every 100,000 Americans were behind bars in 2003, up from 701 the previous year. With recent amnesties for prisoners in Russia, America's reign as imprisonment leader of the world remains unchallenged. (Russia's rate is 584 per 100,000, and by way of comparison with other industrialized Western nations, England's is 143, Canada's is 116, Germany's is 96, and Japan's is 54.)

"You might not fear the Japanese police. But I see where you forgot to mention that they visit each citizen annually."

This is patently false and completely absurd. The police do not visit each citizen annually. In fact, if you considered the logistics of such a notion even for a moment, you'd realize just how outlandish that claim is. How is it possible for the police to visit every single person once a year in Japan, a country with half the population of the United States?

"There is no right to refuse the police if they want to come into your house and search it."

Completely false: Article 35 (Search, Seizure) of the Japanese Constitution:

> "The right of all persons to be secure in their homes, papers and effects against entries, searches, and seizures shall not be impaired except upon warrant issued for adequate cause and particularly describing the place to be searched and things to be seized or except as provided by Article 33. Each search or seizure shall be made upon separate warrant issued by a competent judicial officer."

"The reason kids don't cause trouble is because they would spend years in jail if caught. A friend of mine who lived in Japan for a while knew someone that was sentenced to ten years in prison for merely owning a cane sword. A cane sword is a novelty item you can buy in America in a flea market."

"A friend of mine who knew somebody"? Well, that would hold up in a court of law. I have a friend whose grandmother claims that she saw a UFO once, too! This comment is comical. America, think about statements like this for just a second when your "friends" make them: "A friend of mine that knew somebody…" This is embarrassingly ridiculous and does not even merit a response.

Now, if a person did attack somebody with a *Kendo* stick (a sort of cane sword used in martial arts and which could possibly kill somebody), they would be arrested for assault and battery, which carries a maximum penalty of ten years in prison—the same as in California. This is either a silly cock-and-bull story, or important details are missing. Carrying a *Kendo* stick in public is not illegal. *Kendo* is taught in high school here and you can see kids carrying them on their way to and from school.

"*Kumiai* by any other name is voluntary socialism."

Here is what Libertarian writer, Manuel Miles, wrote to me about my article entitled *"Kumiai"*: "You are the only anarchist I know to recognize that it is the

State, and not 'the collective,' that is the enemy. The community is the natural enemy of and antidote to the State."

"Society in all its forms is a blessing, while even that little government which is necessary is evil."—Thomas Paine

"In America we don't get world news. So are you proposing a law requiring it?"

I don't recall mentioning anything about requiring any laws. Perhaps if you read *Kumiai* and could comprehend what is written, you could understand that. As I am an anarchist, you should know that the only thing I want the government to do is to disappear—certainly not to pass laws.

"We don't have 'real world news' here in America, so obviously the market doesn't want world news."

This is quite humorous. With this kind of logic, there would never have been any new products on the market in the history of mankind. Kind of sounds like what people said about the Wright Brothers: "If God wanted men to fly, He would have given us wings." How could you know that the market doesn't want something that is not available? I suppose we could take this logic to its extreme. For example (in 1970 or so, before cable TV), "There are already four free TV channels. Why would anyone want cable?" followed by, "There isn't any cable TV, so obviously the market doesn't want it." Laughable! This, too, is a bit embarrassing, no? And it's a good example of why Americans need to see themselves from the outside.

(On a side note: One of the purposes of showing news from different nations is that many Japanese, besides wanting to hear a different perspective, also want to study other countries' language. The news-casts are bilingual broadcasts, and just about every TV I have ever seen here had a bilingual switch on it. Since language is the key to understanding a different culture, anyone should know that to understand a different people's way of thinking, you need to understand their language.)

"I noticed you failed to mention anything about Japan's problems like teenage prostitutes or sexual deviants."

Well, I don't understand your point here, but yes, Japan does have teenage prostitutes and sexual deviants, just like America does.

"Why are the taxes in Japan so high?"

Taxes in Japan are much lower than those of the United States. Of course, Japan is not running a worldwide empire, nor does its government run nearly the budget deficit that the United States government does.

"Cutting back on the work the government has to do won't lower your taxes."

This is absurd. How about if we completely cut back on all work the government did? Do you think this would cause the government to cease to exist? I suppose it would. Why is it that village societies had no taxes? But let's imagine that you are correct; perhaps it won't lower your taxes, but working with your neighbors will build trust, understanding and friendships. It also cannot help but to keep the neighborhood safer and the local parks cleaner.

"Sure America is screwed up. There's no question about that. But don't think for a minute that Asia and Europe aren't much worse. You can just look at their standard of living to see that."

Who was talking about Asia and Europe? I thought we were talking Japan and the United States. But I'll play along: Yes, why don't we look at their standard of living? Have you ever been outside the United States? Yes, there are poor people in Asia. There are starving people in Asia. And guess what? There are poor and starving people in the United States. There are very few starving people in Japan, however; there are many more in the United States.

Currently, *the United States ranks 19 in longevity among industrialized nations, according to the WHO. Japan is first.*

If the Japanese are so poor and their standard of living so low, how do you reconcile the fact that Japan has the highest bank savings rate in the world, and the average life expectancy for a Japanese male is six years longer (women live seven years longer) than the average American's?

By the way, to compare Japan with all Asian nations is not only ignorant, but also points toward a white superiority complex. The Japanese, Chinese, Koreans, etc. may have different histories, but hell, they all look alike, right? May I lump together all Germans, Brits, French, Canadians, Australians and Americans, too? Hell, they all look alike.

The above paragraph just shows how ignorant some people are about Asia. Sure, the Japanese and Chinese have some common history and common characters in their alphabets, but don't the Germans, French, Italians, Spanish and Americans also? So may I use the same rationale and lump you all together? Of course not!

"Japan can have *Kumiai* (community) because Japan is a homogeneous society…the white population of America has *Kumiai*. But browns and blacks are marauders and cause the insecurity you write of. Libertarians always ignore the ethnic/racial factor—that is your right—but it is the critical issue, the root cause, if you will—of the problems in America today."

Another incorrect racist stereotype results when folks don't know the great differences between Chinese, Japanese, and Koreans. Well, I'm sure there are many

Japanese who would not agree with you on this point, as there are many Koreans and Chinese living in this country. I believe that the population of Japan is somewhat near 1 percent foreigners—mostly Korean, Chinese and Brazilian—but these numbers do not reflect the actual numbers of "Chinese" and "Koreans" in Japan. Consider that millions of Chinese and Koreans were brought to Japan as forced labor before the end of World War II, and most of them stayed and became Japanese citizens after the war. (Yes, many changed their names, just like many Germans did in America during and after World War I.) These "newcomers" to Japan have a shorter history than blacks do in America or Hispanics in the Western United States. It is impossible to know the exact numbers, but these "Chinese" and "Koreans" are now Japanese, even though many older Japanese would disagree, just as the blacks and Hispanics are Americans.

If you think America's problems are due to blacks and Hispanics, then all I can say is Caucasians should not have brought slaves from Africa, and the United States should not have invaded Mexico in 1840. You might say, "I didn't bring slaves over to America," and you are right, and a black person might say the same thing, but it happened. What are you going to do about it? We all have to do our best with the tools at hand.

You definitely will not have *Kumiai*, or friendly community relations with people, if before you even get to know them, you hate them because of the color of their skin, their religion, or their heritage.

Having a homogeneous society doesn't necessarily mean that a society will have more freedom. What about North Korea? Saudi Arabia? Albania?

Your problems are not due to other people. Your problems are due to you—and US government screw-ups. This "ethnic/racial factor" is just a lame excuse for you to not live up to your expectations. You think the government can wave a magic wand and all your problems will be solved, but that's where the problem lies—too many Americans want the government to control too much of their daily lives. And everyone should know by now that the government can't do anything right. It's too much government interference in the economy, which is causing these great demographic shifts in the first place. If people felt they had a chance to build a good life for themselves and their families at home, they wouldn't leave.

"You don't have a huge immigration problem in Japan like we do in America."

Once again, I'd like to point out that this "immigration problem" is due to US government interference in market/economic affairs. Let's take one example: the minimum wage laws. America has a socialist minimum wage system. Every small businessman, for example a restaurateur, scrapes by on every penny earned. If the government forces him to pay a minimum wage, then he is apt to hire people who will work for less than that wage, especially if business is bad. The people the restaurateur will hire are "illegals." The illegals are able to find employment, so they come.

If you think America has an immigrant "problem," then the minimum wage laws should be repealed. It would put a damper on immigration, and it might just teach American youth the value of a hard day's work.

There are no minimum wage laws in Japan, but in America you want to have your cake and eat it, too, so you have a minimum wage and the immigrants come. The government answer to this is more police and more stringent border patrols. In the end, it is just an endless cycle; more immigrants means more border controls, which means more police, which means more taxes, and that creates the so-called "immigrant problem." Many Americans think, "The government should do something about it!" But you see, the government *did* do something, and that is what created the problem.

Well, that just about wraps it up, but as an extra added feature, here's my own little list of my favorite freedoms here in Japan:

- Public smoking

- Public drinking

- Being drunk in public is not a crime

- Passengers (but not the driver) can drink alcohol in a moving vehicle

- No illegal search and seizure

Sure, these are small things, but small things add up to a lot.

Japan enjoys its freedoms because of what has happened in its history. None of us can change history. Twenty-five years ago I would not have claimed that Japan was a freer country than America, but I'm not talking about history now; I'm talking about today.

So you tell me, considering all the above, which country enjoys more personal freedoms today: Japan or the United States?

Case rests, your honor.

Heading for the Final Word on American Freedom?

The discussion of whether or not Japan is a freer country than America is on going. I have stated my case.

Here are readers' comments from America and around the globe. Is America the freest country in the world?

These are the best of the over 300 e-mails I received. Some are in agreement with me—some are not. I chose these because I felt they were part(s) of well thought-out, reasonable discourses.

I don't think anyone appreciates it when a disagreement breaks down into name—calling. Alas, this is one of the great problems, in my view, with American society today: Americans are quite rude and abusive in their language and tone of voice. It's also one of the reasons (I believe) why Fox News went out of business in Japan. I will explain later on in this book why Japanese people do not appreciate the sounds of people screaming.

I have stated names of writers and locations wherever possible. The jury is still out. Read for yourself what others think. Is Japan freer than today's America?

"I hate discussing freedom in America with someone who patently disbelieves and outright dismisses the possibility that any other country on the planet could possibly be freer than the US. It's infuriating. But, if it weren't so infuriating, we wouldn't have nearly as many people pissed off at our neo-fascist state of affairs and willing to work to foment change. Score one for liberty?"—Richard Dale Fitzgerald

"I am a born-and-raised USA citizen but I am not a fool who will become a victim of US public compulsory education which drills flawed information into children's minds, thinking USA is the greatest nation in the whole world. I read your two articles about Japan's freedoms and I have to agree with you that in practice, Japan does have greater degree of personal freedoms compared to US, while both nations on paper have nearly the same guaranteed freedoms.

"History says, that throughout time in a free society, people will eventually allow the few to take away their freedoms when the people do not take their liberties seriously. That what is happening to USA. People are losing the understanding of political freedoms and how freedoms are key to the prosperity of the republic. I read the italicized words on your second article and I have to laugh how some Americans think USA is the greatest nation in the term of political liberties. They need to have their eyes washed and see more clearly."—Charles

"Just one minor criticism—if you're going to quote Paine, quote him correctly:

"'Society is in every instance a blessing. Government is, in its best state, a necessary evil; in its worst state, an intolerable one.'—The Age of Reason

"I spent a fair amount of time in Yokosuka during my indentured servitude to the US Navy. Socially speaking, you may have a point about the superiority of Japan. I'm just too claustrophobic to ever live there again. Far too many people, far too little space. I like living where I can see a long way.

"I may have to explore becoming an expatriate. It looks to me as if this nation has gone to hell in a hand-basket and there seems to be no retrieving the situation. Besides, engineers like myself can make a living most anywhere—especially given that my Spanish isn't half bad. I see it pretty much the same way as Fred Reed—"I can obey or I can leave—I cannot like it." I'd like my anonymity and autonomy back."—Travis Hunt

"After reading your article and the last 5 of your favorite "freedoms": Public smoking; Public drinking; Being drunk in public is not a crime; Passengers can drink alcohol in a moving vehicle (but not the driver.)

"Hey, it sounds like France!

"I moved to California 5 years ago and I've always wondered why Americans use expressions like "best of the world," "biggest of the world," etc., when most don't even know the capital of Switzerland or Brazil!

"I was in the French Army for a short period of time and a friend of mine was in the 'intelligence' department (in French we say *renseignements*) and he told me that a quick rule of thumb to understanding a country's people was to look on a globe, at the center of that particular country, and check around it and look at what you see.

"If you apply this rule to the USA, what you see is…the USA. It's so big…American people see themselves as the center…. If you apply this rule to France, Switzerland, or even Spain what you see are the other countries of Europe…. European countries always look at each other…"—Antony

"What I find especially astounding, as a twenty-four year citizen of the US who was born and raised in Iran until the age of 12, is the near-absolute inability of most Americans to even imagine a possibly better (and especially freer) system that the current American one.

"I especially enjoyed the "voluntary socialism." I mean, the whole point about our dislike of socialism is the government-enforced aspect of it! Otherwise, people voluntarily getting together to clean or beautify their environment is the best kind of neighborliness I can think of. I have often thought that the crime problem in our inner-cities will not be significantly reduced until the citizens stop relying on the government or the police."—A F

"I find that some of the replies to your first "freedom" article were amusing. I didn't quite expect that sort of thing. Not being from Japan originally, you have a bit more of a perspective on that society and an arms length perspective of American society. I am not originally from America, but from Sweden. And I find that being able to step back a little bit provides a different viewpoint from those who have only lived in this country. Many people don't like others to have a different perspective."—R A in Arizona

"Many Americans are so silly in their myopic nationalism. I don't know how they can keep from being embarrassed while blatantly displaying their ignorance. As for Kumiai, I think it is a great concept and is totally compatible with liberty—you have to be foolish to think otherwise (I've always thought the evils of socialism were due to it's being run as a state-mandated system)."—Greg Puetz

"The way I look at it, different societies have different 'freedoms' and you may need to pick your society if your preferences are much different from the society you find yourself in.

"Some years ago my best friend decided that he could do without certain aspects of American style 'freedom' in exchange for the atmosphere he found in Canada.

"Conversely, several years ago we hosted a young Japanese woman for a year. She was working as a 'visiting' instructor in Japanese at the local high school. She and a number of her exchange friends clearly were in the US because they found Japanese society quite oppressive on a personal level.

"Interestingly, an older Japanese woman who had married and immigrated here many years ago predicted that the young lady would never return permanently to Japan. That has so far proven correct. She returned a year later to continue her studies at a local university, and is still in town.

"So, I guess you need to concentrate on the freedoms that mean most to you."—Christian C. Rix in 'Flyover' country. *(By the way, unfortunately for my friend, Christian, I found out later that this young lady Japanese lady returned to Japan to live.—Mike)*

"I live in Texas where population usually runs about 12 percent or less African origin with the rest split between Hispanic origin and European/Celtic/English origin. Some of us have morphed into Southern origin over the years since our defeat to Lincoln.

"At any rate, even with the communities split as the are, we seem to get along as school mates, soldiers, etc. The problem starts when people trying to gain power use the races as pawns; race baiting if you will. I had occasion to talk to Mr. Nelson Winbush of Florida over the phone one time—his comment was that "they will never allow us to get along". Mr Winbush and I have one thing in common—our great grandpas fought the Yankees. His ancestor was a Black Confederate and mine Welch. The "they" are the politicians and their minions in the press and in our education system.

"So, the fella that stated that libertarians overlook the race issue misses the point—the more government we have the worse the race issue becomes. I have been the only Celt ("white" some people call it) in all-Mexican construction crews where little English is spoken. I have served in US Army Reserve units with nearly all Hispanic rosters and have gotten along fine. Once the political season cranks up, then the tension begins to start.

"I think the bigger divider in the US is rural vs. urban. We in the less populated areas as a whole like our guns, our property rights, and like to drive 80 MPH on open roads. Our friends in the populated areas for the most part view gun owners as dangerous throwbacks to the "Wild West" and would like to use our property for their recreational purposes.

"I don't have a clue about Japan's freedom, and, with an old time Southerner attitude, I wish you all the best but Japan just "ain't" any of my business. But I will tell you, that from my boyhood in the 1950's until now, our freedoms in the US have decreased and fear of the law has increased."—G B

"Most Americans look at America-the-ideal rather than America-the-real. That might be normal, I don't know. I just wish they had a better sense of humor about the country, the politicians, etc."—T H

"I was very impressed on a visit to Wyoming of how community-oriented the people are. Most people I talked to volunteer in the community even as firefighters and paramedics. They are happy to do so rather than pay higher taxes. In many cases they refuse Federal funding because of course: He who pays the bills gets to make the rules.—Melissa

"The only freedom that we still enjoy (for how long?) over the Japanese is firearms ownership. Other than that, they definitely have us beat. I have been to Japan many times and I always enjoyed my visits. Everywhere I went the people were open, friendly and warm. They are great hosts and never made me feel like I was unwelcome or that they were putting up with me because they were told they had to by their boss. Every time I went I had a great time and I would like to go back one of these days."—Bill

"While you certainly bring up good points and I rarely refer to America as a "free country" other than out of habit, your case is not so ironclad as you wish to believe. While you may be able to get a higher count on the Japan column of a tally sheet in a discussion of who has more freedoms, I believe the nature of the question to be far too complex to be wrapped up in two relatively short columns.

"When considering the question of who is more free—a moot point really (in and of itself, though I do understand your point for purposes of this illustration), as America is not free enough, and I am not concerned with the level of freedom in Japan unless you have some examples of previously successful avenues to expand the same there—I think that some freedoms are more valuable than others, and should be weighted in the consideration of the question.

"I believe the ability to possess arms while not completely "free" in the US is paramount to liberty (freedom is granted by government, liberty by God; can't remember who said it) even though we don't have freedom here.

"For my tastes, Americans are not afraid enough of government in general. While it may be a long-shot, the people of the US would still have a shot (pun intended) against a tyrannical government (though when people would realize tyranny and consider it actionable is a true mystery). Without privately held arms, the government is as invincible as Godzilla. With them, there is a chance at liberty."—Jerry Allgood

"(My husband and I)...are both well traveled and have lived overseas in diverse countries for many years. My husband is a Brit. America has become so insular that the population (even the educated) makes wild assumptions that America has the highest living standard in the world—they are sadly mistaken and ill informed."—Jocelyn in Maui

"'2.1 million—719 out of every 100,000 Americans were behind bars in 2003.'

"Yeah, but the statistics purposely do not reflect the illegal aliens in US prisons which account for 1/3 of the prison total population (2.1 million seems low) and that 1/3 are Hispanic illegal!

"Kids in Japan don't get in as much trouble because of a cultural-sense of "non-state sponsored" community. 'Volunteer socialism' is not socialism, it is community!

"Carrying a stick on your person in the US is illegal...The police call it a concealed weapon.

"'Being drunk in public is not a crime'.... In the US my friend was arrested and jailed for public intoxication when the police saw him on the front porch of his house drinking alcohol from a bottle. They came onto his property said he was in public and a danger to himself and to others...I believe that he was totally drunk But in public? And on his own property?...And a danger?...I don't think so!

"While the interest rates have remained almost non-existent, it is Japan's taxes that has kept it in recession for more than ten years...It's also been happening in the US for ten years. The US spends more than it receives in taxes but taxes continue to increase due to welfare programs domestic and now, ever increasingly, abroad.

"Not enough press is given to US citizens who are starving in rural US areas.

"Race relations should be taught on an anthropological level not a cultural level. Cultural aspects should be taught in post graduate studies not undergraduate or high schools or elementary schools...etc.

"The "root cause" is the fact that the US constitution is skewed to further the fascists' cause in the US!"—Barry

"As for the earlier comments by readers in your article, I believe folks were confusing Japan with China, which doesn't surprise me since I find most Americans are incredibly ignorant on geography, world events, and their own constitution (thanks to our government indoctrination centers, a.k.a. public schools).

"In other comments, concerning the standard of living in Japan, it goes back to basic American arrogance and ignorance of the world. Again, they've bought into the mantra they are fed at school. A patriotic mish-mash of material that breeds nationalism, not patriotism.

"The US is no longer the republic our founding fathers started. It is more socialist than it is a free market society. It's 'bread and circuses' for the masses so they can't see their republic is an empire and it's going to hell.

"If you are happy in Japan, then I'm happy for you. I couldn't do it, but that's only because I love the South too much to leave it (unless someone discovers a new land mass where we could move and start all over again, like the early American settlers. But only as long as we don't have to kill off any current inhabitants.)"—Jeff Adams Humble, TX

"...it sounds like you've had to dodge a lot of knee jerk reactions...There are those who are still of the "America...love it or leave it mentality."

"I have spent a lot of time in the last year thoughtfully considering becoming an expatriate. I've come to the conclusion that the USA is too far gone to save, and sooner or later, the house of cards will fall. I have decided that Panama offers me, my family and my businesses, what we need. I can hardly believe that it has come to this, but I don't want to be in the US when things go to hell. We'll do great things in Panama.

"In my research, I surprisingly found lots of places that are more free than USA 2004. I'm glad for you and your family that you are not in the US."—R L

"I have lived in the United States for over 8 years (I was born and raised in Japan), but I have not even for a single second thought that America was better than Japan while I was over there. Every time I got off my airplane at Kansai International Airport, I felt like kissing the soil and screaming*tadaima*! (I'm home!) Although America has sunk into my blood as my second home, it's still my "second home," and my first home is still Japan."—G C

"Thank you for pointing out a truth that, I think, many Americans would not accept as true. And that truth is that "The Land of the Free" is more a line of propaganda than a true description of the US and that in comparison Japan offers a freer culture."—Todd

"Those of us that want world (foreign) news in the USA can get it. Some cable and satellite services offer foreign news services. I have watched CCTV, *Deutche Welle*, BBC, and many others. I can't always understand much, but I still watch sometimes. We can even pay extra to get *Al Jazeera*. I don't have it on my cable system, but I think they're occasionally on the International Channel (They broadcast an hour or so of programming from different foreign networks).

"I don't know if Japan or any other country is becoming more free, but the USA is definitely becoming *less* free. In the not too distant future the case can be made that many countries are freer than the USA. No one of any significant influence is doing anything to stop it.

"'None are more hopelessly enslaved than those who falsely believe they are free.'"—Goethe

—J D Hammond, Indiana

"Everybody claims to be for freedom. I love the people who claim to be Libertarians and pro-peace, but support the Iraq invasion. The world is crazy. Have you heard about my freedom project, the Freedom Summit? It seems like the type of event you would enjoy."—Marc J. Victor, Esq.

"I'm glad that you included the part about the US imprisoning the highest percentage of its citizens that any other county. To me, it's always seemed be a paradox that a nation that imprisons so many people can also claim to be the "Land of the Free." Then again, those words were written by Francis Scott Key in 1814…It probably WAS true then. Not anymore.

"Maybe a few more people will 'wake up and smell the coffee'!"

Government Expenditures and Taxes in Japan v. The United States

Taxation: government budget (per capita)

Rank	Country Budget	(per capita)
1	Vatican City	$19,045.05 per person
27	United States	$6,702.42 per person
52	Japan	$3,466.58 per person

Five Lowest Income Tax Rates Comparison of taxes in the 29 nations belonging to the Organization for Economic Cooperation and Development (OECD).

Single-Worker Average Tax Rate as a Percentage of the US-Equivalent Wage of $29,076.

Rank	Country	Rate
14	United States	18 percent
28	Japan	1 percent

Source: OECD report, Taxing Wages, 1998–1999

"Why does Japan have such a low income tax?!

"Of course, some would just argue that Japan benefits from lower defense cost, since the US bases forces in Japan to "provide" the military deterrent in the area. As I understand it, most Japanese would respond by asking the US to just leave."—Elvis

"Some of your more humorous stuff has been hit-or-miss for me in my readings of lewrockwell.com, but this one and the one leading to it were just very nicely done. Your more serious topics definitely come across better, in my opinion."—Glen *(Ouch!—Mike)*

"I live in Venezuela and it is infinitely freer than the US. Yes it has insecurity and poverty. However, there are no property taxes. There is no income tax. There is a sales tax and there are corporate taxes.

"You can run a red light if there is no oncoming traffic. Yes it is illegal, but commonplace. No seatbelt laws. No helmet laws. You can drink inside of a liquor store.

"The criminal code is a small, large-print book of about 100 pages. And on and on."—M T

"...it is natural to man to indulge in the illusion of hope. We are apt to shut our eyes to a painful truth." (1) I fear this quote is an accurate characterization of a vast majority of the American populace. How any man living and working in the United States of America can consider himself "free" is beyond my understanding. Free to do what? This is the first question I ask people when the topic arises. Without your government issued permit, license, registration, insurance, inspection and tax to name a few, you are not allowed to do anything, much less own anything. 40 percent of everything you earn is taken from you under the threat of prosecution and incarceration or worse, even if you have literally done nothing illegal, vis-a-vis Waco. The Constitution is a dead letter. The great Republic ceased to exist in 1865. "It is an established fact that the United States Federal Government has been dissolved by the Emergency Banking Act, March 9th, 1933, 48 Stat. 1 Public Law 890719, being bankrupt and insolvent." (2) Believe me I could go on for hours. The point being We the People are not "free" and have not been for a long time."
(1) Patrick Henry (2) James Traficant

"Liberty and Justice for all is dead—Long live Liberty and Justice for all."—B. Thair-Boortz

"We do a lot of things very well, and we do a lot of things miserably. But everyone complains incessantly no matter what.

"That's the part that kills me. We're burning up an incredibly disproportionate percentage of the world's resources and we can't stop complaining about the inconvenience of it all. The village I was staying at in Mexico had a well pump go out. A half a dozen people got together to fix the well, and everyone else went about making sure that the old and young had at least the basics for drinking water. And there was a lot of smiling and laughing. I came back to the states a month later and from the sound of it, the world had ended—postage stamps had gone up 2 cents!

"I'm not making that up. People were talking about the government getting their hands deeper and deeper into our pockets, and what a lazy bunch the postal workers were and ad nauseum. Genuine hardship had befallen this country!"—Dawson Barber, Great Lakes Science and Novelty (www.greatlakesscienceandnovelty.com)

"I've been in Japan for four months and after a week here I knew that I was more free here. Why? Because I felt so, that's why. I drank a beer on a train, built a fire down by the river without some cop arresting me, and then I smoked a cigarette anywhere I damn well pleased. Sure, we're talking about recreation here, but is there anything that I can't do here that I CAN do in America? I guess recycling laws are a problem, but who invented that damn recycling in the first place?! America can certainly be blamed for the drug laws here, although they aren't much more harsh in reality. Bars don't even have to close if they don't want to…and daylight savings time be damned!

"It's beautiful watching the US from the safety of a (more) free country."—Mike in Ise Japan

"I agree about the state of American society. It's been such a sad thing to watch. My grandparents are very patriotic and it can be frustrating at times. They're diehard Republicans and are 100 percent for the war in Iraq right now, which causes me a lot of grief when I visit them.

"Americans have gotten more and more dependent. It's really pathetic in a lot of ways. Parents can't be bothered to raise their children properly. Any misbehavior is blamed on ADD, violent games and TV, or "bad”" music like Eminem and Marilyn Manson. I work at a video game store in a mall, and it always amazes me to see how irresponsible parents are. I've had a person come in and complain because I sold a "teen rated" game to her 12 year old. She ignored the fact that her kid was unsupervised with over $50 in cash (and the fact that any parent that prevents their 12 year old from playing a game rated 13+ is going to raise a whiny child anyway.) And then there was the lady who was going to let her 8-year-old kid play Grand Theft Auto (kill people, steal cars, etc.) until she found out it had "bad language" in it, because in America it's WAY worse to call someone a profanity than it is to just kill them.

"Also, one thing I was very happy to see lacking in Japan (when I went there) was the ultra-patriotism. I didn't see a single Japanese flag bumper sticker, shirt, hat, cup, or anything else. I also didn't see Japanese flags hanging anywhere other than government buildings. It's beyond irritating to drive to work every day and see American flags on at least 50 percent of the cars, with such catchy slogans as "These colors don't run" and "Freedom has a price". *It's amazing how everyone in this country thinks that terrorists flew planes into the trade centers because they hate our freedom.* That's just such an utterly ridiculous concept I just don't grasp how so many people think that way."—Derek

"It's a marvelous time when Mexico belongs to the Mexicans…

"Even overhearing the conversations of the "Gringos" at nearby tables at a restaurant can cause one to want to leap to one's feet and scream: "Are you people totally blind and ignorant?" Fortunately for my wife and I, this is a tag team event. When I'm livid, she's calm—and vise versa. Or maybe I can hear them and she can't. Thus we continue drinking, and smoking (the incarnation of evil for most US tourists) and if you drink enough, why, you don't even know they're there. Often we will speak our poor but improving Spanish just to enforce the separation. I was appalled, but not surprised by the comments you received. Sadly, my bet is that all of your valid points concerning ignorance, hypocrisy, the lack of cultural interest or understanding, the lack of any desire to learn the language of the country one is visiting, along with the lack of any desire to meet the real people that ARE the true country that one is visiting, will all be lost to the fact that you dared to mention the acceptability of public smoking with a dash of drinking in a car."—an Embarrassed Gringo

"…you gave a very logical rebuttal to those who e-mailed you about American freedom, although they've never been outside of the USA. I am an immigrant from East Europe, and lived in 4 different countries, so I just laugh at American ignorance."—Peter

"My wife of 37 years is from the Philippines and I have lived in the Philippines for nearly 20 years of that time in various capacities including that of a private citizen for 13 years straight.

"I lived there during the martial law years of the Marcos administration and I experienced the revolution and the various coup d'etats and through it all I would say that, on a personal basis, I felt freer there than I do living here in the US. Not to say there aren't a lot of problems and a lot of some really bad stuff goes down, but overall, life goes on fairly comfortably.

"Americans in general are absolutely the most propagandized, self-righteous and sanctimonious group of people on the face of the earth (with exceptions of course). It seems they really believe that they and their way of life are superior to all others. They have no basis of comparison nor do they want any."—B E Bishop, California

"Of course, you do run into the instinct people have to defend their own things and relationships, no matter how awful they are. For example, you might complain about your mother-in-law, but when I join in and agree, you back off and defend her. Taken to a ridiculous extent, you get the 'my country, right or wrong' crowd. Still it should not be easy for anyone to argue the facts, but the average person believes that somehow America has a corner on the freedom market. Isn't that why the rest of the world hates us?"—Rodney Boyd, "The 21st Century Key to Health And Wealth"

"I am often challenged by the ridiculous argument, "We still have our freedom. If you don't like this country, why don't you leave!" As a writer, perhaps you might list the losses of "freedom" in a chronology through the 20th century and the latest losses in the 'war against drugs, terrorists, immigration, etc'".—P K Fort Wright, KY

"The *Kumiai* mentality would work, and in many cases does work, in small towns in the Midwest and New England, where they have generations of history."—John Young

"In fact, one of these days, when I have the time, I'm going to do a freedom comparison of my own between Vietnam and the US.

"Now before you form a conclusion, let me say that, "Oh, of course Vietnam does not have the freedoms that America has left."

"However, if we were to do a comparison with regards to "direction," it's going to be interesting. For example, what is the highest income tax rate in the US in comparison to Japan? (You never did mention a government stated rate and the real "rate"). Ditto on Vietnam—You know that evil communist, totalitarian place?

"It's illuminating actually when you do an "actual" comparison. And of course as a "guest" or ex-pat in Vietnam, what they (the government) does to me is quite a bit different than what they do to the average Vietnamese.

"The highest tax rate in Vietnam, sans deductions, is about 48 percent after reaching a certain level of income. That's NOT what anyone actually pays though. In fact if one has a discussion about this with a higher income level person in Vietnam and you tell him that the US government "gets" 28 percent after a certain point he will look at you in virtual shock and say, "that's too high!, I thought America was free!"—Tom Pilitowski, US Rare Coin Investments

"I was stationed on Okinawa with the Air Force in the early 90's and traveled through Japan quite extensively. I agree with everything you say. I lived off base and was amazed at how many American service families were scared to even leave the base in their three years on the island. I never locked my apartment when living there, and would often leave my keys in the car. The only time I ever had anything stolen was on base by Americans. A friend of mine once had his car stolen off base at a restaurant, and yes he did leave his keys in his car. However, later we found out it was a couple of teenage kids that had taken it for a joy ride. When they were done with it, they parked it in front of the gate to the base, had not removed anything, and even filled up the gas tank!

"My friends and I would often go camping around Okinawa. We could set up tents, build bonfires, swim out in the ocean and catch a few lobster, all without any restrictions, regulations or busybodies extorting us for money under the guise of 'needing a permit'. We always cleaned up our campsites before we left so that we could come back to it some time. Since I have been back in America I have longed for my days of freedom in Japan."—Hal C.

"'Passengers can drink alcohol in a moving vehicle (but not the driver.)' We can do this in Virginia. And what about owning a gun? Can you do that in Japan?

"Otherwise, I liked what you wrote. Americans think everyone else is a slave when we are the ones who are regulated, taxed and shoved around by government agents."—D F

"It has also been argued that the USA's 2nd Amendment has been rendered null and void in this century with things like multi-million dollar tanks, cruise missiles, attack helicopters, laser-guided bombs, and stealth combat drones. How much of a chance does a Black-Helicopter-fearing Montana resident with his shotgun and stores of grain have against Rumsfeld? Not very much would be my guess."—A Sake-drenched little bird that just flew by

"I enjoyed your article on Japanese freedom. In fact, I feel a need to print it out and go over it step by step, so as to know where I agree and where I disagree.

"I get the strong intuitive sense that you're not looking at the whole picture though. As I recall, the Japanese of, about 20 years ago used walk-mans to deaden their feelings, suicide rates were quite high, and they did not have the kind of alphabet we have, having hundreds of ideographs versus 26 letters.

"They were ritualistic to a high degree, with obligations going back to their ancestors of God knows how many years. I don't know how much of this goes on nowadays, but I suspect the picture has not changed dramatically since then.

"Anyway, I still loved the vigor of your thinking, even though I feel it's more than a little one-sided."—M (R)

"...based on the high level of militarism (falsely being called patriotism) among Americans, and the fact that the American people are required to support a global military empire, it is difficult to claim that the US is a freer place than Japan."—Mark Siano

Well, those were the letters that I felt were the most thoughtful and thorough. I'm sorry I couldn't include more; I still get some, even to this day. I would like to point out one obvious thing about these last few articles—that is, the debate they have stirred.

Think about it, America. If I would have made such a claim as "Japan is freer than America" a few decades ago, I would have been laughed at. Now, it seems that no one is laughing. No, the ones who got the most angry about my claim, I think, are the ones who most fear that this has, or soon will, become the truth. Instead of spending time arguing whether or not the fruit from this farm is more delicious than the fruit from another, shouldn't we, instead, be tending to the crops?

With so many thoughtful people writing in, I still think there's hope for America, and I want to continue the fight to make America free again. I mean, what other option do we really have?

When a conversation occurs that can even debate the notion that, "America may not be the freest country in the world," then America, you truly do have something to deeply consider—perhaps even to fear.

Summation on the View of America from Japan

Now that we may have a better understanding of how the United States looks from Japan, let's take a look at one of the big reasons that people around the world—not just in Japan—have lost much respect for the States and its people.

Probably the biggest reason for this loss of respect is that the Japanese hear much from American news sources that a great percentage of the American public actually supports attacks on other nations. This the Japanese find beyond comprehension.

Japan has been an empire and a nation for over 2,700 years. In that time, Japan had never once been defeated until World War II. They had defeated China (several times), the Mongols, Korea, and they shocked the entire world in 1904 and 1905 when they crushed both the Russian Pacific naval fleet and the Russian Atlantic naval fleet at the Battle of Tsushima Straits, as well as the Russian army. Defeating Russia finally put Japan on the world stage as one of the great military powers.

It must have come as quite a shock to the general Japanese populace to see airplanes bombing their cities in World War II. These attacks occurred, even though the Japanese mass media kept telling the public that Japan was winning the war. It must have been unfathomable to the Japanese, who like today's American believed that their military was unbeatable.

As an American, I see what the US mass media keeps telling the American public about what is going on, and I am appalled at the brazen lies that are being openly touted on American TV and radio today.

Many Americans think that most of the world's countries supported the invasion of Iraq. This is completely false. Even Japan, America's biggest ally in Asia, was against the invasion.

The average Japanese cannot understand what the American public is thinking about the wars in Iraq and Afghanistan. The people I talk to all ask the same question: "Why don't the Americans just get out of Iraq and leave those poor people alone?"

That's a very good question. Perhaps it could be answered by the fact that American cities have never been bombed, and America has never been occupied. The Japanese and their cities have, and they remember it quite well.

In these next few chapters, I'd like to give the reader a few examples—snapshots if you will—of how the Japanese view war, and their experiences with it. Through this, I hope that more Americans will understand the future that today's America is setting up for the children of the America of tomorrow.

Also, I hope that the reader would come to understand that things are not always what they seem. As Robert Heinlein said, "A generation which ignores history has no past and no future."

What is happening today in America, the Middle East, and Japan, has happened before. Sure, the places and dates are different, but the end result will be the same. Unless we can view it from a different perspective, a more objective viewpoint, we are doomed to repeat the same mistakes as those who came before us.

So just how do today's Japanese view war?

The Super Bowl and War Crimes Trials

After working in the mass media in one context or another for almost 30 years now, I can tell you that there is very little, or almost nothing, on TV that is not planned in advance. I'm even beginning to suspect that about all professional sports events, too. One of the biggest, most ridiculous scandals that hit America in 2004 was "Nipple-Gate"! Did Justin Timberlake and Janet Jackson conspire to rip off her top during the Super Bowl halftime show? And what did the execs at CBS know, and when did they know it?

There is no spontaneity anymore. Pssst! Don't tell anyone, but it was all planned.

While I'm on that subject, don't you find it odd that a team that was the door-mat of pro-football for 40 some years suddenly starts winning the Super Bowl when George W. Bush becomes president? And that that team's name just so happens to be "The Patriots"? Call me paranoid, but something just doesn't seem right there.

I'd also like to point out that in the 2002 Soccer World Cup that was co-hosted by Japan and Korea, both Japan's team and Korea's team made it into the final four. Neither team had ever even made it into the qualifying rounds before that (Final 16). The soccer world governing body is called "FIFA." FIFA is as cor-rupt as they come. Rocked by scandal after scandal, there was talk about FIFA collapsing before the 2002 World Cup.

FIFA needed money. How to get money? Well, they had to promote soccer in countries that had money. Those countries just so happened to be Japan, Korea, and the United States. The USA team, by the way, made it to the final four for the very first time in 1994—when the games were held in the United States. Funny, that.

France, who was well entrenched in FIFA and had won the World Cup four years before, were knocked out in the very first round and *failed to score a single goal in four games*. Germany, who will host the next World Cup, came in second in 1998. They made the final 16 in 2002. Give you one guess who is probably going to win the 2006 World Cup held in Germany in 2006.

The World Cup is a scam. The very first World Cup was held in Uruguay in 1934. Uruguay won.

In 1938, the World Cup was held in Italy. Mussolini wanted to win so badly that he hired the entire Argentine team, gave them Italian passports and made them Italian citizens. Guess who won the World Cup in 1938? Italy.

In 1958, the games were held in Sweden. Sweden made it to the final championship game, only to lose to Brazil. I don't believe that Sweden's team had ever made the final 16 before or since. Brazil was the dominant team in world soccer.

In 1966 England held the World Cup. Where was Brazil's team? I don't know, but England won the World Cup over an economically re-energized West Germany.

1970? Mexico. Hey! There's the Brazilians winning again. How about that? Who could have thunk it?

West Germany won in 1974. I'll give you one guess as to where the games were held.

1978? Argentina wins it all in Argentina. Amazing!

Well, I just use the World Cup as an example of just how corrupt professional sports are, but this isn't really about sports. It's about a different kind of "fixed" entertainment event.

No, I wanted to write about a minor story in the news that's probably buried on or about page 19 of your local newspaper. It's just after the section about cooking eggplant for that special someone and caring for your pet's teeth: the upcoming trial of Saddam Hussein.

Just like everything else nowadays, this whole thing will be fixed. There's no way the Sadster can get a fair trial, unless, of course, he has Bobby Donaldson from "The Practice" as his defense attorney. Nope, it's crying time for our former guy.

Besides all the other nonsense that will be going on with this charade, I'd like to point out a few observations I have made about a similar trial that happened about 60 years ago: The Tokyo War Crimes Trial.

I've come to think that that trial was, in many ways, a sham. I'm not saying that those Japanese military leaders were not bad guys and that they didn't do some very bad things. They certainly did. But they also did not get a fair trial.

Why? Lots of reasons. The biggest ones have to do with a cultural perspective. Here's an example. Long ago, I worked for the TV Asahi Broadcasting Network here in Tokyo. I could not speak Japanese that well at that time and I was placed as one of the younger creative staff for a new music program called "Music Station." (Unbelievably original name, eh?)

Anyhow, I was the token foreigner on the staff. TV Asahi wanted to make a very "Western-style music program," like MTV. The management figured if they had me on the team, they could get that debonair foreign flair that a well-dressed, worldly guy like me would bring.

We had our very first meeting. This wasn't my first experience with a Japanese-style business meeting, but it was the first time that I began to understand how they work—or don't work, depending on how you look at it. All of us went into a meeting room. We sat down for a while and talked. Some people talked about what kind of a show it was to be. Some talked about who should be the main personality. I mostly talked about what kind of music we should play. The big producer mostly talked about the weather in Taiwan and how popular Japanese cartoons were over there.

After about two hours, everyone grew quiet and we just sat there, for probably 15 minutes. Me, being a junior staff member, I thought it wasn't my place to say, "What's going on here?" So I, too, sat silently. Then the chief producer slapped his hands on the table and said, "Thanks for coming to the meeting. We'll meet again next week. Thank you." And everybody got up and walked out of the room!

I was dumbfounded. I asked one of the other junior staff, a Japanese guy who was fluent in English, what was decided at that meeting, and he just shrugged his shoulders and said, "I don't know."

A week later we met again. This time my jaw bounced off the table when they announced the make-up for the entire show! They told us the format, the style of music to be played—they even told us the name of the two main personalities. I asked my buddy again, when was all this decided? Had I missed a meeting?

He replied, "Who knows when this stuff is decided. Most things in Japan are not decided at meetings. They are decided after or between meetings as the boss talks with various people who attended the meetings. The meetings are kind of a 'show' in Japan."

That was it! No wonder! I have been to many meetings since then, and whenever the meetings end, I am always sitting there wondering, "What was this meeting all about? What was decided at this meeting?" And, "Why am I here?"

Now that I am older, if I am at a meeting, I always run the meetings and we always decide whatever it is that we met to decide. Before I adjourn the meeting, I double check to make sure the Japanese staff in attendance understands what it is that they are supposed to do. Otherwise, meetings with Japanese businessmen are just about always a huge waste of time, especially if the meeting is held in the Japanese language.

Every year around mid-August, on the anniversary of the ending of the war, Japanese TV will broadcast the Tokyo War Crimes Trial. Of course this show is edited, but still it runs about 10 hours straight, with no commercials.

I've watched it many times. Every time I watch it, I understand more and more of what the Japanese military leaders were saying. Since this is Japan, there are only subtitles for the English-speaking people, like the Australian judge of the war crimes trial, Mr. William Webb.

The Japanese guys have no subtitles, of course. That's why it has taken me a long time to understand what it is these people are saying. They speak a very old dialect of Japanese, and I have to hear it over and over before I can understand what is said.

There are two parts of the trial that especially stick out in my mind as examples where there was no way that the Japanese leaders could have gotten a fair trial; both had to do with culture. Since language is the key to culture, I believe that it is impossible for a non-Japanese-speaking person to preside over a fair trial concerning the actions of a person in this society.

At one point in the trial, the judge asks then Japanese Prime Minister Hideki Tojo something like, "On (such and such a date), you and the Japanese military high command held a meeting. Did you decide to invade China at that meeting?"

Tojo, who was a very intelligent man and could speak some English, tried to explain to the judge how meetings in Japan are conducted.

The judge interrupted him. "At that meeting, did you, or did you not, decide to invade China? Yes or no?"

"I'd like to explain," said the former Prime Minister.

Once again, the judge, quite perturbed, stopped him and ordered him to answer. "Yes? Or no? Mr. Tojo!"

This little exchange went on for a while and has stuck in my mind ever since I finally understood what it was that Tojo wanted to say. Finally, Tojo had to answer. "I cannot answer that question satisfactorily if you will not allow me to talk!"

Somewhere around this time in the trial, Tojo stopped answering questions at all. He probably figured that the judge was not interested in communicating with him.

This prompted the prosecuting attorney to point out to the judge that this was proof that Mr. Tojo was indeed completely corrupt and had absolutely no sense of remorse and deserved the death penalty, as he was nothing short of a mass murderer!

I thought, "Here's a Japanese guy who has been raised and conditioned by the strict rules of Japanese society for 65-some years, and this foreign judge thinks that he can just throw away all that conditioning just because he's been talking to that judge for 30 minutes. Absurd!"

There was one more thing that Tojo said that has left an impression upon me. This will be difficult for people who haven't studied enough history to understand, but if you realize that Japan is a country over 2,700 years old, and in that period Japan was almost always at a state of war with someone, this might make sense to you. It never made sense to me before. I still don't condone it, but I can understand how some people would think this way. Tojo said, "Japan is an imperial nation. And as is the case of all imperial nations, whether they be British, French, German, Russian, or American, it was my duty to my country as prime minister to keep that empire healthy and to make it grow." (I'm paraphrasing here.) Kind of sounds like some big company CEO!

That was the way people thought many years ago. Hopefully, human society has gotten wiser and this idea of empire building is past. But, I fear, with the actions of the United States recently—hell, since 1840—that it has not.

I know Hideki Tojo is probably responsible for war crimes. I know he bears responsibility as a Head of State. But I also know that this was not a fair trial. This was a case of "victor's justice," and a very shaky, poor, and inadequate exercise in international law.

And guess what? When Saddam Hussein goes to trial, we will have not learned a single lesson from it. And you'd think that, if anyone could, Americans would be the most sympathetic to the trials and tribulations of someone who was trying to build an empire.

Why? Because no country has ever been better at building an empire than the United States has.

"The United States of America. Established in 1776...and still growing."

War Insanity, a View from Japan

One of the most well known early TV dramas in Japan was a show called "I Want to be a Clam."

The show first aired in 1959 and was the story of a small-town barber named Shimizu, who was forced into military service in World War II.

During the war, Shimizu was a lowly private, guarding American POWs. One day his commanding officer ordered him to kill a particularly troublesome prisoner. Shimizu reluctantly followed orders and murdered the American soldier.

I am not making excuses for Shimizu's actions, but in this case, had he not followed orders he would have been executed himself. That's the way Imperial Japan was.

Such is the insanity that war brings.

When the war ended, Shimizu went back home, but soon thereafter he was arrested by American MPs and sent to the Tokyo War Crimes Tribunal and sentenced to death by hanging.

In the final scene from the drama, Shimizu walks up 13 steps towards the gallows and says, *Heitai ni torareru koto mo nai. So da, watashi wa kai ni naritai*—"If I were a clam, I wouldn't have to be a soldier."

Much like French, Japanese is a very romantic language. In Japanese, the above statement sounds like poetry; it is full of double entendre. It could also be translated to mean "If I were a clam, I would be under the ocean, where there is no war." Or "If I were a clam, I could say nothing."

This drama carried a serious anti-war message, but it also brought up several complaints from the Japanese that, over these years, I have come to agree with.

How could the USA and England try and execute low-ranking soldiers when high-ranking Allied commanders were guilty of much worse war crimes and were deemed not guilty? How could the Atomic bombing and murder of 200,000 people at Hiroshima and Nagasaki not be called a "war crime"? How about the firebombing of Tokyo that killed 140,000 civilians in one night? How about the daily bombing raids on homes, residential areas, civilian-use railroads and trains during the war?

None of these places were military targets. Perhaps someday the history books will call these crimes what they really were—genocide.

Until then, we have to live with what Garry Wills said. "Only the winners decide what were war crimes."

Now America grapples with the daily incessant news and stark reality of "war crimes" committed by US forces and their mercenaries: the torturing of prisoners in Iraq, Afghanistan, and, of course, Guantanamo. That is not to mention the bombing and killing of old men, women, and children everywhere in Iraq and Afghanistan. Someone must take responsibility. Americans are shocked and upset.

Strange, though, all the Japanese people to whom I've talked are not surprised that this ordeal of torture and war crimes were delivered by the hands of Americans. No, I haven't met one Japanese person who was surprised. They had all seen it before—from both sides.

The more-than two dozen Japanese I asked all said the same thing. "War makes people do crazy things."

Perhaps Japanese people think this way because they have seen war up close. Most Americans haven't.

If those Iraqis who were tortured and forced to watch as well as perform sex acts were religious people, they probably thought that they had landed in Dante's Inferno. And I read that 50 percent of all Americans claim to be Christian. Hypocrites!

Steven Weinberg said, "With or without religion, you would have good people doing good things and evil people doing evil things. But for good people to do evil things, that takes religion." I wonder what that says about American people who claim to be Christian, all the while being pro-war?

George W. Bush says, "This is not the America I know."

Now we have some low-ranking MPs and soldiers who will have to be penalized somehow, but, as usual, the guys at the top get away. Just like in the story about Shimizu. But that's not the problem viewed from over here, America.

Sure, some very ill American soldiers were caught on film, torturing Iraqis. Sure, there are thousands of other, even more horrendous photos that we will probably never see, and many more acts that were never recorded on film, but the prevailing opinion from this side of the Pacific is that the real responsibility for this entire mess lies far above people like these lowly soldiers.

Sure, those soldiers are sick and they need serious psychological help. Sure, their lives are ruined. So are the lives of untold numbers of Iraqis, Afghanis, and yes, Americans, too.

War is madness. War makes people do insane things.

So are these people who committed these war crimes counter to the Geneva Convention relative to the Treatment of Prisoners of War *worse* than the people at the top who started this war who are in violation of the Nuremburg Tribunal, article 6(a), namely: planning, preparing, initiating or waging a war of aggression, or a war in violation of international treaties, agreements or assurances? I don't think so. It's not even a comparable crime. It's like comparing apples and oranges.

It seems like common sense, to me, that the people who created this deranged war are by far the most guilty parties concerning crimes against peace and crimes against humanity. In turn, *all* who supported or did not speak out against this revolting, perverted war from the start are accessories to mass murder. But, don't worry. It's small potatoes, America. When you are constantly waging war, you can always plead insanity.

Sir Isaac Newton and the
Coming Invasion of Iran

Near my apartment, a man by the name of Faramarz runs his business. Faramarz is a nice, friendly guy—one of the nicest guys you could ever hope to meet. Faramarz has been in Japan for over 22 years. He is one of the few foreigners I have met who has been here longer than I have.

Faramarz

Faramarz is married to a Japanese woman, and his business sells exquisite, handmade Persian Carpets. These are some of the largest and most beautiful carpets I've ever seen. They are the kind of things you would see on the floor of a palace or the office of the CEO of some huge Japanese company. I imagine that carpets like these grace the floors of places like Buckingham Palace or the Imperial Palace. Faramarz's handmade carpets are as beautiful and detailed as any you will ever see.

Faramarz has two employees, Ramin and Aribizu. These guys impress me a lot. They are very friendly and intelligent. They can each speak more than three languages, and their English is superb. It's amazing that they come from what many of us in the West would consider a "backward, third-world country."

Aribizu and Ramin

Every person I have ever met from their country has been extremely intelligent, and proficient in several languages. One of my best friends in college was from the same place, and he could speak English, French, Russian, and *Farsi*. *Farsi*, as some of you may know, is the native language of people from Persia—or what we now call Iran.

Last night, Faramarz invited me over to sit and chat in his office for a few minutes. It was fun. Faramarz and his two employees had a wager on a sale they were working on. The sale didn't go through; Faramarz lost the bet, so he had to buy ice cream for everyone. I thought, "What a bunch of sincere, easy-going, peaceful people."

Faramarz and I started to discuss world events, and I spent my time trying to explain the thinking of my countrymen. Faramarz and his friends all seemed to feel sorry for me. Well, not for me exactly, but for you, me, all of us whom we call "Americans."

You see, this kind of thinking I have found quite common over these last few years when I meet people from other countries (and I meet quite a lot due to my job). It all boils down to this: "Everyone all over the world likes American people. We just hate your government."

In the last year I have met people from Bulgaria, Romania, China, Thailand, Korea, Australia, England, Scotland, New Zealand, France, Afghanistan, and Kenya, and they have all said basically the same thing: people everywhere are beginning to despise the United States.

The talk then went into the Chinese concept of "Yin and Yang." Faramarz explained to me that what is going on in the Middle East all fits in perfectly with the concept of Yin and Yang. In Japan, this concept is described as "Dark versus Light."

I was a bit surprised to hear Faramarz explain his take on this concept to me. I would expect to hear something like this from someone from China or Korea, but someone from Iran? Then again, when you realize that the Middle East has always been the road to the Far East, it shouldn't be too surprising to hear them speaking of a philosophy that mirrors Eastern Asian thought.

Simply put, Yin and Yang represent the balance of everything in the world: dark and light, good and evil, you and me.

Yang is the spirit of "light." He has the side of good and light—us and everything else that is not dark. Yin is, of course, the complete opposite. Yin is the "dark" part of the spirit—evil and darkness. Defeat is on his side of the balance.

In this Eastern philosophy, balance is everything. If something falls, something else must come back. That means that if one manages to become the most powerful, the entire universe will be out of balance. So if Yang won, everything in the world would be happy, but not for long, for the balance would be upset. For as long as Yang is in power, the reverse effect must come into play, and Yin will dominate after that for an equal or longer period of time until the cycle reverses itself again.

Of course many Westerners might just chuckle at this silly "Eastern" notion, but last night it dawned on me. I realized that this concept of "Yin and Yang" is exactly the same as in Sir Isaac Newton's Third Law of Motion, called "Principia Mathematica Philosophiae Naturalis," published in 1686. Isaac Newton stated, "...that for every action (force) there is an equal and opposite reaction."

All actions are "forces," so this indisputable law says every force has an equal and opposite force. For every action, there is a reaction. For every behavior, there is a consequence. Like the rock thrown into the pond, the ripples radiate out, eventually hitting the shore, and then again returning to its center. For every act, there is a consequence.

One might take issue with my interpretation of how Yin and Yang and Newton's Third Law of Motion are, ultimately, the exact same thing, but I think anyone can see where there is a correlation. Furthermore, could any educated person in the entire Western world argue with Newton's Third Law of Motion? I don't think so. Agreed? Whether you want to call it Yin and Yang or Newton's Law, it is an undeniable fact that every action has an equal reaction.

That's why now I'd like to tell you folks a little more about Persia (Iran). Did you know that Persia is one of the oldest civilizations in the world, and that Persia was once one of the largest empires the world had ever seen? Did you know that, even though Persia has lost battles, arguably, it has never been completely conquered and held under complete occupation in over 3,000 years? Did you know that Iran has more than three times the population of Iraq, and 63 percent of that population is under 30 years old? Did you also know that, geographically speaking, Iran is more than four times larger than Iraq? Did you know that Iran's economy was more than twelve times the size of Iraq's, as of 2003? Did you also know that, although no one is sure of the total casualties during the Iran-Iraq war of 1979 to 1988, estimates range from 800,000 to 1 million dead, at least 2 million wounded, and more than 80,000 taken prisoner? That there were approximately 2.5 million who became refugees and whose cities were destroyed? That the financial cost is estimated at a minimum of $200 billion dollars (in 1980 dollar amounts)? And even though, according to some estimates, Iran lost about one million soldiers, it was still *not* defeated by Iraq, which had massive US and British backing?

Of course, you do know that now the Bush administration and the neo-cons are setting America up for a war with Iran. Right?

With George W. Bush as president, go ahead, America, attack Iran. But, as sure as the sun will rise tomorrow, you *will* be forced to pay the piper. And it will, most certainly, be a catastrophically heavy price.

Please don't send me e-mail arguing with me about this observation. Argue instead with Yin and Yang—or, better yet, argue with Isaac Newton's Third Law of Motion, "…for every action (force) there is an equal and opposite reaction."

2003 Facts on Iran: http://www.cia.gov/cia/publications/factbook/geos/ir.html
2003 Facts on Iraq: http://www.cia.gov/cia/publications/factbook/geos/iz.html

Becoming a Kamikaze for the State

There's been lots of talk recently about America reinstating the military draft in order to shore up its over-stretched military. I don't think we need more people in uniform. We just need no more wars and no overseas bases. How's that for an original idea?

Of course, with the talk of the Selective Service there's also talk of "How to run away from the draft."

During the Vietnam War, I know that thousands of American youth took off to Canada and elsewhere. I would have done the same.

I remember watching the war on the news when I was a kid and seeing helicopters drop off soldiers who were being shot at. Some of the soldiers fell. Everyone ran. It was chaos. I don't ever remember seeing "the Enemy." Those scenes terrified me. My mom, being Japanese and having her entire family killed in World War II, not to mention being married to a Marine who was training guys to get killed in Vietnam, would have approved of my taking flight to another country to avoid going to war.

I already mentioned that since war is insane, it makes people do insane things.

My mom told me that during World War II, when she was an elementary school girl living in southern Japan, that army soldiers would visit her school and teach all the little girls how to use a sharpened bamboo pole in order to kill American invaders. She told me the soldiers would tell the little girls, "You are going to die, but you are going to kill one American before you do."

Can you imagine? A bunch of little 7- to 10-year-old girls standing on some beach as the US Marines land and these little Japanese girls trying to stab the Marines to death with bamboo sticks? And the Marines mowing down these little girls with machineguns? If this isn't total insanity, I don't know what is!

Americans can run away to a neighboring country, but Japan is an island. I wondered how the Japanese "escaped" from the war. Surely there were those who did. How did they do it?

I have heard stories about young Japanese men drinking entire bottles of Soy Sauce for days on end in order to destroy their health and be deemed "unacceptable, due to health reasons."

I heard that if you drank an entire bottle of Soy Sauce, if it didn't kill you, the salt and ingredients—straight, just like that—would cause you to become violently ill and vomit. If this were continued for a period of time the person would have a serious weight drop and become deathly ill.

I had also heard that, towards the end of the war, Japan was so short of supplies that the Soy Sauce was so watered down that this method was no longer effective. Unbelievable! Those guys couldn't even kill themselves quietly to avoid the war.

I talked to my wife's grandfather, who is now 92 years old, and got some ideas of how the Japanese of his generation perceived this problem. He served in the Imperial Navy and is a very intelligent man and became a well-respected university professor and writer after the war. Probably, because of this, he is very careful to choose his words.

It's difficult to explain what he said, because even more than today, Japanese people of his generation do not say things directly. I have to admit, I had to hand the phone to my wife and then have her talk to him. I am not completely able to read into his words what he means, but I'll try as best I can to relate to you what he said.:

> "I cannot speak for anyone except myself. I did not want to go to the war [he never said this exactly, but he meant it]. But, at that time, no one in Japan could say such a thing. The government told the people, and the people believed that 'the war is for the good of the country, so it is for the good of all.' The public mood was such that it would have been quite shameful and 'anti-patriotic' for anyone to say anything different. There must have been many who did not want to fight. Just as there were many who did want to fight. Those who wanted to fight wanted to do so for the glory of their country and for their families' honor. In war, a man can kill in order to gain social status. The more he kills, the higher his social status will become. No one could possibly say plainly, "I do not want to fight." That would have brought much shame to that person's family. There must have been many who wanted to run away; there must have been some who did. But it was never spoken about. Even after all these years to say that 'So-and-so ran away from the military,' would be to bring disgrace upon that family, even if that person is no longer living. So this is a very difficult subject for me (our culture) to discuss. So I cannot help you, Mike, with the information about the Soy Sauce that you want."

"All I will say is that 'War is inhuman. Therefore, the only ones who wish to be associated with it cannot be human at heart.'"—*Shigeo Numata*

Young boys getting ready for Kamikaze missions.
When others are dying around them, could they say, "No!"?
And, ultimately, what was it all for?

My grandfather and I said, "Good-bye," and we hung up the phone.

"Gee, Grandpa. All I wanted to know about was the Soy Sauce," I thought.

But then, I thought about it; he's right. Think about it. Do not let something as ridiculous as "the mood of the country" or "what others say" force you to throw your life away. It's not worth it.

If there is a Selective Service, don't sign up for it. If you are called, don't go. Do whatever you can; run away; get sick, drink Soy Sauce. Do whatever it takes, but do not join the military. Do not go to war.

Due to social pressures, your mother or father may not be able to say it, but I'll bet there are lots of people (including them) who would rather have you around—even if it's in another country—than to be visiting your grave or wheeling you around in a wheelchair in ten years just because our federal government tells us, and we believe that "The war is for the good of the country, so it is for the good of all."

When you really stop to think about this notion, it is completely crazy. How could killing and being killed be good for anyone?

Hell, rather than go fight and die in another country, I'd rather go live in one. I also know that living in another country is not so bad. In fact, I like it. I've liked everywhere I've lived...

And isn't that all a part of being a human? Living with people and liking where you live?

"What if they had a war and no one came?"

(For more expert information on avoiding the military draft, see "How To Stay Out of the Military," a primer on draft resistance by David Wiggins: http://www.lewrockwell.com/orig4/wiggins5.html)

Chicken-Hawk Down

"Artificial intelligence is no match for natural stupidity." ~ *Unknown*

One of the things that Japanese people find so curious about America and Americans is the perception that Americans are very gung-ho for war. There were constant news reports—before the invasion of Iraq—from the US mass media that claimed that 98 percent of all Americans supported; or that even after these disastrous last two years, 50 percent of all Americans still believe that attacking Iraq was the right thing to do.

Japanese people are dumb-founded by this type of thinking. I gave a speech at one of the top universities in Tokyo at the start of 2005, and a student and a professor came up to me after the speech and asked me, "Are Americans really that dumb? Why?"

I told them that all Americans are not that way, but the trend is quite worrisome. Americans have never experienced the horror of seeing planes bombing their own houses. Of course the Japanese have. And there are still many who quite vividly remember it.

I'm sure there must be some Japanese who are extremely right wing, but I've never met one. I have never met a pro-war Japanese, but I have met many pro-war Americans. Funny thing is, I have never met a pro-war American who was a combat veteran, and I have never met a pro-war American who had family in the military.

Chicken-Hawk Down is the true story of two modern day gung-ho armchair American generals who are sent to cyberspace on a critical mission to capture the hearts and minds of intelligent book-reading people. When their mission goes terribly wrong, due to incompetence and forged papers as well as a lack of knowledge of their own troops in the field, the men find themselves outnumbered and illiterally fighting for their lives, credibility, and stock-folios.

These are the true adventures of those two great armchair commandos. Two brave men who, even though they had never met before, find their lives intertwined in a mutual case of ignorance, braggadocio, and fibs, in a vain attempt to cover their asses and continue with their daily facade of intelligence.

I know about this story because I was there. It isn't pretty, but then again, when is war ever pretty?

The initial invasion attempt

It was a bright, sunny morning. Commando Rich had been drinking coffee and watching too much TV, as usual, in his suburban American apartment. He was restless. He would have to wait for hours before Commander Drugged Limbaugh would come over the airwaves, cheering the troops to fight on and to give guys like Commando Rich their reasons for living, as well as their American History lessons, for they certainly didn't learn any in school.

Things looked bad in Iraq. Fallujah was being blasted to the ground all the time other cities in Iraq were falling to the insurgents. As with any guerilla war, the enemy had melted away before the invading American forces. Commando Rich, who had gotten his war training through reading Sgt. Rock comics in his youth, had a burning desire to support the troops. But how? He could go down to the Army Recruiting station and sign up, but that would be dangerous and risky. Not only would he lose his job as a short-order cook, he might wind up actually getting shot at himself! And actually, he didn't really want to *personally* go into Iraq; it was much more of a fulfilling and vicarious thrill watching people get killed on TV, and he sunburned so easily with his delicate and sensitive skin. No, going to Iraq and actually fighting was out of the question.

"It's hot over there, and besides, I'm the best omelet maker at the Bun & Breakfast. Who could possibly take over? Who could possibly make a better breakfast than me?" he pontificated in his mind. "No! Joining the military was out; I have other, more important, priorities."

Commando Rich leapt to attention. Suddenly, General Idea came into the room. It wasn't a particularly good general idea, but it was the best Commando Rich could do with the tools at hand: a PC, some cool soldier photos, and no girlfriend to keep his miniscule upper-works occupied.

Commando Rich set off on a cyberspace propaganda mission that he was sure would turn the tide of the war toward the Americans favor. He created a mass e-mail that had a photo of an American Army soldier who, on his sleeve, had insignias that said, "(USA) Doing the work of…" And was followed by three decals of French, German, and Russian flags. The script read:

> *Look at the black patch under the US flag—you gotta love them and their humor. This **should** be on the front cover of Time, Newsweek, etc. But it won't be. Let's you and me 'put it there' by forwarding this all around the world (so to speak)! (The flags are France, Germany, and Russia—in case you don't know.)*

Commando Rich figured that he had to explain to his dim American compatriots what countries those flags came from. He was an expert—an old pro. Rich figured that if even he didn't know what those flags looked like, if he had to look them up, the receivers of his e-mail certainly wouldn't know what they were. Here is where Commando Rich's Psy-ops training from the Sgt. Rock manuals came in handy.

As sweat poured down Commando Rich's face, he gritted his teeth and kept hammering away at the keyboard. Altering photos to look real was no easy task, and Rich knew that. Soon Rich became famished; he had been working on altering the photo for several hours now. The apartment was hot. It must have been 80, maybe 82 degrees in that room. Commando Rich thought, *Well, if the boys in Iraq can take it, so can I.*

Even so, he knew he'd need his energy for the night shift at the Bun & Breakfast later that same evening. He popped a couple of "C" rations (chicken pot pies) into the oven range.

Forty more minutes! he thought. *Forty more minutes until I can take a much needed break from the front lines and chow down.* He wiped the sweat from his brow. He opened the fridge and pulled the pin on a Diet Coke and took a few big swigs. He wiped his mouth with his shirtsleeve and swaggered back to the computer.

After several more attempts at making the photo look like the real thing, Rich had to call it a day. Besides, the bell on the oven range had rung over 10 minutes before, and it was just about time for Commander Drugged Limbaugh to come over the air, exhorting the troops to fight on. Rich hurriedly sent his propaganda bomb into cyberspace.

He clicked the "enter" button and put both fingers in his ears and shouted, "Fire in the hole!" The mail was now blasted into cyberspace.

He was satisfied with a job well-done, two overcooked chicken pot-pies, and a Diet Coke.

The plan unfolds

Meanwhile, on the other side of cyberspace, General Bob had received the propaganda mail. He, too, was a crusty old veteran of watching other people's wars on TV. He was a supposedly well-educated person, and yet he was a hardened *modern day* American patriot through and through.

When General Bob received the message, he knew exactly what to do, for he was a member of a "patriot cell" operating on the West Coast of the United States, he sent the mail out for his contacts to disseminate.

"Humph! That'll fix them!" General Bob twittered. He tuned into Commander Limbaugh, all the while watching *Temptation Island*, with both hands down the front of his pants and the TV volume turned down.

Japan enters the fray

When the photo came up on my surveillance computer, I knew that the dorks were up to no good again. I sent a short reply that said, "Yeah, and 1,545 (and counting) US Dead and over 21,000 US Troops wounded & crippled for life; they and their wives and children must be laughing their asses off." (http://antiwar.com/casualties/)

After dealing with fools my entire life, I always try to keep in mind an ancient Chinese saying: "The only one to argue with a fool is a bigger fool."

So I left it at that, or so I thought. The e-mails began going back and forth between other people at a furious pace, each side struggling to get an upper hand. I attempted to stay out of the fray, but was dragged into the fighting as the e-mails kept getting forwarded to me. *Why* is anyone's guess.

But as any intelligent person knows, you can't argue rationally with a Chicken-Hawk; they will keep changing their stories. Perhaps it is due to too much television; perhaps it's due to Attention Deficit Disorder; perhaps it's just plain stupidity. But, hell, I'm not a medic, how should I know? All I knew is that there were two Chicken-Hawks invading my world, and I was beginning to get pissed off.

First off, I proved that the photo was a fake. I referred all of the guilty parties to a copy of the Army Regulation 670-1 concerning uniforms and insignia. Of course, anyone with any common sense, military experience, or even a basic knowledge of military history would know that such insignias are a sign of disrespect to the uniform. But these weren't people with any common sense or any of these other vital points of interest; these were Chicken-Hawks!

General Bob meets heavy resistance and takes return fire

Upon being blasted by another person, General Bob wrote "Oh My God, you are blind! The footage in Fallujah shows us cleaning out scumbags. And how can you even talk about France in anything but utter disgust?" He then went on to add, "I sent you that photo because I am proud of our soldiers."

Hmmm? He says he is proud of our soldiers, yet he sends around a photo disgracing their uniforms? Typical, twisted logic of a Chicken-Hawk, I thought.

General Bob also wrote, "Check your history and tell me when France last won a war. If we aren't involved, they get their assed kicked. If we weren't involved in saving their quiche-eating asses in WWII, they'd be speaking German now."

The past comes back to haunt General Bob

General Bob's lack of manners, as well as his poor knowledge of history, especially American history, really irked me, as he, in typical armchair General fashion, acts like he knows what he is talking about—but he doesn't. Slagging off the French after they helped save the United States from the British at least twice, I could not hold my fire any longer. That was it for me.

I knew what I had to do. I had two big juicy Chicken-Hawks in my sights; I had several batteries of SAM missiles loaded up and ready to go. First up, General Bob had to go down in flames. I hit him with everything I had. I wrote:

"In 1974, General Bob was an honor student in high school. I believe he was captain of the swimming team (anyway, he was one of the top guys on a very powerful squad). He was a straight 'A' student and honors all the way.

"Every year, the President of the United States appoints two students per year per state to go to the United States Military Academy at West Point. (I reckon that means nominees could go for free to get a university education at a very respected school.) Richard Nixon was president of the United States at the time, and we were out of Vietnam by then. One of the two people nominated from California to attend West Point was—you guessed it—General Bob!

"General Bob's father was an ex-career Marine, and he was ecstatic! His mother, having lived in a country that was heavily bombed in World War II, didn't like the idea at all. Also, one of his mother's best friend's husband had gotten killed in Vietnam.

"Anyway, our own gung-ho General Bob gets appointed by the president of the United States to go to West Point. To hear General Bob today, you'd think he would have jumped at the chance to go! But, nope, he didn't go.

"General Bob and his father had several massive fights about West Point. Of course General Bob's father wanted him to go; he was a marine. General Bob's mother was a bit negative-ambivalent. But good old gung-ho General Bob—the guy who we all hear cheering the troops on—was dead-set against it. I clearly remember one night when General Bob and his father were fighting about it, and General Bob said, "There is no way that I'm going to put on a uniform and go and kill people."

"Ultimately, after many fights, his father gave up and General Bob went to some hippie university on the West Coast.

"Now, to hear General Bob talk today, you'd think that he would have volunteered for military service, never mind the West Point nomination, but he didn't go. Heck, just like all these other big-talking Chicken-Hawks, if they really wanted to support the troops they'd go and sign up today. But they don't, because it's all just that: "big-talk" from people who are full of shit.

"General Bob is a war hypocrite; a 'Chicken-Hawk.'"

It was a direct hit! General Bob went down in flames! I'm sure he has lost respect among his group of Chicken-Hawk friends. They'll never let him forget this. Why? Well, of course it is a characteristic of Chicken-Hawks to always try to divert attention away from their own disgraceful shirking of duty and big-mouths. So now General Bob will be on the receiving end of their boots. What a shame!

I find it appalling and quite disturbing that General Bob would be so "rah-rah" about war—any war. After hearing this incredible true story about him, you might feel the same as I do. But is it really his fault for not having a basic grasp of American history or current events? Is it this poor man's fault for being so igno-rant and blind and getting his information solely from stupid morons like Com-mander Drugged Limbaugh? Shouldn't I be more kind and forgiving to this poor man? Shouldn't I show more compassion? Nope. No way! Not when the USA is bombing and killing children in other countries for no good reason, and guys like General Bob call those kids "scumbags" and support their killing.

He deserves what he gets.

Commando Rich falls into the trap

Not being a person who likes to leave any job undone, I began my own little Psy-ops operation onto the creator of this insolent "joke." I noticed an e-mail address on the bottom right hand corner of the photo of the soldier and "borrowed" a name and rank and wrote:

This is a degrading slap to the men and women in uniform. I demand that you cease immediately the dissemination of this photo. This is a God-damned dis-grace."

Blake Rogers
Sergeant, "A" Company, 1st Battalion, 7th Marines
Korea 1951–1952

To which Commando Rich responded:

Get a life. It's an editorial composite that was created for an international mag-azine.

Sheesh.

Regards,

Rich

P.S. You shouldn't use the Lord's name in vain; it doesn't make you more of a man and it offends people.

"Aha!" I thought. "I have already caught Chicken-Hawk Commando Rich in a lie…That was fast!" In Rich's first piece of propaganda he writes,

"This SHOULD be on the front cover of Time, Newsweek, etc. But it won't be. Let's you and I 'put it there' by forwarding this all around the world (so to speak)!"

Now he says, "It's an editorial composite that was created for an international magazine." Oh really? Gee, does it sound like someone is lying to cover his ass?

Commando Rich Goes Down in Flames

After receiving Rich's reply, I wrote and told him that I worked in the mass media and was located in Japan. I requested that he tell me the name of the inter-national magazine because I didn't believe him and I wanted to check his story—easy to do. I also told him that if he ignored my request or didn't write an explanation or apology and launch it into cyberspace to all of the usual suspects, I was going to write this—let's call it "a little promotional exposure" for Com-mando Rich and his activities—so any time you see from now on any sort of photo like doctored US soldier photo in this chapter, you'll know it is a fake. And you know now that Commando Rich is, well, not a truthful person.

Commando Rich doesn't want to write back to me anymore. Gee, do you think he is a Chicken-Hawk?

I guess there's no doubt about it. And that's what's wrong with the modern-day American Chicken-Hawk: they all talk a big game, but when it comes right down to it, they have no guts, and they lie. And they'll keep lying to you, telling you that they are not lying, just like 10-year-old little boys, because that is the psychological level these people are at. Kind of like his lying fat assed teacher Drugged Limbaugh or President George W. Bush—chronic, habitual liars. I suppose they can both be forgiven, though. Of course they are liars; they both have a drug abuse problem.

Does Commando Rich deserve our contempt? Yes. He's a pathetic little worm.

The Chicken-Hawk Down Epilogue

What is the point of this entire story, you may ask? Well, that's where I show you my easy plan to eliminate Chicken-Hawks everywhere. That's right. Do you realize that if all these gung-ho Chicken-Hawks had a back-bone instead of a jaw bone, we probably could have had sufficient troops in Iraq and Afghanistan today and had those countries free and on the road to democracy and prosperity a long time ago! Yep! (Well, at least according to Chicken-Hawk logic).

So all you pro-war people are now called Chicken-Hawk unless you have served in the military. You may avoid being called this by joining right now or by forcing your 18-year-old sons and daughters to join the military. I know the Army would just *love* to have your children, probably just as much as you Chicken-Hawks would love to kill rag-heads, scumbags, and camel-jockeys. So you join, or send your kids, and everyone's happy! No more name calling—no more lack of troops. A free Iraq! A free Afghanistan! *You or your kids get killed*, but you can be happy! You can be proud! No problem! No more evil! We're there.

I do have better things to do than argue with ill-informed, supposedly educated people who are painfully ignorant on the topic that leads to their own uncouth, boisterous behavior. So sign up for the military today! But until you do sign up, please don't send me your ignorant pro-war Chicken-Hawk e-mails; I don't want them.

Besides, I already eat chickens for dinner.

Notes on Chicken-Hawk Down: Many people have written to me and asked me how I know so much about General Bob's history. Well, you see, General Bob is a close member of my family. After I wrote that message about his disgraceful actions and avoiding West Point—all the while being so hypocritically gung-ho for war today—he wrote me an angry message that said, "You are an asshole. I'm just enjoying some 'ribbing' with some friends and you have to take things personally. Why do you always have to take these things so personally?"

Besides being a self-righteous dim-wit, he was furious. One of his other friends wrote and told me that he was getting ready to volunteer to go to Iraq. Bet you a donut he still hasn't. General Bob got angry at me, and we haven't spoken to each other since.

He's mad because I exposed him for being a war-mongering hypocrite. He wonders why I take "it" so personally.

For myself, I wonder how any true American—the supposed flag-bearers of justice and freedom for the world—could *not* take what is going on personally. A true American patriot would dedicate their life to the truth first and the flag second. America cannot have its freedom protected if the flag comes before the truth and justice.

Why do I take it so personally?

How could anyone who *really* loves their country not take it extremely personally when their country is committing mass murder on innocent people and children and committing war crimes?

My brother may have gone over to the wrong side with the idiots and killers. I cannot stop him, but I'll be damned if I will lose my country without a fight.

I ask you a question: Do *you* take your country murdering innocent children personally?

When Animals Attack

"Our country is now geared to an arms economy bred in an artificially induced psychosis of war hysteria and an incessant propaganda of fear."—*General Douglas MacArthur*

War is and always will be the result of hysteria. This hysteria infiltrates the very fiber of society and causes a sort of mass hallucination. America is experiencing it now. Japan has experienced it before. How about World War II? How about when many countries seemed to be on a bad-acid trip at the same time?

Documents recently revealed to a reporter show a clandestine effort on the part of all combatants in World War II to make every attempt to win the war, with the help of pigeons.

Formerly labeled as "Top Secret," recently released documents from the British War Office and MI-14 show that efforts to stop Nazi pigeons from passing British war secrets was such a wide concern among senior British officers that even wartime Prime Minister Winston Churchill authorized Herculean government funding for an anti-pigeon defense force called "The Pigeon Committee."

While the British were secretly developing their own pigeon forces in order to spy on German troop movements, this effort often met with failure, as English-speaking pigeons were unable to pass on important intelligence to their French-speaking pigeon underground resistance counterparts, and vice-versa. While the French birds did speak Pidgin English, that was still incomprehensible to the Brit birds who were hampered by having brains the size of a half a peanut.

In order to shoot down Nazi pigeons, Churchill authorized a huge ultra-secret government-spending program on training British "Falcon" and "Hawk" class feathered vertebrates. It is unclear to this reporter, at this time, exactly how successful this program actually was, but it seems certain that this effort was much more successful than using conventional anti-aircraft fire to down the Nazi birds.

Fighter falcon squads were stationed near the Cliffs of Dover, under the command of RAF Wing-commander Sir George Williams. Hawk units were usually stationed on the Isle of Lucy.

By the summer of 1940, Jerry's vaunted "blitzkrieg" had smashed French resistance and Paris was in Nazi hands. But with the help of the Royal RAF Carrier Pigeon 3rd Brigade, the British expeditionary force was able to escape the Nazi claws at Dunkirk. 8th Army General Barnyard Montgomery posthumously awarded the queen's highest honor to a French pigeon named Cher Ami.

On the other side of the world, Tojo's henchmen got a nasty surprise when British birds showed their mettle and may have been instrumental in General Mountbatten's defeat of the Japanese army in Burma.

When the war ended, the British War Command continued research into RAF pigeon strategic war planning by investigating how our fowl friends could be used to deliver devastating blows to the Red Army and "change aerial warfare forever."

Documents that have now been released to the National Archives reveal that the War Office intelligence section MI14 warned, "Pigeon research will not stand still; if we do not experiment, other powers will." (http://news.bbc.co.uk/2/hi/uk_news/3732755.stm)

Several ideas tossed around by the top tossers in MI-14 were "borrowed" from the Imperial Japanese Air-force "Kamikaze" squadrons. One plan called for equipment and training for an entire 1000-bird squadron of pigeons to carry 2-ounce explosive charges and to suicide-bomb a selected enemy target. This plan fared poorly, as after just one practice session, the pigeons were usually nowhere to be found. And thus, training was terminated.

But the MI-14 were not to be discouraged so simply. Another plan called for pigeons to dive-bomb and suicide-charge into enemy searchlights, thereby clearing the way for Allied bombers to hit their targets.

British soldier experimenting with a kitty-piloted artillery shell

Funding for this plan ran into trouble as another top secret RAF section involving moths for the same purpose of blocking enemy anti-aircraft spotlights demanded all the funding for their project, thereby deadlocking the war office as to which project deserved the money and the blessing of the queen.

With the Cold War growing more and more tense by the day, the British decided to expend massive amounts of money in research and development on a pigeon project whereby the birds would be used to deliver bacterial agents and nerve gas on enemy targets. However, the internal security service MI5 branded the commander of this air unit, Wing Commander WDL Rayner, a "menace in pigeon affairs," and he was summarily dismissed.

In related news, it was also revealed from the British National War Archives that post-war plans for a "chicken-warmed" nuclear landmine that was planned for use in Germany to halt any Soviet advance had been shelved. The plan called "Operation Blue Peacock" was hatched in the early 1960s. (http:// news.bbc.co.uk/1/hi/uk/3588465.stm)

The plan called for a live chicken to be placed inside a two-ton nuclear device that would be buried under the ground, and the heat of the chicken's body would keep the warhead hot enough to avoid a misfire.

As the U.K. could no longer afford a large military force, rumor had it that these plans—as well as other details of top secret military projects—had been handed over to the Pentagon as the United States military had the funding, White House backing, and American public support for such projects.

Unnamed Pentagon sources said that the US military had been looking into ways to counter the Iraq insurgency's terrorist donkey carts.

One possible idea was to have pigeons carrying 2-ounce mini-nukes suicide-bomb all donkey-carrying carts in Iraq and other Middle-Eastern countries.

Several doves and pigeons in the local park were questioned by this reporter, but he was unable to get any comment—official or otherwise.

(Pretty funny? Yeah? Unfortunately this is a true story…Think about it.)

Vietnam, Iraq, the Dishes, and Vacuuming: A Household Analogy

Of course, looking back on the Vietnam War, it was obvious that the United States could have never won that war. Not in 10 years. Not in 50 years. Not in 100 years.

Now-a-days, many pundits compare Vietnam and Iraq and claim that the US government is missing out on all the lessons that we should have learned 40 years ago. The problem with this kind of comparison is that the people running our government have never been in the military, so they cannot relate to any knowledgeable person's experiences. Hell, we all know the closest George W. Bush ever got to really playing army was going to the department store to buy a really neat-o flight jacket with cool patches on the sleeves and stuff.

The opposite side of the argument says that Iraq and Vietnam cannot be compared to each other.

I am not going to argue either side in this article. I am here merely to state the results of my scientific studies and how, over these last several months, no matter how many times the experiment was repeated, the results have remained the same.

I will set out to explain in incredibly simple terms—terms that anybody can understand—the reasons why we lost the war in Vietnam, and why we can never win in Iraq.

My explanation holds up to the scientific method, in that it can be reproduced at any household, anywhere in the world, and the results will remain the same—no matter the season of the year, time of the day, or the location. Anyone can repeat my experiments, and the results will be consistent.

This explanation is going to be so simple that even George W. Bush can understand it. And believe me, I am not mis-underestimating him here.

Let me start out by giving you my daily schedule: I usually wake up by 5 a.m. everyday. I make some coffee and do some "work" work. The "work" work is my duty as part of a living organism in a consumer society. If I don't do it, I don't get any money, and if I don't get any money, I don't eat.

Besides "work" work, I also must complete some "house" work. My "house" work duties require that before my wife wakes up I wash the dishes, vacuum the living room, and scrub the bathroom. After my wife wakes up, I vacuum the hallway and bedrooms.

This hypothesis shall consider vacuuming the living room, washing the dishes, and scrubbing the bathroom as analogous for The Vietnam War. Vacuuming the hallway and bedrooms shall be synonymous with the war in Iraq. The vacuuming of the living room will be the quashing of the dirty communist insurgency; the dishes and the bathroom will be the "winning hearts and minds" part.

Since I had to do the vacuuming, I went out and bought one of those new high-tech vacuum cleaners called "Cyclone." Let me tell you, this baby really sucks! Bad joke, but right on the money. The "Cyclone" is the newest super-powerful vacuuming device that has come out in Japan. I was told by the salesman that the "Cyclone" is "the most powerful vacuum cleaner in the world!" Japanese manufacturers always use Japan as a testing ground for new appliances that will go on sale in the United States and foreign markets later on. If it's a hit in Japan, it's a pretty safe bet that it's going to be a hit in America.

Keeping with our scientific model, we shall now consider our super-duper high-tech vacuum as analogous with an American-made Apache attack helicopter, which was used in Iraq. Or in the case of the living room (Vietnam), it will be switched to low-power mode, thereby replicating a 60's model Huey attack helicopter.

The dirt and dust in the living room are Vietcong that have to be rooted out.

Cleaning the enemy out of their dirty hideouts in the nooks and crannies of my living space is an everyday job. At first light, I flick on the power switch and my high tech gadgetry goes into attack mode. It's really cool! Kinda like that movie "Apocalypse Now," where Robert Duvall plays Wagner's "Ride of the Valkryes," as the US helicopters go in to blast out those dirty V.C.!

But damn! War is hell! Everyday I go in there, blasting the hell outta them with the high tech stuff, and the next day they come back, just like cockroaches! It never ends. And since I have to do it every day, day after day, I have come to realize, though personal experience, that the Vietnam war was indeed unwinnable. No matter how much firepower I bring to bear, the communist dirt returns to their hideouts the next morning! It's like they actually *live* there!

How many days more will this carnage go on? How much longer will this senseless cleaning go on? How did I ever get myself into this kind of no-win situation in the first place? An even more pressing question is, how do I get out of this?

Winning hearts and minds is also a "damned if I do—and damned if I don't" prospect.

To save time and effort, I usually take a shower or bath first, and then I clean the bathtub area. I figure it is more efficient that way. What with water bills, gas, and electric bills, it's just logistically better to bathe before securing the bath area. If I scrub the enemy grime from the bathroom early in the morning, my daughters get pissed off because they are in a hurry for school and want to use the shower. They tell me that I'm interfering with their plans. Never mind that I am also busy trying to keep them away from each other's throats as they struggle with each other over control of vital power supplies for use with hair drying devices! It's very much like the Shiites and Sunnis in Iraq.

It's the same thing if I am blasting out remnants of old food and hostile bacteria from the dishes in the kitchen sink! The kids will say they want to eat something before school! They tell me to get out of the kitchen! They tell me that I'm in the way! Don't they understand that I am cleaning the kitchen and bathroom for them? Don't they understand that I am washing the dishes for their happiness? Don't they understand that I care? Don't they see that I just want to help them? Don't they realize that this is a life or death struggle?

No they don't. They just want me to give them money and they just want me outta there…fast!

If I get outta the way and don't finish my tasks, then when my wife wakes up she'll be pissed off and severely reprimand me that the room is a mess.

So you can see, by the results of my scientific experiment in the living room; the bathroom; and the kitchen, that the Vietnam War was indeed unwinnable from the start.

I have learned my lesson. Sure, I am a good soldier and will do my commander's (my wife's) bidding. But I won't like it. And I now know how futile it really is.

I'm not as dumb as these people we have running the US federal government. I have the experience. I have the knowledge. I know the area like the back of my hand. So don't even get me started on the filthy Iraqi insurgency in the hallway and the bedrooms. I can't win. I don't even want to think about it.

Sure, this model is simple, yet very precise. It is so crystal clear that even a small child can understand it. And that, my friends, is where I have also come to realize the really tragic part of all this.

Even this simple model, I fear, is too complicated for our commander-in-chief. You know, George W. Bush has probably never washed a dish or vacuumed a room in his entire life.

Who knows when was the last time he took a bath.

Summation of How the Japanese View War

In August of 2004, I went to see the Hiroshima Dome. The dome is the site that stills stands today at what was the epicenter of the atomic bomb blast. It is quite a surreal place. It doesn't look as if it is of this world. I felt like I was looking at a prop for some kind of horror movie set. The walls that are still standing and the frame of the dome are stark reminder of the ultimate weapon of instant genocide.

There are places on the ground where the sand had been turned to glass due to the immense heat. The grounds are surrounded by a fence, because with time and weather the structure continues, to this day, its unrelenting decay.

It is a ghost house. A visitor can hear screaming when viewing the building. It is a place that can make one feel physically ill upon looking at it. The Japanese who live there seem to want to ignore it, but they can't. The Hiroshima Dome seeps into every person's thoughts, and I, for one, cannot erase the image out of my head. I'm sure many Japanese people feel the same.

I have asked many Americans if they would take up arms to protect America in a war. I have met many who have made statements like, "If America were invaded, I'd get my gun and fight." When I would pose the same question to a young Japanese, I would be surprised to hear, "If we were invaded, I would put my hands up and not fight."

Could this be a part of the modern-day Japanese psyche left over from the war and having two atomic bombs dropped on civilians cities? Could it also be a part of Buddhist philosophy that teaches "All things will pass."

That Japan is such an ancient country and has such a very long history, it doesn't surprise me anymore that young Japanese think this way. Perhaps this type of thinking is truly the key towards world peace: no fighting.

The United States has not fought a war to protect America since the 1800s. Americans today need to study their history and to learn just how they have been tricked into believing that what goes on in Europe or Asia or the Middle East affects them. It doesn't.

The Japanese today know the way to peace and prosperity, and that means to have a good economy and to trade freely with every country. In this way, and in only this way, war can be avoided.

Take World War I, for instance. What difference did it make to Americans whether a Kaiser or a king was running nations in Europe? None. It's just that France and England had borrowed too much money from US banks that the banks pressured the US government to get America involved in the "War to end all wars." And the American public bought into it, hook, line, and sinker.

America's involvement in World War I indirectly led to the rise of Nazi Germany, and Japan (who had been our ally in World War I) was now our enemy. Because of Pearl Harbor? No. Because Japanese imperial interests were beginning to conflict with US imperial interests in China and the rest of Asia.

The American public was sold on a war against a madman, and they bought into it—hook, line, and sinker.

Today we have Saddam Hussein and Osama Bin Laden—madmen who, we're told, want to destroy our civilization. Guess what? The American public has bought into it again, hook, line, and sinker.

My grandfather summed it up best. "War is an in-human activity, so the only ones who wish to be associated with it must be inhuman at heart."

The Japanese have learned their lesson. What will it take for Americans to learn theirs?

And now comes the fun part of this book. These are the stories of various true experiences I have had in Japan. I have met many unusual characters in this place. I have met people that would be impossible to meet face-to-face in the west. I've drank with many world famous rock musicians, was buddy-buddy with George Herbert Walker Bush for a day; and have done things in Japan that would be unimaginable in the west. These are my recollections of some of those events. (By the way, if you want to read about George H.W. Bush selling Amway in Japan, go here: http://www.lewrockwell.com/orig4/rogers2.html)

Perhaps after reading this, you'll agree that I have met some very unique people and had some unbelievable experiences. I hope you laugh. I also hope you don't think that the weirdest person in Japan must be yours truly…I mean, come one, there has to be *at least* one more.

America's Field of Dreams

"The one constant through all the years…has been baseball. America has rolled by like an army of steamrollers. It's been erased like a blackboard, rebuilt, and erased again. But baseball has marked the time…. This game is a part of our past…. It reminds us of all that once was good, and that could be again."—*Field of Dreams*

I went to my favorite Italian restaurant for lunch a while back. I go there quite often; the food is great, it's cheap, and the atmosphere is relaxed. They also have one of those large screen TVs that must be five feet across. They use it sometimes to show sports events like the Olympics or American professional baseball.

The big topic in Japan right now is the Seattle Mariners right fielder, Ichiro Suzuki. In the summer of 2004, the Japanese people were are all concerned and wondering if Ichiro would break the American baseball single-season base-hit record. Ultimately, Ichiro broke the record by five or six hits. But I was absolutely sure he would when the season still had 14 games left. Why?

It's because of the way Americans think when it comes to baseball. This is one beautiful part of America and American society that, I feel, must be recaptured in all aspects of American life in order to straighten out the societal problems in today's United States.

Baseball is supposed to be fun. I like to believe that life is supposed to be fun, too.

I watched the game on the big screen and was impressed by how the fans gave Ichiro his reception every time he came to bat.

You know, if that situation were the other way around—with a foreign player in Japan—the foreign player might not get the chance to break the record held by a Japanese player. Herein lies the basic reason why Japanese baseball will never become competitive on a world level with American baseball.

A lot of it has to do with the fans; a lot of it has to do with American and Japanese culture.

On the American baseball diamond, everyone is considered an equal, whether you come from Japan, Taiwan, Cuba, Mexico, Australia, the United States, or wherever. Whether you are black, brown, red, white, or yellow, when you get on that playing field, no one cares where you are from, they only care about whether or not you can perform. That's the beautiful part of the "American Way."

I don't believe that this kind of open-minded thinking exists in any other field when it comes to how Americans perceive people from other countries. I get the impression, in the fields of politics and the military, Americans think, "If you don't like our way, we'll bomb you!"

This kind of thinking and these kinds of actions are definitely not good ways to make friends.

When Ichiro comes up to bat, do you think American pitchers disrespect him and think, "I'm going to strike out this slant-eyed S.O.B!" Of course not! I would imagine that the pitcher thinks, "Oh, Lordy, I've got problems here."

And that's that. Strike Ichiro out! Feel good! He gets a base hit and the pitcher thinks, *Dammit! He did it to me again!*

Professional baseball players are professionals because they act like professionals and show each other mutual respect. That is a heck of a lot more than I can say for the way many Americans treat each other in public, or many Americans' attitudes towards foreigners.

Of course in Japan, too, there is racism. There are ill-educated, xenophobic people in all corners of the globe. Japan has them; America is no different. But one would hope that America, billed as the "land of the free," would, and should, be more open to ideas from foreign lands.

In 1995, Japanese baseball star Hideo Nomo became only the second Japanese ever to pitch in the major leagues. His debut with the Los Angeles Dodgers was closely watched by fans in both the US and Japan. Before Nomo went to America, he pitched with a team named the *Kintetsu Buffaloes*. When he announced that he was going to America to play, he became the target of much derision from the Japanese mass media.

"How dare such a pompous young fool think he could make it in the American big league?" was the talk among sports columnists and fans alike. Nomo was hated in Japan at that time. I was rooting for him to succeed. That was, I thought, the only way Japanese baseball could begin to reform itself and throw off the rules, which remain to this day—the rules that cause Japanese baseball to be second-rate.

Nomo was named the National League Rookie of the Year in 1995, and he threw a no-hitter against the Colorado Rockies on September 17th, 1996. Nomo also grew famous for his unorthodox "tornado" delivery, twisting his body around with his hands held high before each pitch. On April 4th, 2001, he threw another no-hitter, this time while pitching for the Boston Red Sox. The feat made him only the fourth pitcher to throw a no-hitter in both the American and National leagues, along with Cy Young, Jim Bunning and Nolan Ryan.

Nomo became a star in America and only then did the Japanese press hail Hideo Nomo as a super-star. Because of this, he became very popular in Japan.

In many ways, in Nomo's case, the Japanese were like children. I've heard it said before that people don't like it when their friends try to succeed. Hideo Nomo succeeded in America, and then became accepted in Japan. All Japanese people have an "American Dream."

Now we have Ichiro Suzuki. Suzuki plays for the Seattle Mariners. Long a superstar in Japan, where he played for the *Orix Blue Wave*, Suzuki moved to the American major leagues for the 2001 season. That made Suzuki and New York Mets outfielder Tsuyoshi Shinjo (where is he now?) the first non-pitching Japanese to play in the American major leagues since the 1960s, sparking intense interest in both the US and Japan.

In an era of power hitters, Ichiro stands out for how he controls the game by excelling in virtually every area except home-run hitting. He uses a unique batting style that allows him to hit the ball while he is running.

Once on base, he is a threat to steal. Ichiro was one of the best hitters in Japan. His first professional batting coach told him that he'd never make it unless he changed his batting stance, but Ichiro proved that coach wrong. Upon deciding to leave Japan, once again many Japanese sports writers and critics attacked him as "lacking the power and size to make it in the big leagues." But once again, Ichiro has proven them wrong. In his first season in America, Ichiro batted a whopping .350 and led the Mariners to a record 116 wins, winning the Players' Choice, MVP and Rookie of the Year Awards in the process.

He went on to break the single season hit mark set by George Sisler with the St. Louis Browns, way back in 1920.

Here is where American baseball, American fans, and America excel. While my Japanese friends here are all wringing their hands, wondering if Ichiro would break the record, I laughed and told them that he most certainly would.

Americans have a big heart when it comes to sports. In many ways, the Japanese do not. The thinking is completely different. If there were a foreigner in Japan, that player would probably not be allowed to break the record. In America, the pitcher who throws the pitch that Ichiro hits to break an 84-year-old record will forever have his name added to the history books. In fact, a big league pitcher would probably want to be the one to throw that pitch.

I doubt that a Japanese pitcher would do so, and that is why I—and a lot of other people in Japan—have lost interest in Japanese baseball. Let me explain:

In Japan, the fans' favorite team is the *Yomiuri (Tokyo) Giants*.

Some of you folks may have heard of a home-run hitter named Sadaharu Oh. Oh wore uniform #1 for the Giants, played first base, and batted left-handed. Oh's father was Chinese, and his mother Japanese.

In 1964, Oh set a Japanese record for 55 home runs in a single season. That record has held until this very day, but it shouldn't have. It should have been broken by a foreign player named Randy Bass.

Randy Bass started his career in the American big leagues with the Minnesota Twins. He played several years for the San Diego Padres, until he wound up on the Texas Rangers, and then moved to Japan.

Randy played six years for the Osaka team known as the *Hanshin Tigers*. In 1985, he stood at 54 home runs for the season, with four games left to play. I believe he probably would have set a new homerun record. But this is Japan, not the United States.

Like I said, an American pitcher would most probably want to have thrown the ball that hurled Randy Bass into the record books, and with it the pitcher himself, but not a Japanese pitcher, and especially not a pitcher for the *Yomiuri Giants*.

In the final three game Tigers vs. Giants series, Randy Bass was intentionally walked every time he came up to bat. I was disgusted, and so was every other pure baseball fan in Japan at that time. One time Bass came to bat and he was holding the wrong end of the bat at the plate. They *still* walked him! This one episode led me to the point where I now have absolutely no respect for Japanese baseball. This incident is just one little microcosm as to why Japanese baseball is, and always will be, second-rate.

By the way, guess who was the Tokyo Giants' manager that season and during that series? Why, none other than Mr. Sadaharu Oh himself!

In the eyes of the world, America has lost much of its shine these last few years. I know it. You probably fear or suspect it. As for me, looking from the outside in, I can tell that it seems that many Americans are living in fear and confusion; many hold a sort of self-righteousness that has made America the scorn of many formerly close and friendly nations.

Like any type of relationship between people, it takes years to build trust; it takes but just one action to destroy that trust. I fear the trust that people around the world have had for Americans has been destroyed over these last 3 years. That is why you folks live in fear. Why should anyone trust you more than you trust them?

The people I live with, the Japanese, seem to still feel warmth for Americans, but they are deeply concerned. It's much like the worry a person has when they see their friend destroying themselves with self-destructive behavior like drinking too much or abusing drugs. It's also a sort of resignation; you want to help, but if your friend won't listen, what can you do?

That is why, when I see Ichiro come to bat, even if he is not playing at home, Americans stand proudly and give him a standing ovation. It is a showing of pride and respect. Ichiro shows his respect back by playing the hardest and best he possibly can. This happens regularly, day after day, on America's field of dreams.

American basketball, football, and especially baseball have done more for creating a positive image of Americans for people around the world than the US government could ever do with hundreds and hundreds of trillions of dollars in aid, not to mention the damage to America's image done by the current US administration waging its wars.

You see, America, you can have the peace, respect, and love you so desire if only you'd all play with mutual respect on the "field of dreams" in your daily lives. If you do, you will be reminded of all that once was good, and all that could be good once again.

The Poor Gerber Baby in Japan:—The Murder of an American Icon

It's almost too much to bear. These days, some of the most disgusting news originates from the United States. Again, I heard some of the most revolting news I have heard in a long time. The only thing that was not shocking to me was that the news came from America.

My wife wanted me to go to the store to buy some Gerber baby food for my kid. She especially wanted the prunes. I guess my kid had been constipated and the Gerber strained prunes worked the best for unclogging the kid's plumbing. She told me that she had been everywhere, and no one was selling it anymore.

Nonsense! I thought. I grabbed my backpack and walked twenty minutes to the nearest super drug chain store around. They didn't have it.

I went to another large chain drug store, *Seijo*. They didn't have it.

Finally, I went to *Higuchi Drug Store*. *Higuchi* is a little more expensive, but they specialize in baby goods. *Higuchi* always has everything. I walked to the baby food section and, sure enough, no Gerber strained prunes. I asked one of the store clerks about it and she called the store manager. I asked about the prunes and he told me, "We are no longer going to sell any Gerber baby food. Once our stock is gone, that's it." There were only about 8 jars left of whatever Gerber food was on the shelf. I bought them all. I threw them into my basket and stared at the rows of empty shelves that all said "Gerber this" or "Gerber that." The shelves were empty, white, and lonely. The most famous baby food company in the world, and they had no products on the shelf of one of the biggest drug stores in Japan.

The Gerber baby had been killed. It was the murder of an American icon. The murder of a defenseless baby. You and I—everyone—knew this baby. We grew up with this child. My children grew up with this child, and so did yours.

Long ago, many people thought that this baby grew up to be Humphrey Bogart or Elizabeth Taylor, but this baby's name was actually Ann Turner Cook.

The Gerber story began in the late 1920s. It was an American success story. Dorothy Gerber had been straining solid food into baby food for her 7-month-old daughter.

Dorothy's husband worked at a canning company called Fremont Canning. One night, after work, he came home, and like a good husband and father, helped his wife to strain food for their child.

Later they both had an idea that straining the food would be much easier and much more efficient at the canning factory. After a few tries, strained peas, prunes, and carrots were canned and ready for sale.

As Paul Harvey would say, "And now you know the rest of the story."

And now this baby is dead.

And why? Because some nutcase in America was putting notes in baby food jars saying the food was "tainted." What kind of a monster would even consider harming an innocent baby? Luckily, all of the children whose parents unknowingly fed them the tainted baby food are safe. Whether this was just a prank, or some kind of effort to extort money, there is something terribly morbid and grotesque about the mere notion of poisoning a baby's food.

But then again, there is also something terribly wrong and grotesque about bombing innocent children in other countries, too. Perhaps not. Perhaps Americans have become used to it. But to me, an ex-pat American who has been away for a long time, this is vile beyond description.

All of this came hot on the heels of the inept handling of the Mad-Cow scare by the US government. Japanese people are afraid to buy American beef.

Now, do you think a Japanese mother could trust her child's welfare to another American product that has lost its good reputation? Should a mother do so? I doubt that I would.

How about the mothers of children in European countries? How about the Germans, or the French? America has been treating them like dirt since the invasion of Iraq.

How about Asian countries? I don't know what the Chinese think about this, but I do know that several babies in China died in the spring of 2004 because of tainted baby food. I don't know where that baby food was manufactured, but with this news, do you think the Chinese will trust American products?

It takes a long time to build trust. It just takes one action to break that trust.

I think very few Americans will realize fully the ramifications of this Gerber baby food scandal for America and the American economy. The Gerber baby was an American icon. Maybe not as big as James Dean, Marilyn Monroe, Elvis Presley, or even Mickey Mouse, but just as American. Anyone who knows those

American idols must have shared a meal with the Gerber baby more than a few times in their lives.

And now the Gerber baby is dead; at least in Japan she is.

Is it just another scratch on the paint of the American dream? Or are we nearing the final straw that will break the camel's back?

Thanks, Gerber baby, for sharing so many good times with my loving mother and me. I will miss you.

Alexander Graham Bell Was a Thief—And Other Rude Awakenings

When I was a young man, I used to hang around some pretty wild characters near Los Angeles. That was great. I like people who are part of the "lunatic fringe." They make life interesting.

There was this one guy named Ron E. Fast. Even to this day, I don't know what Ron E.'s real name was. The last time I heard about him was several years ago; I guess his rock band had a performance somewhere near the Mojave desert, and after the show, Ron E. ran down the street outside of the venue in his shorts, shouting at the top of his lungs, "The infidels! The infidels!"

He soon disappeared. The police found his car a few weeks later in the desert, abandoned, somewhere outside of Barstow, California, on the side of the interstate on the way to Las Vegas. The car was filled with soiled men's and women's underwear. Ron E. was nowhere to be found. Some people might think that sounds like foul play. I think it just sounds like Ron E. Fast.

Then there was another guy named Tim Foley. Tim had a sort of a crazed "mad professor" look to him, and the very first time I met him, he came up to me, beer bottle in hand and with a deadpan serious leer, and accused me, "Everything you know is wrong!"

Who is this guy? I thought. Then I noticed him running about in the crowd of people, presumably saying the same thing to everybody there. He must have really freaked a lot of people out. What a trickster! How could he have ever known just how close to the truth he really was?

I'm not making this stuff up. Some people might find people like these two cards frightening. I don't. They made me open my mind more. They made me laugh. And actually, once you got to know them, they were really nice chaps after all.

Living in another country is another good way to get oneself out of "thinking inside the box." Japan has done that for me. Learning another language is the best way to get a better understanding of another land, and surprisingly, a better understanding of one's own country.

Since I started living in Japan, so many of the myths I was raised up on and taught to believe when I was a child and student in America have gone by the wayside. Of course, for most people, living outside of the United States is impractical, but it is a great way to get some intelligent views and a real eye-opening education—destroying myths that the state-run American educational system have engrained in you—is by checking out www.lewrockwell.com.

One reader said it best for me. "I've now read approximately 1200+ articles during the last year on Lewrockwell.com and the Mises Institute (http://www.mises.org/). It's interesting how one's beliefs and even way of thinking can change after having one's previous beliefs shattered with a wave of information. It wasn't comforting and I confess to some initial hesitation when I first encountered the two websites. In fact it was exceedingly shocking considering what I was originally brought up to believe."

Yes, finding out the truth can be initially shocking. I suppose it would be normal for anyone to be hesitant at first. He continues, "It wasn't easy to have practically every belief I once held challenged and eventually destroyed but its preferable to believing a lie (I absolutely hate being lied to)."

Yes, I would agree that it is much more preferable to know the truth than to live a lie. If the person prefers to live a lie, that is their sad choice, but the truth is the truth. As Mikhail Gorbachev once said, "A lie told, even ten thousand times, never becomes the truth."

It takes an open mind and a curious heart to find out what's really going on in this world. In chapters two and three of this book I tried to point out that, as Elizabeth Gyllensvard succinctly summed up for me, "…there is never a justification for 'the final solution.'"

I tried to illustrate that in order not to repeat the mistakes of the past, we first must study them and then acknowledge them for what they are. I used an example (that I consider somewhat absurd, actually) of the massacre of the American Indians to show that the rationale for crime can find no end if one is to always look for excuses for them.

But some people still fail to grasp the basic point. One reader even wrote, "The massacre of the Indians is not as simple as it seems. Even the Indians had inter-tribal conflict." As if the Indians not getting along with each other was an excuse for wiping them out!

I suppose the next time this person has a fight with his sister, that would be justification (using this rationale) for the eradication of his entire family. Nonsense!

From living in Japan and traveling many places in the world, I can tell you an obvious truth: wherever you go, to whatever country in the world, you will find the local people very proud of their heritage, as they should be. Americans certainly don't have any exclusivity on this.

I would also like to show you all how something we were all taught in school is completely wrong. In doing this, I hope that some folks might wonder: if this is wrong, then what else we have been taught that is wrong?

In American schools, students are taught that Alexander Graham Bell invented the telephone. This is patently false. An Italian man by the name of Antonio Meucci—not Bell—invented the telephone.

This is an undeniable fact. Of course American schools will teach differently, for whatever motivation the government has. There will be those of you who will dismiss what I have written here as just mere propaganda, but it's not. Don't believe me? I will allow you to prove it to yourself.

Look at what your own US government had to say about this during the 107th Congress of the United States of America, 1st session. Resolution #H. RES. 269 on September 25th, 2001 (10:41 AM): http://www.esanet.it/chez_basilio/us_congr_res.htm

"Expressing the sense of the House of Representatives to honor the life and achievements of 19th Century Italian-American inventor Antonio Meucci, and his work in the invention of the telephone."

Incredible! Not only this, but the House of Representatives go on to not-so-subtly say that American icon Alexander Graham Bell actually stole the plans for the telephone from Meucci!

If I were a poker player, I might say, "Read 'em and weep." However, I think it would be more apt, in this situation, to say

"How about that? You can learn something new everyday."

It is indeed a frightening notion to consider that everything you know might be wrong. It actually sounds somewhat humorous, if you ask me.

I guess Cullen Hightower was completely right when he said, "Wisdom is what's left after we've run out of personal opinions."

*(By the way, what **was** Congress doing, discussing the invention of the telephone exactly two weeks after September 11th, 2001?)*

And Now a Message from My Sponsor

"With most men, unbelief in one thing springs from blind belief in another."—*Georg Christoph Lichtenberg*

There is something that I think has really become terribly distasteful about American society today; that is the abusiveness and the angry tone often used in daily conversation by many folks, especially those on TV. Of course, not all Americans are guilty of this; it seems to me that this lack of self-restraint and inability to provide some self-anger management is getting worse every year.

I have seen this with my own eyes. I'm sure I am guilty of it sometimes too, but I always make the daily conscious effort to never raise my voice. It seems to me that many people in America today are constantly angry and just plain rude for no reason at all. I wonder if it has anything to do with an overall tension that seems to permeate American society today. I remember when I lived in the United States, I never really thought it so extraordinary to see a couple shouting at each other on the street, or strange to see "friends" or family members arguing to the point where fists start flying. Could it be that people take themselves so seriously that they can no longer enjoy even a small debate that leads to a minor disagreement without losing their tempers?

When you look at the "big picture," does it really matter what one single individual like you or me think?

Perhaps it is just my imagination, but whenever I watch old American black and white movies from the 1930s or 1940s and see gentlemen disagreeing about something, they always end up slapping each other on the back and deciding to "discuss the matter at another time" as they walk off together as friends into the dining room and leave their discussion at the doorway.

Nowadays, I have many times heard Americans who were getting ready for a particularly ugly disagreement say, "No! Let's get this out in the open right now!" It didn't matter if strangers were about; the fight would begin. When you see this

108

type of thing in public, doesn't it occur to you to wonder, "Don't these people have any discretion? Aren't they embarrassed?"

This never happens in Japan. I am not saying that the Japanese are better than the Americans. I'm just saying that the Japanese, or all Asians for that matter, "don't usually wash their dirty laundry in public."

I wrote an article once that brought me a very large share of e-mail from people who were extremely angry at me for writing that I liked Ted Rall's work and that I admire the guy (www.tedrall.com). Well, I do, and I am not ashamed to admit it for a second. You know why? Because I work in the "mass media" too, or more exactly, I should say, "I work in show-business." I do know what I'm talking about here when I say, "Ted is very successful at what he does."

Do you know what makes this success so very special? Because he is doing what he wants to do, and he is getting paid to do it. How many people can actually say that they are working, doing what they dreamed about doing as a young person, and making a good living doing it? Not many, I would guess.

How many people dreamt of becoming a professional sports player or musician, for example, when they were young, only to throw that dream away and take some corporate McJob? I'd reckon that at least 99 percent of the people are that way.

Guys like Ted Rall are like professional major league baseball pitchers; if Ted keeps "throwing strikes," he can continue to play another day. If he starts tossing up bad pitches, he could be cut. The day he stops hitting the strike zone is the day he might have to look for another job.

There is no difference, in this sense, between a professional athlete, a professional writer, a successful actor or actress, or a musician. If there are people who love you, there will be those who hate you. That is a successful formula. If people don't care, you're gone.

Several other readers wrote to me complaining about some nonsense comparing Ted Rall to Rush Limbaugh. "Would you, Mike, write an article praising Rush Limbaugh?" they'd ask.

Well, I'll tell you what; in many ways I do admire Rush Limbaugh too. Why? Because neither Rush Limbaugh or Ted Rall work "for the man." They are both self-employed. Ted works for himself; Rush works for himself. And isn't that the "American dream?" How many people in America can say that today? I wish I made as much money as they do, doing what I want to do. Don't you?

Ted and Rush may call it something else, but I call it "show-business." And, *in show business, there is no such thing as "success"; there is only survival.* Pretty profound, eh? Should be; Diana Ross is the one who said that.

In Rush Limbaugh's case, I may not like what he says and I know he doesn't know his history well, but only a fool would not admire the fact that he has a long-running popular radio show, makes a pile of money, and he can talk non-stop on the air for four hours straight, by himself, and keep his audience. Now I know from experience that this requires some very special talent.

Only an imbecile would not recognize this talent for what it is. Ted Rall is the same way. Ted could have been an executive at a large international Japanese bank, but he decided to dump that and go for his life's dream in the late 1980s. How many people over 30 can say that? Not many!

Now, Ted is world famous and has written many books and is syndicated internationally. Sure, Ted may write or say things that I don't agree with; hell, my wife says things I don't agree with! But that doesn't mean that he deserves my hatred or scorn. And neither does Rush Limbaugh.

Many people have written to me, calling me all sorts of names and saying that they "…will never read [my] articles again!" or "remove me from your mailing list!" For what? Because I wrote an article about a political columnist and cartoonist that I like? Oh, please, give me a break! Shall I only write articles to please certain readers, or articles that I want to write? It's fine if folks don't want to read my articles any more, because they shouldn't do what they don't want to. But I would hope that even readers who disagree with me will understand that they are more than welcome to continue reading as I try my best to write something provocative, or at least funny.

One guy even wrote to me, "Frankly, it disgusts (me) how you and Lew Rockwell and other self-proclaimed champions of freedom keep turning to avowed socialists and communists (Michael Moore, Ted Rall, Noam Chomsky, etc.) to make the case against Bush."

So, what's this guy saying? He wants Lew Rockwell to censor me when I'm merely making an opinion? Wait a minute! Who sounds like the communist here—me or him?

I'll let everyone in on a little secret. In a supposedly free society, if you hear something on the radio or see something on the TV that you don't like, take the remote control and change the channel! Amazing! It works every time! I know it's a bit more difficult if the offending material is on the Internet or in a newspaper or magazine. In this case, you may have to point and click a mouse or *manually* turn the page.

Many times I use a similar method when I get hysterical e-mails from people who, instead of writing me silly mail, should be studying English; I use a button on the keyboard that has the word "delete" written on it. It never fails either.

Whatever happened to the America that said, "I may not agree with what you say, but I'll defend to the death your right to say it"?

Of course I do not make editorial policy at Lewrockwell.com, but I've come to the conclusion that if you really don't want to take the risk of reading articles that are specifically intended to cause you to think or re-think your policies or beliefs, then perhaps you are in the wrong place and should stick to Reader's Digest. Literary materials such as Reader's Digest are an excellent place to read articles that are scientifically tested to insure that even laboratory mice will not become offended at content.

"One's first step in wisdom is to question everything—and one's last is to come to terms with everything." ~ *Georg Christoph Lichtenberg*

Confessions of a Professional Pro Wrestling Announcer

"When you are in politics and depending on somebody to keep you in, you really ain't able to act like real life."—*Will Rogers*

Well folks, I hate to make this announcement, but this just might be the last book I will ever write in my life; it might even be the last time I ever touch a keyboard, for that matter. My life has changed too much over these last few months.

There are some things in a man's life that he knows he can depend on: his dog, his horse, a good Kenny Rogers song, and his pickup truck.

Lord knows we can't depend on a woman to stand by her man, to give him two arms to cling to—especially when nights are cold and lonely.

Some things in life are sacred to a cowboy, and I have some of those sacred thingies too.

But after what happened to me the other night, I am now questioning everything I have ever believed in: God, my family, the government, love, flowers, children, and other pretty things…Sniff…

Shoot! Okay, I suppose I'd better start off by tellin' ya'll the truth about life and all the things that really matter to you, because once you've finished reading this you'll realize as I do that nothing really matters…Nothing really matters, to me (any way the wind blows).

I'd been keeping it a secret and not telling anyone, but times have been hard on the Rogers family. The music business is going down the shit-can faster than you can say "Brittany Spears supports George W. Bush for president." And since the music business has been going so badly, I've fallen on hard times. So hard, in fact, that when some folks from the Pacific Professional Wrestling Foundation and the WWF asked me to ring announce the world heavyweight title match in Tokyo, I had to take the job. I had no choice; I had to come out of retirement. I needed the money. Yes, it is true.

Now some of you folks out there are probably thinking that Pro Wrestling is all fake, and I can understand that. That's what I had thought for my entire 49 years, and that's why I did not want to do this job. I thought it was way below my dignity, but after what I witnessed the other night—after I saw with my own eyes some things that I just cannot explain—I am now certain that Pro Wrestling is real; it's as real as real-life. When it comes to Professional Wrestling, everything you know, or think you know, is wrong.

Some people have some weird idea that professional boxing is real and pro-wrestling is fake. I can't figure that one out. But as George Foreman said when asked what he thought about today's professional boxing, his answer was, "It's just a big joke." I suppose Big George would know more about it than anybody.

Like I said already, I have always thought that Pro Wrestling was fake. Well, of course I did—and so did you. You know why we thought it was fake? Because it was always on TV. That's right! Because everyone knows everything on TV is fake!

I mean, come on! Does anyone actually believe that Big Bird is a big bird, and not just a man in a bird costume? Does anyone actually believe Star Search is not fixed? (Oh, the stories I could tell you about Star Search and Survivor!) Does anyone actually believe that there is absolutely nothing going on between Fox Mulder and Dana Scully, even though they are no longer on the X-Files? Is there even an X-Files anymore? Does anyone actually believe that The Boston Red Sox won the 2004 World Series?

How many times have you heard conversations like this recently (between the average man on the street and his friend)? "I can't believe that the Red Sox came back from three games down to sweep the Yankees and sweep the Cardinals to win the World Series!"

"Neither can I...Unbelievable!"

See what I mean? We all know this stuff is all real or fake because we have either seen it with our own eyes or we watched it on TV. Now who you going to believe? Your own eyes, or TV? Your own eyes, right? Great! Now you and I are on the same page.

On October 31st, 2004, at the Tokyo Ryogokukan Sumo Arena, I was the ringside announcer for the 20th Anniversary of "The Great Muto" Special Pro Wrestling match.

Throughout his long career, The Great Muto has fought for the World Championship against the likes of Hulk Hogan, The Rock, Antonio Inoki (who lost in his bid to unite the boxing and wrestling world championships to Muhammad Ali), Giant Baba, Bob Sapp, The Gladiator, Andre the Giant, Sting, Abdullah The Butcher, Day-Lo Browne, Scott Norton and many more.

I arrived at the Sumo arena for a sound check and rehearsals at two o'clock. The bouts were to start at five. The Sumo arena holds 12,000 people and the tickets at about $90 each were all sold out well in advance. (You figure it out—$90 dollars multiplied by 12,000—plus TV revenues, merchandising, etc. Now that's not fake, that's *real* money!)

We did our sound checks and made sure our match cards were correct. (This was, after all, a Pay-per-view national TV broadcast that was bilingual, as several famous American wrestlers were on that night's card).

After the sound checks, I had a few hours to kill so I sat by ringside and watched these wrestlers warming up. Man, I couldn't believe it! Besides doing the usual stretching that all athletes do before their race or event, these guys went through their moves.

Like a ballerina dancer warming up by doing pirouettes and what-ever-you-whatcha-call-its; these guys would roll over repeatedly on the ring, practice falling, practice getting slammed down, practice being flipped over judo style; they even practiced the *Ju-Jitsu* art of being tossed and rolling so that you do not get hurt in that falling process. I was shocked. Even though these were only warm-ups, they still required a huge amount of strength and stamina, and man did they have to hurt! I cringed every time one guy would come slamming down on the ring and the sound of the crash would explode all the way to the roof!

I checked the ring's surface a little later on and it was not soft; it was hard like plywood.

After sound checks and announcement rehearsals, everyone went backstage to prepare for the doors to open, and when I was called back the place was packed with people. The seats all the way up into the back of the 4th floor rafters were packed with paying customers. What a sight!

There were a total of 8 or 9 matches that night. I sat ringside with several other ringside announcers. There were three stadium announcers, two radio announcers, and three groups of TV announcers from three different TV stations. There were also at least 50 professional sports photographers there.

Some of the fights started and I could hear the comments of the audience from behind me. There was one old lady who was saying things during the first few matches like "Oh! No one believes this!" Or "That's ridiculous!" Or she would just laugh.

Odd thing is, though, by the time we got to the final three or four matches she was going berserk and screaming louder than anyone else around us. This lady was in a shark-feeding frenzy! She would scream at various wrestlers who were down, "Get up! Get up! Get up! Get him! Hit him! Hurt him!"

She was jumping out of her seat and screaming bloody murder when some wrestler she liked got pinned. She'd cry foul and be bashing the metal protection railing that was around the ring. I was glad that the railing was there. I wasn't worried about being bashed by wrestlers who came crashing out of the ring so much (which they did a few times). I was glad that the metal railing was there to protect me from people in the audience like her.

The weird thing about it was just about all the customers were this way—at first laughing and jovial, but as the night grew on they could smell blood and they were out to get some. Oh, the savagery! Man's inhumanity to man. I felt sick.

Former pro wrestling champion and now president of the Pacific-World Wrestling Federation, "The Lariot" Stan Hansen. Stan was also known as the "Unsinkable Battleship" in Japan and is the only man ever to defeat both Antonio Inoki and Giant Baba!

There were a few bouts where wrestlers would cheat and three guys would bang up on one guy over and over. They'd kick him when he was down and hurt him in every possible way you can imagine. The worst part was that even though the wrestler wanted to give up, they wouldn't let him, and they'd just keep beating him senselessly. It was brutal. It was a kind of torture, and the crowd loved it.

I think I now know the atmosphere of an ancient Roman coliseum when gladiators fought. The two warriors are battling it out in the ring; they are doing their best to entertain the audience, all the while attempting to get out alive, but the audience will accept nothing less than repeated, senseless, and severe punishment, meted out to the perpetrator of some crime committed against them as a collective self. What that crime was, I don't know. I didn't see the previous matches, but they wanted to see pain.

The people demanded the head of the criminal, and they were furious when they were denied. They were denied either because the criminal won the fight or the referee stepped in and stopped the execution of the criminal from being carried out.

I didn't feel ill at what was going on in the ring; I was ill by the reaction of the audience. They went as wild as animals, foaming at the mouth, and they wanted more and more violence.

They got their blood and violence in the next tag-team grudge match: the local clean-cut fair-fighting Osamu Nishimura versus the Legendary King of Bloodshed, Abdullah the Butcher.

Abdullah the Butcher's schtick is that he always cheats and pulls a knife on his opponent and cuts him up real bad. Sure, it's all fake! Yeah, fake. Well, that's what I thought until Abdullah the Butcher pulled the knife he had hidden and began cutting this guy right in front of me with it. Folks, he wasn't six feet in front of me and I could see it clearly; he was cutting this guy's forehead and the guy was bleeding. There were no "blood balloons" or anything like that. It was real! Now don't forget that I have worked in broadcasting for over 27 years, but I had never seen anything like this.

If I had seen this on TV, I wouldn't have believed it, but it was right in front of me. I saw it with my own eyes. The crowd was furious. They were throwing things at the Butcher. Eventually the match ended with the Butcher either being disqualified or his partner being pinned; I'm not sure which. But I had seen enough. I felt sick to my stomach. I wanted to throw up. I knew then that this Pro Wrestling business was not a joke; it is, indeed, all real.

Sure, some of you reading this are thinking, Mike has really gone off the deep end this time, but I want to ask you a question. Have you ever sat ringside at a Professional Wrestling match? No? Have you ever been a professional Professional Wrestling announcer? No?

Well, if you answered "No" to either of these questions, then isn't it just a wee bit possible that I might know a little bit more about this than you do? Well, I suppose I do and I'm telling you that it is all real!

I'm sure there will always be unbelievers amongst you, which is laughable when you stop to think about it. I think many readers are involved with finances such as stocks and bonds and the horse races, and they will be the people who will most claim that the stock market or money markets aren't "fixed" either! Ha! Okay, let's say it's not real; it's all fake. Fine. Then all I can say is that following your logic (and mine), that means that everything we see on TV could be either fake or real.

I say that if it's on TV, it's fake. If you are there, it's real. Life is just one big *Truman Show* and you are in it, even though you fail to realize such.

People pay big money to go watch pro wrestling: it's a spectacle. But I'll tell you what, it's no more or less fixed or a spectacle than any other professional sport. It's no more or less fixed than any other "game."

The most amazing thing about this entire business is when you realize that American politics are just one huge spectacle too. The outcomes are already decided; everything is fixed; the bookies make their odds. People pay big money, watch, and get overly excited over who wins and who loses. Family members even get into fist fights over politics! Sometimes it gets so bad that some families are destroyed by arguments about American politics, and this game goes on and on, year after year. Everyone knows it's a joke. Everyone knows it's fixed, yet they still come back, paying their money, screaming for more! Unbelievable!

Oh, the savagery! Man's inhumanity to man. It makes me sick.

A Nose for Shit and Money

Japan is such a safe place that I am often completely dumbfounded. I sometimes hear about people who lose their wallets, bags, purses, what-have-you, and they get them back—intact! When their wallets are returned, there are no credit cards missing. The cash is all still there. It is truly mind-boggling.

This sort of honesty is contagious, too, just as I believe dishonesty can be contagious. In America, I've rarely heard of anyone losing their wallet and ever getting it back. It's sad, when you stop to think about it.

In Japan the old saying, "Do unto others as you would want them to do unto you" is true. In America, unfortunately, I get the impression that the saying has become, "Do unto others *before* they do unto you." It is a pathetic situation, at best, that can only lead to mutual distrust and suspicion in American society.

The following experience is completely true. Unfortunately, the only proof of this I can offer you is to give you a quote that my father—a hillbilly boy from North Carolina—used to say all the time: "So help me God, this is true. Strike me dead if it's not!"

I moved to Japan in 1984. Since being here I have found money more times than I can remember. In 2003 I found more than 211,000 yen (about $2,100 US dollars), just lying on the street.

My wife, on the other hand, is good at winning contests, as well as stepping in dog shit. I guess you could say the good comes with the bad.

When my wife and I got married, she wanted to have a wedding in Hawaii. Fine. Any girl who would marry a twice-divorced loser like me can have anything she wants. That's the way I saw it. I figured I'd have to pay for it, but that was not a problem. Money is never a problem when you don't have any.

So she gets this ticket for some kind of drawing. You know, the typical contest type of thing: fifty thousand people will win nothing, a thousand people will win a free cola (with any purchase of a large fries), ten people will win a Walk-man, five people will win a brand new-fangled 20-speed mountain bike, and one person will win a trip for two people, all expenses paid to—you guessed it—Hawaii!

Like most contests, people who enter try to get as many entry tickets as possible. My wife had one. But, of course, you do know who won the trip to Hawaii? That's right—my wife!

I was at home when she went to the final drawing. The phone rang. I answered and my wife was screaming, "I won! I won!"

"That's nice, dear." I calmly replied. I asked her when she was going to come home, 'cause I was hungry. She was surprised that I wasn't shocked at her winning the contest. Of course she won. I just knew she would.

I also expect her to step in dog crap whenever we are walking around. You might say, "It's a 'dung' deal." My wife is a very beautiful girl. She has all these fancy clothes and expensive shoes. Looks like a beauty queen. Me? I always dress like a bum, I never shave, and I never comb my hair. Kinda like Beauty and The Beast—except the Beast was actually a prince. I was a punk.

And that's why my wife always trips; it's those ritzy, high-heeled shoes. And whenever she is walking on the street, unless I stop her, she'll step in dog dung. It could be the tiniest piece of dog dung around, it could be the only piece of dog dung on the whole block, but my wife will step in it.

But not with me, or should I say not with "my nose" around! I always stop her before it's too late. Like I said, I have a nose for dung and money. It's kind of like a built-in radar. Don't ask me why, but I never step in dog shit, and I always pick up money on the street. Sure, most times the money I pick up is just a yen or five, but many times it has been more—much more.

Several years ago I found 70,000 yen ($700) lying on the street—twice—in a span of about three months. I would say that I find money on the ground about twice a week now. I also find unused telephone cards, subway cards, etc.—things like that. I have come to expect to find money on the street as I walk around.

One night, in mid-2003, I had to work late. I grabbed a taxi and headed home at about 4:30 in the morning. When I got home, I saw some trash on the street. This usually pisses me off because my knee-jerk reaction to trash being on the street is because I figured my 18-year-old daughter or some of her friends left it there.

We had gotten a new guard man at the apartment about a year ago. I don't know his name, but he is a really nice guy. Does a good job, too! Every morning he's out there in front of the building, sweeping up trash. You know these door guardsmen guys don't get paid a lot, so I kind of feel sorry for him; whenever I see trash in front of this building I pick it up. You know, help the guy out.

There was a manila envelope. I picked it up, but it didn't feel "right." It felt like money. You know, the feeling of a big wad of money? It doesn't feel like paper. My nose went into action. I opened the envelope and inside it were twenty 10,000 yen bills! I couldn't believe it! Upon closer inspection, I saw that the bills were entirely in serial numbered order. The envelope had nothing written on it.

What was this money doing on the ground at this time of the morning? My mind raced. Two-hundred thousand yen! Imagine all the guilty pleasures I could buy with this money! I could gamble, drink, and eat until I got sick. I could go out and have the "special" Asian massage (both gambling and prostitution are illegal in Japan, but the police "look the other way"). I could go out and be a really "bad boy" and buy drugs! *No!* I thought. *My wife would be mad about that.*

First off, women know if you have been "sleeping around." They either have their own "built-in radar" or they can smell perfume on your clothes; I don't know which it is. Drinking or doing drugs, while sounding fun, meant that I would definitely get caught, because my wife can tell within one second if I am high or not. Then I thought, *Pachinko! That's it!* But then again, that was no good cause if I went to *Pachinko* and lost (which I surely would); then finding this money would mean nothing.

I went into my apartment and my wife was sleeping like a baby. Of course I woke her up. I told her about the money and asked her what I should do. She said, "Do whatever you want! Go to bed!" She's grouchy like that when she just gets up. She fell back to sleep immediately. My mind raced back to all of the lovely decadence that money would have bought. The devil was sitting on my left shoulder, saying, "You stupid jerk! I told you not to say anything!" But, now it was too late. My wife knew.

The next morning, when I got up, my older daughter was in the living room. I told her about the money and she exclaimed, "Let me have fifty thousand yen!"

"Nah, I can't do that," I answered. Then I explained to her what was going through my mind: Should I keep the money? Or should I take it to the police? I was sure this was dirty money—you know, some underworld type dropped it out of his pocket. But what if it wasn't? What if this money was meant for some poor mother whose husband had run away from her and her child? Wouldn't they definitely need that money? I know; I'm divorced and I pay child support, so I know how tough that would be on that family. If that were the case, they should have their money.

At work, I told my two closest friends about the money. Both told me to give the money to the police. I figured they were right. An angel was sitting on my right shoulder and said, "You're a good boy, Mike."

When my kids found out that I had decided to turn the money over to the police, they thought I was nuts. But think about this: what choice did I have? None, really.

I mean, as a father you always try to teach your kids to do what's right—to live honestly. They knew I had found the money. What would they think if I just kept it? Wouldn't they think, "Daddy says 'be honest,' but Daddy doesn't do what he says." And then there was my wife; I need her to trust me completely. She knew I had the money. What would she think if I just "pocketed" it?

So the day after I found the money, I went down to the police station and walked in. Japanese police are really nice guys usually, but a bit suspicious towards foreigners. Two cops were at the front of the police station.

"Yes, what do you want?" they asked me.

"Here, I found this." I threw the envelope on the desk.

"What's this?" they asked.

"I found this. It's money…" I calmly replied.

They still did not seem to understand. I pulled out my identification and tossed it on the desk and went through the entire story I have just told you.

"Where was this money?" they asked again.

"On the street, in front of my apartment."

There were about eight policemen all around me, looking on in disbelief.

"So you found this money? When? This morning?" they asked.

"Uh, no, not really. I found it yesterday," I admitted.

"What? You found this yesterday? Why didn't you bring it here yesterday?" They all blinked in confusion.

"Well, I thought about what I should do with this money, then I decided to give it to you guys. I figured I might just get it back anyway."

"You did the right thing." said the top policeman. "You are an honest man."

"Well, I'm not that honest!" I replied, "I did think about it for a whole day."

I then drew a map, showing them where I had found the cash.

"Wait a minute!" one cop said. "That's not on the street. That's inside of the apartment building!"

What? I thought. *He's right!*

The policeman added, "Because the money was found on the steps of the entrance way into the complex, it is most probably property of the owners of the building."

Dammit! I thought. *I could have kept the money and kept my mouth shut and no one would've known!* I signed some documents, the police took the money, and I went home.

Nice guys, I thought. The police probably thought, *Crazy foreigner!*

At least my kids and wife knew I was honest, and that is worth much more to me than two hundred thousand yen, right? At least I could live with the knowledge that my wife trusted me just a bit more and my kids either thought I was just a little crazier or more honest than they did before. Anyhow, that's how I tried to rationalize to myself that I had just voluntarily given up $2000. *What an idiot!* I thought.

A few days later, I saw a poster inside of the apartment building alerting people to the fact that a "large sum of money" was found in this building, so if it's yours, go to the police station and claim it. I felt like crying. I thought, *I'll never see that money again…Easy come, easy go…And, I need a drink!*

My wife told me that if someone didn't claim the money within six months, it would be mine, and that was probably the last time I thought about it. I did, though, talk about it on my late night radio show, in an incredibly vain attempt at making myself feel better.

Sure, I'm an honest guy. Sure, I can look my kids straight in the eye. But $2000 would have also bought me some very spiffy stuff, like a pair of gold-framed Versace Sunglasses so no one could see my pupils!

I told people that being honest was the best way to live. I have really been trying these last seven or eight years to be a completely honest person. Sometimes it's hard, though, especially when I have a huge wad of cash in my hand. Being honest? Sure it's great, but sometimes, when I thought about giving the money to the police, I would get all "misty."

Time passed. The long, hot summer days turned into fall, and then into winter.

One day my wife and I came home from lunch and we checked our mail. My wife said, "You got a postcard from the police! You got the money!" She smiled broadly.

"Really? Wow! Japan is a great place!" The card asked us to go to some lost-and-found police station downtown and collect the money. We went there. I gave the policeman the postcard, my identification, and within 3 minutes I had the money.

"Incredible! I can't believe it!" I said. I opened the envelope and counted the money. Sure enough, it was all there: two-hundred thousand yen. We walked out of the lost and found. I thought, *Easy come, easy go*, and I handed the money to my wife.

Pretty cool, eh? I know that if this happened in the United States, the police would have "found" someone to claim the money—if you know what I mean.

I always hand all my money to my wife. I never carry a lot of cash. Why? Because money is evil and will cause me to do evil things. St. Paul said, "The love of money is the root of all evil." And he's completely right, it is. Well, at least it is for me. Whenever I have lots of cash in my pocket, I find some way to make some trouble for myself.

If I want to be happily married, I have to give all my money to my wife. And, if you are a guy, and you are married and/or thinking about getting married, take my advice; be smart. Give all your money to your wife and let her handle it all the time. Never carry large amounts of cash with you. If you are like me, cash will make you irresponsible and immature. Guys often think not with our brains, but with our hormones. Thinking with your hormones is a sure-fire way to get into all sorts of trouble. So be smart—use your brain.

Now there are probably lots of men reading this right now and thinking, *No way, Mike. I am the man. I will handle the money. My wife is not smart enough to handle the money.* Well, if you are thinking this, then I can tell you that you are either confused or an idiot. Why? Well, if your wife is not smart enough to handle the money, then you must be an idiot for marrying a stupid girl. Or if you think that men are smarter than women, that just proves you are a fool, and only a fool will allow a fool to handle his money. Get it? So if you want to be a happily married guy, give all your money—all of it—to your wife. When you need money, ask her for it. This is a well-known secret to all happy marriages.

Another thing I'd like to point out to all you guys reading this is that up until now, who was the most important woman in your life? 99 percent of all guys will say that the most important woman in their entire life was their mom, of course. Now, the next question is when were you guys the happiest in your entire life? Wasn't your childhood the most wonderful time of your entire life? And why was childhood so wonderful? Two things: We had no money, and we had no responsibility.

Ah, yes! No money! As any Buddhist Zen master will tell you, "Nothing" is happiness; the key to happiness is no money! If you have no money, you will have no responsibility! That's right. When you were a kid and you wanted something, how did you get it? You asked your mom to buy it for you. And, basically, she always did, right?

The happiest time of any guy's life was when he was a kid and Mom took care of everything. And that's how you guys should treat your wives; they are the boss. They handle all the money. You do what they tell you to do (well, sort of), and whenever you want to buy something, you ask your wife for the money. Absolutely let her handle it—always! I cannot stress this point enough.

There is another good thing about giving all the money to your wife and making her the "Accounting Chief." (Hell, titles are free! If it makes her happy, make her "Accounting President"! Or how about "Accounting Princess" since most women have fantasies about being a Princess?) After putting her in charge, you can do what I do! When it comes around to tax time—God, I hate doing taxes!—you tell your wife, "Well, honey, I'd just love to help you with the taxes, but since you handle all of the money here, I guess you'll have to do it by yourself, especially since I have no idea how the money is spent." Then when your wife is waist deep in papers for the tax office, don't forget to ask her for some money so you can go down to the bar, drink some beers, and watch the baseball game! Wooo-Hooo! Isn't life just wonderful being a kid again?

Also, when you were a kid you tried to do right. You tried not to lie, cheat or steal. As we get older, there is really no one to watch over us about these kinds of things, so we have to watch over ourselves. "Honesty is its own reward!" And I can prove it to you!

Just about a week after getting back the two hundred thousand yen and giving it all to my wife, I headed out for work. It was about eight o'clock in the evening. Near my house is a discount liquor store. I am a "regular" there. Anyhow, I walk out of my apartment and down the street when I walk by a Catholic sister coming out of the liquor store, and she's carrying two cases of beer! A bit unusual, to say the least. She stopped at the street crossing and waited for the light to turn green. She looked at me and smiled. I said, "Oh please, let me carry that for you."

"Oh no, no, no. It's quite all right," she said.

"No, no, please!" I grabbed the two cases of beer and walked across the street with the nun. She was a very short, old woman, but she was tough! I mean, those two cases of beer were heavy, even for me! I don't know how she carried those by herself! Perhaps the Lord was helping her. Probably. Doesn't the Lord always hang around nuns? I think so. That's why nuns scare me to death.

Catholic sisters are some of the most terrifying people I have ever met in my life. I don't know about you, but I have never met a Catholic nun who didn't look like she was the "Wicked Witch of the East"—or born in the fourteenth century. Forget those stupid Whoopie Goldberg movies! I have never met a young Catholic sister in my life! They don't exist. I think Catholic sisters have some sort of contract with God that allows them to live for several hundred years without anyone else knowing about it. I mean, look at Sister Theresa! She looks the same now as she did when Elvis Presley was skinny! How do they do that? Well, don't think about it too much, because if you do you probably won't sleep tonight and you'll have nightmares for a long time to come.

So I'm carrying these two cases of beer for this sister. We start walking the opposite direction from the train station. About 100 meters down the road was a car with the trunk open and another Catholic sister waiting there. I think she was praying. She was probably praying something like this: "Oh dear God, please help Sister Mary carry those heavy boxes! Oh Lord, show us a sign that you are taking care of us and that our prayers will be answered!"

Then I show up, start carrying the boxes, and it's "A miracle! Our prayers have been answered! Thank you, Lord!" Not, "thank you Lord; thank you, Mike Rogers" is more like it!

I said to the sister, who was walking with me, "It's not often that I see sisters buying beer! A pretty amusing sight!"

"Well, we are having a party on the 16th. Won't you join us?" she asked politely.

"Oh no, I can't. I have to work that night." Also, going to a party with lots of "church people" and nuns hanging around sounds a bit frightening to me. I'm sure they are all wonderful people, but I would feel like Satan standing in a nest of baby chickens.

"Uh, no thanks, really. I promised my wife I wouldn't drink before work."

The nuns insisted that I come to their party, but I kept saying, "I'd love to go, but I can't." This went on for a while; they kept insisting and I kept declining. Finally, they said, "Well, if you can, you are more than welcome, young man."

Young man? I thought. And with that, we all smiled.

"Thank you. God bless you," they said.

"Well…Uh…Don't drink too much…Er…Have a nice party," and I turned around and walked back towards the subway station. I felt good about myself. I had done a good deed. Not only did I do a good deed, but it was a good deed for one of "God's assistants"!

Pretty cool, I thought. *Damn! I mean, darn! I wish I'd had a camera.* I continued walking to the station. I was thinking about the nuns and how good my life had been recently. Things were going fine. I was happy. I had found the two-hundred thousand yen. Now I had helped some nuns!

Life is funny. "God works in many strange and wondrous ways!" I've heard. I kept walking. I walked up to the signal just before the station. There were about forty people waiting for the green light. The light changed color. They all crossed the street. I was about ten meters behind them. Then, there on the crosswalk, right in front of me was a ten thousand yen bill (about $100) lying on the street! Right out in the open!

Wow! I thought. *Why didn't any of those people see this? It was right under their feet!* Then I realized that if I hadn't walked four or five minutes out of my way, if I hadn't have helped those Catholic sisters with their beer, if I hadn't chatted with them I would have never found that money! I would have walked by that crosswalk too soon, and I would have missed it!

Oh, thank you, God! I thought.

So I don't ever want to hear any of you young people saying, "There is no God." That's nonsense! I know there is. And if you live right, be honest, don't lie, you will be rewarded! Heck, I got ten thousand yen for carrying two cases of beer for some nuns who were on a beer run! And it was all tax-free!

Of course I gave the ten thousand yen to my wife when I got home...Hey! Why ruin a good thing, right? If you realize that with money you can do and buy all sorts of "good shit," then you will realize that money and shit are basically the same thing. So, like I said, I have a nose for shit and money. Because—and they really do—they smell the same.

(Since the writing of this article, my wife has continued to win contests. She won a $1200 Peugeot racing bicycle as well as a folding bike in the last 2 years...I've been pretty consistent at picking up about one cent everyday. Honesty does pay.)

Snoring—Nature's Own Home-security System

I went to visit my wife's mom and dad's house the other day. It's been a while, and they wanted to see our new baby. He's three months old now and has just about gotten to the point where he recognizes people and doesn't freak out when my father-in-law holds him. He likes that—my father-in-law, I mean.

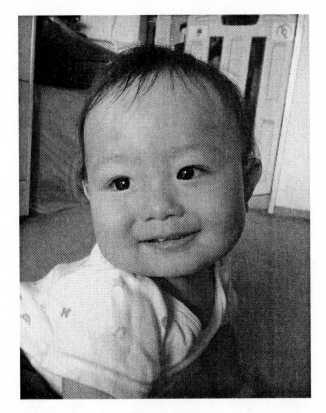

My kid—Wray

Anyhow, the in-laws are old rich people. They live in a rich folks' neighborhood full of other old rich folks.

I guess recently there have been a few burglaries around their house, and all the folks living around there have gotten pretty nervous. The talk is that the *Triad* (Chinese gangs) are busting into people's homes when they are not around and stealing everything. At one home, the bad guys even stole the roofing off an outdoor car garage!

My mother-in-law doesn't like it when I walk around the neighborhood by myself. Why? I guess she thinks that the neighbors might call the cops because some sneaky-looking foreigner is hanging around, smoking cigarettes. Maybe the neighbors will think I'm a Chinese gang member! You know, all foreigners *do* look alike!

The other day I was going outside to have a smoke in the morning and she said to me, "Aren't you going to shave before you go outside?"

I was crushed. I thought that my in-laws didn't like me for a minute there! But I guess when I walk around the neighborhood, wearing my sweat-shirt hood on over my head, unshaven and looking like something between Yassar Arafat and one of those rappers in *Boyz from da Hood*, she worries about what the neighbors will think. No wonder my mother and father-in-law took me around at New Years and introduced me to as many neighbors as possible!

Anyhow, the in-laws live in the country here in Japan. There are no foreigners around where they live. It's so bad there that if I hop into a taxi and speak Japanese, the driver will just look at me and blink and say, in bad English, "Pardon me?"

The taxi drivers, and anyone else around there, for that matter, do not expect anyone with a foreign face to speak anything but English, so when you speak Japanese to them, their minds just cannot register it. I really hate that. Makes me feel stupid.

Okay, maybe I have an accent. I'd like to think that my accent in Japanese is kind of like Ricardo Montalban's is in English: "Cordoba—it's a bootiful car!" Maybe not!

So I am riding in a taxi, and behind the driver's seat they have all sorts of advertising for this and that: travel tours, medical services, home security systems—you name it, they've got it! I mentioned to my mother-in-law that they should hook up a home security system at their house. She doesn't want to do that.

Why? Well, Japanese people are always very concerned about neighborly relations and keeping *wa* (harmony) with their neighbors. I tell her that if she has a home security system, it won't stop burglars from breaking into her house; it just will force the crooks to rob the neighbor's house instead. Well! We can't have that! She absolutely doesn't want that to happen! What would the neighbors think?

"What if the neighbor's house does get broken into because we had a home security system in our home?" she asks.

Yeah, yeah, I know what you're thinking…Westerners can't even try to dissect this logic. This is Japan! These are the ways of the Japanese. So I drop the subject about home security systems.

Also in the taxi they have ads for stuff like laser surgery to remove excess fat, cataracts, liver-spots, acne; laser surgery for sinus relief; laser surgery acupuncture. You name it, they've got it. They now have surgery that will repair your vision back to 20/20. They even have laser surgery to stop men from snoring at night!

My wife grabbed the pamphlet for the snoring laser surgery. I got nervous.

Laser surgery for snoring? Never! Now that's where we real men have to put our foot down!

The last straw came for me the first night at their house. In fact, every night it was the same thing: I can't sleep because of all the noise. That kid is driving me crazy! Even worse than the kid is my wife! She won't let me sleep! Everyone complains about my snoring.

I feel like one of the Three Stooges. My wife slaps me while I'm sleeping and says, "Wake up and go to sleep!" She says my snoring is going to wake up the baby! She says if I can't control my snoring, to go by myself and sleep in the next room!

"My God! Wake up the baby? Heaven forbid! But what about *my* feelings?"

So I slumber off by myself in the next room, cold and alone, cast off by a wife and child who don't realize that my snoring is actually a product of natural selection that evolution has given me! God saw to it that all men could protect their family by the use of snoring!

Then it dawned on me! That's it! It's all a scam! We wouldn't need any sort of home security devices if the guys were at home snoring all day!

Think about it. Who in their right mind would break into some house if they heard some monstrous snoring at the place? No one, that's who!

There are evil people and predators everywhere! Millions of years ago, when the ferocious wild animals came prowling around, what did Bambi and the wimfolk do? Why they either hid or ran away, just like a bunch of girls! We men don't do that!

First off, we protect our woman and young-uns at night by snoring. Then if we should be awakened while snoring, we shift into our secondary stage of natural selection: a bad mood!

Besides the natural built in home security/family protection that an awakened male offers—usually called domestic violence—we also offer snoring at night, and for free!

For example, let's go back to caveman times. We have a caveman that we shall call "Fred." Fred finishes his job at the rock quarry and scurries home. Wilma, the wife, has prepared dinner for Fred and their baby. After that they go bowling, then they come home and sleep.

At night, while terrifying dinosaurs prowl the neighborhood, how does Fred protect the wife and kid? By snoring at night, that's how! The sound of loud snoring warns predators that there is a male of the species sleeping in that particular abode and that to awaken that male is a dangerous proposition. It's been this way for millions of years, and it will continue to be so in the future.

Let me ask you a question. It's dark. You and your wife and kid are driving on the interstate, looking for a place to sleep at night. You see a dark motel at the side of the road. You pull into the parking lot. The neon light is off and all you can hear is some sort of wild animal's snoring off in the distance.

Are you going to stop the car there and stay at that motel at night? Hell, no! You are going to hop back onto the interstate and go back to that Motel Six you saw a while back! $49.95 doesn't sound too bad anymore for the three of you when you compare it to the "Motel Hitchcock Psycho" you had just been to!

It was the same way, way back when. When Fred, Wilma, and their kid were walking around, looking for some place to sleep, do you think they'd walk into some dark cave where there was some animal snoring at night? No way!

So I've had it with all this whining from the female half of our populace. It's time for all "real men" (just like me) to draw a line in the sand and be proud of our slobbish, so-called uncouth, bestial behavior! No more manby-panby garbage about how the "Y" chromosome is degrading, and that men are doomed to extinction in 125,000 years! Nonsense, I say! I have to seriously wonder why people are so worried about a few hundred thousand years from now when the sun is going to burn out in 35 million years anyway!

"Kind of like tripping over the quarter to pick up the penny!" I'd say.

We shouldn't take this lying down! Well, okay, maybe we should take it lying down, because that's where we do our duty, regardless of whether we are sleeping or awake!

Surgery for snoring? Never! That's what the female of our species wants us to do, because if we do, we will have really given up on our last vestige of male dominance! It's a duty, and it's a duty we do best!

So when your boss or wife complains to you that you are "Sleeping on the job!" you tell them, "No, I am *protecting* this place!" You are not sleeping on the job! It *is* your job! So snore away, my brothers! The louder, the better! It's not only your birthright; it's your God-given gift! It's also a lot cheaper than some home security system! And even better, a hell-u-v-a lot easier to install!

Feeling Frisky? Please Make an Appointment

Well, it's started happening to me. I had an appointment with the little woman and I forgot about it...

I had my suspicions a while back, but this morning sealed it: I must be going senile. When I woke up, I spent five minutes searching all over the house for my glasses, when all the while I was wearing them. I guess that's absolute proof that I'm over the hill. It truly is a sad day in the Rogers' household.

Up until today I had always attributed my forgetfulness to various factors: hangover, wild youth, mania. But no! Not anymore! The proof of the pudding is in the eating.

Why, it seems like just the other day that I was a jumping, skipping little boy, chasing butterflies. Never mind that I was doing that while I was supposed to be playing baseball for my dad's Little League team! Ah, those memories!

I remember one special game. I think I was about 7 years old. I was in right field. That's where the coach (my dad—or your dad, as the case may be) always put their most hopeless player.

In the middle of the game, nature called. *What the heck!* I thought. *No one ever hits the ball into right field!* And so I turned around and "watered" the grass. I'll never forget the shouts of joy and the cheering on from my team-mates and my dad as some kid hit the ball into right field as I was busy and looking the other way!

My baseball team. Dad as head coach.
My older brother, Bob (front, second from left) the best player on the team.
And me (front row, far right) the worst player on the team.
Wonderful memories...We lost every game that year!

I quickly tinkled down my pants leg. I searched for my glove—all baseball players have to have a glove; can't touch the ball without a glove! Just as I was about to make the game-saving spectacular long throw to get the guy out, just as he slid into home plate on an in-the-park homerun, the centerfielder stole my thunder and picked up the ball and hit the "cut-off" man.

What a waste! I could have picked the runner off! Oh well! There's always tomorrow! I wonder what mom's making for dinner? I thought. But those days are long gone.

I used to have a memory like a steel trap! Names! Numbers! Anything! You just tell it to me once and I could remember it. But not anymore. I suppose I should have seen it coming a while back when I stopped waking up "feeling young" every morning.

When we guys are young, we can get "motivated" at a mere moment's notice. Sometimes we get motivated at very embarrassing times! But as we get older, we have to make a schedule and add it into our appointment calendar.

"You've got that 'lovin feeling'?" We answer our better half…"Fine…I understand…. Let's see. Today is Tuesday. I think I could schedule you in by Friday at, say, five-thirty? How's that?" Then we write it down in our schedule book. We don't drink for the next few nights. And we go to the sports gym the next two days and try to watch some "Bikini-Beach Trash" garbage TV show sixty minutes before the scheduled time in order to get "mentally prepared."

Then we try to relax, and we pray.

I hear from some of my older guy friends that even watching "Bikini-Beach Trash" on TV loses its effect over time. It's not only you watching the girls! It's them watching you, too, that has a huge effect on your, um, "positive self image."

When you are a young buck, beautiful girls look at you and you can see a twinkle in their eye. I call it a twinkle. You know, kind of like that twinkle that your favorite fishing lure has. You know—the twinkle of that large-mouthed bass "killer" lure? Those large-mouth bass just can't resist that twinkle! Kinda like us large-mouthed guys. We can't resist that twinkle either!

But, as with all things, we must try to gracefully give up the treasures of youth: the good looks, the girls, the wild nights, the disco inferno…Those days are long gone.

Of course I was going to end this with some snappy, funny little remark that would bring a smile to you, my dear reader, but I can't remember what it was.

Oh well, it'll come back to me later on…

Ah! Now I remember! Now that I've found my glasses I have to find the TV tuner! I want to watch that TV show. Um…what's it called? You know—that "Bikini-Beach Trash" show. What channel was that on? I need to watch it. I think I have an appointment.

Rock and Roll Repudiation

The one thing that is very consistent between the governments of Japan and the United States—all governments for that matter—in spite of what they tell you is that they waste our tax money on all sorts of ridiculous things all the time.

There is nothing the government can do that is not a huge waste of money and a boondoggle. It is in the very nature of the government and the people who work for the government to first, always protect their position. That's the number one priority for any government worker. The success of a given project will be the second objective to the bureaucrat; they must retain their jobs first. Corporations are often guilty of the very same thing, but corporations do not tax us. And second, the government must utilize every penny allocated for a project. Have you ever heard of a government-sponsored project that was completed on time and under budget? I never have.

Let me give you a good example. During the Apollo space missions, the US government bragged that they had overcome the lack of gravity in space and had designed a ballpoint pen that would write in zero gravity. Great, eh? No, not exactly. They spent $13 billion dollars of our tax money on this idiotic project. They touted it as a great achievement for science. I don't think so. But perhaps it is. Perhaps I will need a ballpoint pen that will work in zero gravity next time I'm writing a check to buy groceries on Mars. Who knows?

How did the Russians get around this "space-writing" crisis? They used a pencil.

Well, score one for Democracy and your tax dollars at work.

I don't know about you, but I still have a problem finding a pen that writes at my home every time I need one.

The government will continue to grow and waste money; that is the purpose of all governments. And they will all tell us that every project, every penny spent is for our own good.

We've all heard about government-funded research into the effects of Rock music or Rock music versus Classical. Millions have gone down the drain into this absurd research. Is it millions well spent? I'll let you be the judge.

Many have claimed that rock music is one of the key causes of the troubles of today's youth; the medical what-nots and reasons why. Now I will once again come to the rescue of the United States government and the US taxpayer in saving at least hundreds of zillions of dollars of research money into why today's youth are so messed up.

There have been many excellent articles written on the subject of children with Attention Deficit Disorder; Linda Schrock Taylor comes to mind. I admit that I do not have the training or education to be considered an expert on this subject, but after 4 children—the oldest being 20 and the youngest being 6 months old—yesterday it dropped on my head like a ton of bricks. So here it is. I do think that Rock and Roll music causes brain damage in very small children. There, I said it.

Lead vocalist for The Rotters in 1978—www.therotters.com

I can hear you right now, "Mike is a Rock and Roll hypocrite, turncoat, and has definitely lost his mind this time." That's plausible, but I don't think so. Let me explain.

In the late 1970s I played in a "real" Rock and Roll band. What is "real" Rock and Roll? Well, it's not played on the "Hit Parade of Hell" on the radio, that's for sure.

Most people do not listen to real Rock and Roll. Most people listen to commercial pabulum.

Aerosmith, The Eagles, Sheryl Crow, Billy Joel, No Doubt, just about any Top 40 hit artist, are not "real" Rock and Roll. That being said, I don't think you should play this type of trash to your small children, either.

Rock and Roll is supposed to be dangerous music. The music of protest: social disorder and unrest. Stuff your parents don't want you to listen to. There used to be lots of it. The last Rock and Roll boom was Punk Rock, which started in the late 1970s.

I suppose today's dangerous music would be Hip-Hop or Underground Rock. I also would not expose very small children to this type of music.

Now, I don't suppose anyone, especially anyone who really does like real Rock and Roll, would argue the idea that Rock and Roll music is supposed to be dangerous music, right? And, if it is dangerous, then it seems logical that small children should not be exposed to it.

Look, I'm serious here. This is not a comedy article. I'm not going to give you any of that "Rock and Roll is the Devil's music" nonsense, either. I love *real* Rock and Roll music.

I just realized yesterday that small children should not be subjected to it. That's all.

Drinking alcohol or taking drugs can be dangerous. Should small children drink booze or take drugs? Hell, should very small children (babies) drink coffee, Coca-Cola or eat sugar? Of course not!

I never set out to research this subject, and had I read something like this myself a few years ago, I would have dismissed this article as complete and utter nonsense. But I have seen what has happened to my own children, through their and my own experiences, and it doesn't look too good.

My oldest daughter was brought up on Rock and Roll music, in a Rock and Roll household. (I know. My fault.) Her daddy is and was a Rock and Roll DJ. She liked "The Rocky Horror Picture Show" and David Bowie when she was five.

Now she is 20 and has just recently been able to hold down a job for more than a few months. Usually she gets bored very quickly and quits. She quit high school, too. Need I mention that she has had some troubles with the local police? I thought it was all part of wild youth. Would this be called A.D.D. in America?

I don't know. This is Japan. We don't have an A.D.D. problem here; at least I've never heard of it.

My second daughter was basically brought up in her first 5 years by my mom, since my first wife and I were getting a divorce. My mom and dad don't really listen to music too much anyway, but if they do, they listen to Harry Belafonte, 101 Strings, or Hank Williams.

My second daughter graduated from junior high school in 2004 and is going to a high school overseas. She's pretty straightened out and never gets into trouble. She didn't really start listening to Rock music until she was 12 or so. Is there a connection here? I think there might be.

My third daughter got very ill as a young child and spent a lot of time resting in a hospital. Of course no Rock and Roll was allowed there—only Classical music. She is now in 5th grade, a top student, and a very popular kid in school. She lives with her mom and grandparents, and they definitely do *not* listen to Rock music.

My third wife wanted a baby boy. Fine! My wife is a classically-trained pianist. She graduated from the most famous classical music university in Japan. She hates the rock music that is played on the radio. Like I said, If it's on the radio, then it's not "real" Rock music.

Before our son was born, my wife played Arthur Rubinstein's Chopin, Van Cliburn on Tschaikovsky, and Mozart for him. I also threw in some very cool (but not Rock) Perrey & Kingsley, "Soothing Sounds For Baby" by Raymond Scott, and "Switched on Bach" by Wendy Carlos. We continue playing this kind of music for him to this day.

We have also been teaching our son Baby Signs—a sign language for babies. According to the Baby Signs book, parents should start teaching baby signs after 6 months. We started early. This kid already knew 5 signs at 5 months. He loves playing his toy piano. (It plays classical tunes) He is very calm and smiles a lot.

We also don't let him watch TV. Yesterday, after he was playing his piano, I asked him if he wanted to listen to music. I played some Rock and Roll for the first time for him. I played some Pop-Punk Rock—I think it was the band "Green Day."

His reaction was almost instantaneous. He began to get very nervous and agitated. He almost started to hyperventilate. I turned the music off and he calmed down instantly. I was quite surprised at his reaction to the music.

I had only seen him get hysterical once before that. That was when I watched him for 5 hours by myself while his mom had an appointment. He went nuts (taking me with him) when his mom wasn't around.

Of course I am proud of my son—seems like he is really smart,—no thanks to me—thanks to my wife, I'm sure. I love all my children. But if I could do it all over again, I would not play loud Rock and Roll music to my babies.

I've seen it with my own eyes. When you stop to really think about it, I guess this makes perfect common sense.

People who love Rock and Roll music will call me an idiot or whatever. Like I said, I personally love loud Rock and Roll music, but I don't need some US government multi-million dollar sponsored research to tell me one thing that should be obvious to anyone with a lick of sense: *Loud and aggressive sounds are **not** good for babies.* Of course! Isn't that obvious?

A Disguise, a Name, Free Speech
& No Smoking, or How I Keep
Myself from Being Killed

I see from the recent news from the West that the American and British police are going to throw "terrorists" and anti-war protesters into jail. Sure would be a good idea if they'd actually define exactly what a "terrorist" or "anti-war protestor" is.

I guess these sick people—the anti-war protestors—were actually out exercising their rights to free speech and making a public disturbance! They thought they could go out, carrying dangerous placards—"Hey you could poke someone's eye out with that!"—all the while disturbing the environment with their loud-speakers and ruining the economic livelihood of the Homeland with their traffic-stopping public displays of disorder and unruliness. Perhaps these dolts actually considered themselves to be living in a "Free America"?

Fools! How anyone could be under such delusions and be such simpletons is beyond me. Being arrested and treated like a common pickpocket, burglar, thug, or even worse! No, my friends! This would never happen to me! I am smart enough to know who "butters my buns," and I know well enough to stay in a designated "Free-Speech, Smoke-Free Zone."

Those who would knowingly disturb the peace and blatantly attempt to ruin the harmony of society must be dealt with by the most extreme means. Those who break the law must be dealt with by equal measures.

That is why I am not foolish enough to mess around during some sort of public disturbance. This is why you will never see my face at any public demonstration or event protesting the actions of our beloved government.

Of course we had some anti-war protests that a "friend" of mine helped organize and which I may or may not have attended. Either way, like I said, you have no proof that I was at such a public altercation, nor proof that I was even aware that such an event may or may not have occurred.

141

2

Schizophrenic in Japan

You see, I am a foreigner in a foreign land. That makes me stick out like Michael Jackson at a Toy's 'R' Us store. So what do I do? I don't play with fire! That means I don't smoke cigarettes at public disturbances, and I always wear a disguise!

Yes, a disguise. I may have actually gone to anti-war demonstrations here in Tokyo and pointed out the undercover policemen to the crowd that gathered. In fact, one time I may have even told the crowd "Thanks for coming to our anti-war demonstration. I'd also like everyone to give a big round of applause to the members of the Secret Service, the CIA, and the undercover members of the Tokyo Metropolitan Police Department who have risked their lives to come out here to help us protest the war…There they are! Standing over there at the top of the stairs to your right, ladies and gentlemen. Give them a big hand!" And then I pointed out the police to the crowd.

Everyone started clapping and looked at the dozen or so undercover cops who froze like a deer in a car's headlights. Were the under-cover cops obvious? Nah!

Oh, I'll bet they wanted to kill me! But they can't, for they don't know what I look like. Wearing a disguise is the way to go! No one knows what I really look like.

Also, the Japanese Gestapo cannot pick up my vital DNA from a cigarette butt for analysis to link me to the scene of the crime, even though it wasn't me anyhow!

That's it, my friends! Desperate times require desperate measures. You want proof that my "plan" works? Well, you don't see me being locked up for protesting the war, do you? And I *may* have been at every single anti-war protest we held here in Tokyo. I *was* on the FM radio protesting the war. I was a public figure! And yet…no one knows exactly what I look like.

This really was my promo photo for the FM station I worked at!

I believe that it was Tony Blair who said "The lunatics have taken over the asylum." He's quite right, you know. They have. Wearing a disguise and not smoking at public demonstrations is a common sense, self-preservation method.

Even if you suspect that "they" might be watching you, it's best to wear a disguise. I do it not because I'm worried about the Japanese police; I'm worried about those fruitcakes in the White House. I am afraid that they might come looking for me. Oh laugh now, but I've never been in jail. Can you say the same thing?

But I'm pretty safe, I figure. I mean, I live in Japan. Even if those folks in the CIA or FBI wanted to get me, they couldn't. Even if they could read *Kanji* (Chinese characters), they'd never find me in Japan. Two reasons: One—I am a master of disguise. Even I don't know what I look like.

And two—in Japan no one can find any addresses here anyway. The address system used here is incomprehensible to even the locals. Hell, you could live across the street from me and I wouldn't know your address. No one else would, either.

Japan doesn't use an address system like America. There is no "100 block on A street;" "200 block on B street," etc, here. Japan uses a hodge-podge "ward" system. (Don't even ask me to explain it; it's just the way it is. That's all, no point in even thinking about it.)

So, I figure that during World War II, when the US marines were slogging it out in the Guadalcanal and they wrote a letter home that said "Send lawyers, guns, and money," it got there quick—in spite of the US Postal Service!

But when the Japanese soldiers did the same thing, it took much longer. Why? Well, all the able-bodied, healthy, young men were sent off to the "front." That meant all the Japanese postal workers who knew the area were gone. That left the rest of the people here to fend for themselves. New people had to be hired by the post office in Japan, and with the messed up address system used here, letters to the Japanese High Command took several days longer to get there than their American counterparts.

So I figure that's why Japan lost the war. Orders for supplies and stuff were really slow, even worse than your regular mail order! That's how I see it, anyway.

But I digress. The Gestapo in America and Britain want to throw these public disturbance thugs into prison for believing that they have the right to exercise free speech. Those simpletons!

If you want to beat the Gestapo at their own game you have to think like the Gestapo. Forget about the image of a Nazi you've seen in the movies. Those are actors. Real Nazi's don't wear monocles and hold their cigarettes funny. I don't even think real Nazis smoke!

Let me ask you a question. Have you ever seen a photograph of Heinrich Himmler smoking a cigarette? No? Why? I figure he knew, through his "experimentation," that his DNA could be lifted from the butt of a cigarette, so he didn't smoke in public.

He knew that his luck could change as quickly as the Russian winter set in upon the Nazi troops advancing on Moscow in 1941. He knew that the fortunes of war were as fickle as Lady Luck. Maybe that's why he didn't take chances with cigarettes.

I like to think a lot about these kinds of things.

If you are protesting against our beloved government in public, you shouldn't take any chances either.

Some of my "fans" have written to me to tell me that if I were to ever come to America, they would kill me. I find that laughable, at best. I have been going to America at least once a year—every year—and even though I have been indeed "killed" every time, I am alive today, as you may witness from the reading of this book.

I go to Las Vegas every year. I stay at the Hilton. There are two Hilton Hotels in Las Vegas, so I'm not going to tell you which one I go to.

If you want to find me, walk into any casino in Vegas and ask them, "Is Mr. Rogers gambling here?" They'll all look at you like you've lost your mind! They will probably ask you, "Is it is a 'wonderful day in the neighborhood?"

My detractors think they know my name. Perhaps, but "Rogers" is an extremely common name in America. So, tough guys, you want me? Find me! Go to Las Vegas and look for Mr. Rogers at the casino. Good luck! You'll need it.

Let me show you just how impossible it would be to locate me by telling you a true story about what happened the last time I was in Las Vegas. I was playing Blackjack with my wife at said hotel casino. Suddenly, the casino became quite active with the scurrying around of security forces. The background music over the air changed into that very famous country tune, "The Gambler." There were scores of old ladies gathered around a Blackjack table to my left. Then a man with a very familiar face came to the table and began dealing cards to the ladies.

I asked my table dealer, "What's going on?"

"Oh, they are having a Kenny Rogers radio promotion, and all the people who listened to the radio and won, get to play Blackjack with Kenny Rogers as the dealer," she replied.

I looked over to Kenny, waved and yelled, "Kenny! Dude! Hey, Homes! Wassup? Remember me?"

Kenny just scowled at me and gave me a confused, blank stare...

Probably too much Gin and Whiskey, I figured.

Well, with all those people gathering around, it got too crowded for my liking and I called the Pit Boss over.

"Say, would you mind making reservations for my wife and me at that nice Steak restaurant you got over at the other side of the building?"

"Sure!" she said. "What's your name again?"

"Rogers."

"Okay. Rogers for two people then. What time?"

"Right now is fine!"

So we cashed in what few chips I had and walked over to the Steak House. When we got to the restaurant, there were security people everywhere! There were at least ten security guards in front of the restaurant and six or more inside.

"What's going on here?" my wife asked. It looked like the place had just been robbed or something. I hesitated before walking in, and one of the security guys politely waved me to move forward. We went up to the hostess counter and I said, "I have a reservation for two people."

"Yes. And your name please?" She smiled.

"Rogers." I said. The girl froze. She looked at me like she had just seen a ghost.

"Rogers? Rogers, for two?" She quivered.

"Yes, please." I replied in my usual, friendliest manner.

"Just a moment," she said, then she ran into the back of the restaurant. A moment later an older lady came out.

"Yes sir? May I help you?" she asked in a very business-like manner.

"Yes. The name's Rogers. Table for two, please. I have a reservation." I cheerily repeated.

"Rogers? Did the Pit Boss call to make the reservation for you just ten minutes or so ago?" the lady asked.

"Yes, she did, and she's doing a very fine job, I might like to add!" I said.

The lady looked confused. Strange, eh? There sure seemed to be lots of confused people at the Hilton that day!

"Come with me, please." The lady took two menus and walked us into some kind of VIP room at the restaurant. I had been to that restaurant several times before, but I had never seen the VIP room. Such splendor! Such opulence!

"Say! Look at these forks and spoons! Are these real silver?" I asked my wife.

My wife scowled at me and said, "Don't put that in your pocket!"

After we sat down, the lady whispered to some of the security guys and they all looked at me as if to say, "What? Him?" And they all walked out.

Our waitress came running up to our table as if to say, "You're not supposed to be sitting here," but the older lady shook her head and nodded in a message of "knowing" sign language and the waitress started walking slowly to our table. I could read her mind. "That's not Kenny Rogers! Damn! There goes my $100 tip for the night." Depressed, she walked up to our table and scribbled down our order.

Poor waitress lady! I suppose she had envisioned a huge tip, a photo with Kenny, or who knows? Maybe Kenny and she would have "hit it off"?

Isn't Kenny Rogers super-rich? Heck, I'd marry him in a minute!

But oh, little did our poor waitress know just how bad her luck had turned that moment! I had been at the Blackjack table. I knew how Lady Luck could change in the wink of an eye.

My wife is Japanese. We live in Japan. We don't eat those huge portions of food that are served in America. Every time we go to America, we are shocked to see the size of the steaks that people attempt to eat. In America, the portion for one person is equal to the portions of four people in Japan, and that's no exaggeration.

I ordered one small steak, one baked potato, and one side of asparagus.

"And what will the lady have?" asked the waitress.

"Oh, that's all. We'll share. Oh, and could you please bring an extra plate, please?"

"Anything to drink?"

I asked my wife if she wouldn't like to share a bottle of the $200 Dom Perignon.

"No." my wife replied. I looked at the waitress.

"Just two glasses of water, please." I smiled.

The waitress wrote down our order and slouched back into the kitchen. She didn't seem like a very happy camper.

Perhaps she doesn't like her job or she has personal problems at home, I surmised.

Hey! It wasn't my fault this lady was having a bad day! It's not my fault I can't eat a whole half side of a cow for dinner like many Americans do!

The food was great. After dinner, we gave the waitress a pretty good tip as a consolation prize anyway.

But I digress once again…The whole point of all this is this: If you want to fight the power, do it. Just try to make sure they don't know what you look like.

Don't play with fire. Don't smoke at a public disturbance. That way they can't lift your DNA off a cigarette.

Trust me here. I know what I'm talking about. I've done it all, and never been arrested or properly photographed. And since no one knows what I look like and I have such a common name, there is no way anyone's going to kill me if I go to America.

No! Wait! I take that back! There is one who can kill me! They don't need to know what I look like to kill me. They don't even need to know my name! They only need to know what money looks like. They kill me *every time*...at the casino at the Las Vegas Hilton.

What Would Groucho Say?

Things have changed greatly in American society. Were things always the way they are today? Were Americans always so paranoid? No, I don't think so. I have come to the conclusion that Americans have become so jaded to the insanity of American society—especially since 9/11—that many of them can no longer view the world and their own society in a rational manner.

It wasn't that long ago that people in America were always suspicious of the government—a healthy suspicion—and they used their gray matter to think things through. I know it was this way. Now, I get the impression that many Americans are just cheerleaders for the boob tube and the crap being expelled from it.

I studied cinema and television at my university. At that time, and even now, I was a complete Marx Brothers freak. I currently own all of their movies—even the crummy ones—on video and DVD; I love Chico's piano playing. I am even a collector of Marx Brothers and Groucho Marx recordings. I have some extremely rare recordings that very few people have, or have even heard in decades.

One night Groucho came to me in my dreams. He spoke to me. This is what he said, and this is what I saw: It's Thursday night, and the National Broadcasting Company presents America's favorite TV game show host; here's…Groucho Marx on *You Bet Your Life!*

Groucho: Hello, everyone, and welcome once again to "You Bet Your Life"—the game show that brings in interesting people from all walks of life with interesting things to say. All I know is that we have guests in the studio and the doors are locked, so I have to go through with it.

While we're talking to any one of our studio guests, if they say the secret word, out will pop the duck and award them a prize of $1000. Now before our first guest comes into the studio, I'd like to ask our announcer George Fennerman to tell us what the secret word is for today. George?

George (whispers): Groucho, today's secret word is "control."

Groucho: Okay, now that we have our secret word, let's meet with our first studio guest today. You know him as the head of the Homeland Security Office;

he's the guy who keeps us all on edge and has the name to go with it, Mr. Tom Ridge...

(Canned applause. Abruptly stops.)

Groucho: Well, welcome to the studio, Tom.

Ridge: Well, it's good to be here, Groucho, answering the questions. As you know, I'm usually the one asking the...

Groucho: Enough about that, Tom. What have you been doing recently?

Ridge: Well, you know I've been keeping very busy...

Groucho: How so?

Ridge: Oh, just keeping up on messages, cleaning out old files from the file cabinet, making a few phone calls...

Groucho: Who do you usually call, Tom?

Ridge: Well, say for example I get a hot tip that terrorists are about to strike...

Groucho:...A hot tip? Where would this come from?

Ridge: Oh, from our government intelligence services...

Groucho: Government intelligence services? (Pauses and looks at the audience.) Government intelligence? That's the most ridiculous thing I've ever heard!

(Audience laughs)

Ridge: Well, as I was saying, if I get a hot tip that terrorists are about to strike, you can bet that I'm on the phone immediately, calling all the important people that I should call.

Groucho: Such as?

Ridge: Well, first off I get right on the phone to the boss directly...

Groucho: You mean the president?

Ridge: No! No! My wife. I have to tell her that I'll be late for dinner that night.

(More wild, but polite, applause and laughter from the audience.)

Groucho: Making sure the chicken pot pies don't get cold, I'm sure...

(Audience lightly chuckles.)

Tom, who was the barbarian conqueror known as the "Scarge of God"? Scarge...Spelled S-C-O-U-R-G-E? I can't even pronounce it.

Ridge: You mean "scourge."

Groucho: Scourge, eh? Rhymes with "George."

Ridge: "Scourge"? Rhymes with "George"? Hmmm, barbarian conqueror? Groucho, I'm...I'm sorry, I don't know who that would be...

(More canned laughter)

Groucho: So you say you've been cleaning out old files and such. What kinds of things do you keep in those files, Tom?

Ridge: Oh, we have posters and brochures. Things to help people in case of an attack. Things like that.

Groucho: Posters, eh? What kind of posters? Are these like posters for the theater? Do they say, "Starting this Saturday there will be a terrorist attack at Central Park or something?"

Ridge: Oh no, Groucho. The posters are not specific. We made them without dates and times printed on them; that way we could print up a lot of them at once and save money on printing costs. We get a bulk discount for anything over 100,000 posters at once, so we try to make them as non-specific as possible that way they can have varied uses and be used over and over.

Groucho: So, Tom, you've been in the government a long time. Is that how you usually do things?

Ridge: Well, we in the government like to get right on top of things and do it the "old fashioned way." We just keep humping at it until we feel the job is done...

(Groucho stops...Looks at the audience...Audience begins to roar with laughter...)

Groucho: It doesn't matter what anyone says to me anymore; the audience always takes it as a dirty joke. They probably wouldn't be laughing so much if they realized just how bow-legged they really were.

...What do you mean, "the old fashioned way," Tom?

Ridge: Well, Groucho, the old fashioned way means control, and lots of it.

(The cigar-smoking duck drops down along with the confetti.)

Groucho: Well, Tom, you said the secret word. What was that secret word again, George?

George Fennerman: Groucho, the secret word was "control."

Groucho: So, Tom, you win the $1000 dollars. What are you going to do with that $1000 dollars, Tom?

Ridge: Well, first off, Groucho, I'd like to hire a secretary to help me with some of my paperwork. The way things are now they are so backed up that this week I'm still trying to clear out the files from 2001.

Groucho: Oh, so that's the reason for all the commotion?

Ridge: Yes. Well, I feel it is safe to say, "Better late than never!"

Groucho: Yes, and I feel it's safe to say "That the world is a tragedy to those who feel, but a comedy to those who think"...Of which one of us is not doing very much of...

(More laughter)

Groucho: Well, we wish the best of luck to both of you. Just make sure your secretary keeps both her feet on the floor and you shouldn't have any problems. Well, that's all the time we have for tonight. Thanks to Tom Ridge for being here...

Ridge: And thank you, Groucho.

Groucho: I have a feeling that we'll be seeing lots more of Tom and his posters in the days to come. Good-night, folks.

(Canned laughter and applause. Fade to black.)

Patriotic Photos and Other Tips

"Government data. You just have to love government data. Because there is nothing so delightfully absurd." ~ *Charles Featherstone*

Well, it's that time of year again. Things to do. Stuff to take care of. Errands to avoid. Along with all the regular daily affairs that clutter up our minds and schedules with minute details, there are the uniquely important ones that come only at this time of year: new tires for the car, buying gifts for the kids, and making sure you renew your driver's license before it expires…My driver's license has expired!?

Oh, don't forget being a good husband and father and all of the irresponsibilities that go with it.

Our better half seems to find it none too amusing when we, in our haste to avoid getting things done, seem to disregard the little notice envelopes that come in the mail, especially the ones from our friends in the government or the Department of Motor Vehicles. What are those people's problems? Don't they ever write just to say, "Hello"?

Well, as a matter of fact, they don't. While there is legislation pending before congress to approve government distributed "Hello!" letters, there are no federally approved "Hello!" forms as of the time of the publishing of this fine book.

But let's get back to the year-end cheer. If you're like most husbands, you've gotten everything done by now. Well most of what you're supposed to have done: presents for everyone, clean underwear for the dinner at the wife's folks' home, you've even showed up to work on time lately in the hopes that your boss will give you a decent bonus this year. You've done more than what was expected of you. Good job.

But what about the man in your life? What about the most important man on the face of the entire earth? You know of course who it is that I am talking about. That's right, number one: yourself. What do you give the man who already has everything?

Let's face it, God's gift to the women of the world does not need much else. Lord knows that we already look and smell our best without the cologne or new neckties, and why would we want our wife and kids to buy us something that we

153

don't need? Something, I might add, that just winds up costing us cash out of our own pockets. No thanks, right?

How many times have you heard that song that goes, "I wish it could be Christmas everyday of the year"? Probably once too many by now, but wouldn't it be wonderful if every day really could be Christmas? Well, it can be. Today I'm going to give you some super tips on how to make your life more exciting over the coming 12 months and show you how you can add just a touch more pizzazz and adventure to your daily hum-drum. And you can help out our government*at the same time!*

But how? Well, luckily for all of us, this is where the boys down at City Hall come to the rescue. Yep, you read right. How many times have you wanted to live the life of an International Man of Adventure? To always be on the run? To boldly go where no man has ever gone before? To be like me?

Here are a few things to keep in mind for the coming year on how you can spice up that drab and dreary existence, and all with the cooperation of our friendly government!

Your Taxes and Documentation

For example, take the tax office, please! Just kidding. No, really; the tax office guys are your friends. They need you. It's true. Now any true-blue patriot knows that it is your duty to cheat on your taxes as much as possible, as often as possible. That's right. The government guys actually *want* you to cheat! If no one cheated, we wouldn't need a tax office, would we? What would those people do if you didn't cheat on your taxes? Why, they'd all be out of jobs, wouldn't they? So you cheat on your taxes and the government gets to expand its services to stop people from cheating on their taxes. It's the best of both worlds; everybody wins! And you do your part to help to create much-needed jobs for a better America.

So let's all pitch in and help out by cheating on our taxes next year. You'll be glad you did.

I.D. Cards and Photo Documentation

"Great, Mike. But I *already* cheat on my taxes. How else can I help?" Well, glad you asked. Never forget this simple rule: there's any number of ways you can help the government to help you in doing whatever it is the government is supposed to help you in doing—faster and much more efficiently—so don't forget to take a number.

Let's say you do need to go to the Department of Motor Vehicles to get your driver's license renewed. Now this is one of the best and most memorable ways to earn a "present" from a visit to a government office that I can think of, and it's a gift that just keeps on giving the year round.

For example, I had to have my driver's license renewed the other day. For most people this would be a royal pain-in-the-ass. But think about it. Does the guy at the DMV actually want to work? Does s/he want to see your ugly face? Doesn't s/he deserve to pick his navel as much as the next guy? So if this little process is going to be a headache for everyone involved, you might as well try to make the best of it.

Look, I'll be Ernest with you if you are Frank with me. You need that driver's license, and the guy at the DMV wants to "chill" as much as possible. What to do?

Well, do what I do. Make a driver's license that you can be proud of, and one that the people at the DMV won't soon forget. That's right. What could be more treasured than a true "keeper" from the DMV? And what could brighten up the day for a DMV worker as much as having a guy like me come in for his driver's license registration? Not much, really.

The best way to make a driver's license that you can cherish and keep as a family heirloom is by having your photo taken with the most preposterous, ridiculous-looking face that you can possibly make. Now that's what I call a worthwhile trip to the DMV.

"Yes, but Mike, they always tell me not to smile or make a pleasant face when I take my photo for my driver's license." That's right, they do. It's their job. But do you want to be like everyone else? If everyone jumped off a cliff, would you? Are you a lemming? No! You are an individual! You want a photo on your driver's license that you'd be proud to show to your friends all year round. That's why you want the stupidest, most idiotic, most absurd-looking photo you can possibly get away with on your driver's license.

Now, think about it for a moment. Is there anyone who actually is happy with their driver's license photo? I've never met anyone who was. So why not take a photo that will become a conversation piece?

At some places, the government guys will allow you to take your own photo for your documentation—passports, etc.—so those are easy to make stupid faces on. But not at the DMV! There is a secret to getting that super photo with that unbelievable face that will make you the life of parties and having all your friends wanting one too!

What you need to do:

• Plan ahead. Try not to shower or shave for at least 8 days before going to get your picture taken, especially you women! Never comb your hair. When applying makeup, do it in a moving vehicle on the way to the DMV, particularly you gentlemen.

• Always check to see what time the DMV stops accepting applications. Let's say it stops at 4 p.m. Wonderful. You show up at about 3:45. Take your time. They aren't going anywhere, and if you show up near closing time, they'll just want you out of there ASAP so they can go home the usual ten minutes early.

• Always be the nicest, most pleasant, lovingly patient person in the entire world. Say "Hello! Top o' the morning to you!" to everyone, regardless of the time of day. Hold the door open for old ladies and their dogs.

• Always look around and act real confused.

• Chew a few raw garlic cloves just before you go in to the DMV. Boy, does that smell bad! When your name or number is called, always try to get as close to the staff worker as possible so you can blow some of that *fragrance du garlique* right into their faces. You are in no rush; you *like* being at the DMV! They'll love that and will want to help you along your merry way as quickly as possible.

Now I already mentioned that the DMV people won't let you make a scowl or some stupid face just as they are taking your picture, so how do you get around that? Simple. Make sure you are making an idiotic face the *entire time* you are in the DMV. That's right. From the very moment you step in through the door, you should be making a crazed scowl or gritting your teeth. Furrowed brows are a nice touch, too. Don't forget to wrap several bandages on the bridge of your glasses!

I know that there are a lot of crappy method actors/actresses out there (Lord knows we've all seen Mel Gibson once too many times), but I believe in the Stanislavski school of acting. If you want to take a picture that makes you look like a psycho, then your acting has to come from within! You must think, "I am a fruit basket; I am a looney; I am Monty Python." Mind control is the key word here. Mind control the entire time you are in the DMV, not just when you are going to have your picture taken. If you do this, then when the person taking your photo wants to say something, they can't! What can they say? Not a whole heck of a lot! (Preferably, they'll feel sorry for you.)

Let's say you are sitting there with a fashionably twisted look and the lady is about to take your photo. She stops. What's she going to say to you? "Uh, excuse me, sir, can you try to look more normal?" No way! If she does say anything, stay in character! Ignore what she says and ask her if hair is sticking out of your nose or something. Hell, pull at your nose hairs and ask her if you can borrow her tweezers. If that doesn't work, tell them that you haven't taken your medication for that day.

My new driver's license—pretty cool, eh?

Now, I know a lot of you are laughing right now and you think I'm joking. But I am not. Think about it: There are, actually, lots of very strange looking people running around. I've seen them. So have you. Isn't it just possible that they know something that you and I don't?

Once you get the first license with the stupid face on it, it will be easier to get the second, then the third. I know; I've done it. You younger folks can use your license at bars as a "pick-up" line. "Wanna see my driver's license?" S/he will probably immediately fall in love with you right there on the spot. I know my wife did.

Imagine the hours of fun the family will have, too! With grandchildren on your knee, you'll show them the absolutely insane photos you got away with in your youth. The grandkids will all giggle and scream with laughter and say, "And Grandpa, did you ever get better?"

The John Dillinger look—suave, sophisticated, unshaven

The Patriot Act

"Ask not how much money your country can pay to you, ask how much you can pay to your country." ~ *John F. Kennedy*

I've noticed recently that several "famous" writers have complained that the Patriot Acts allow for "them" to check through our garbage, see what kinds of books and magazines we read, accumulate all sorts of information on us as to where we go and what we do, things like that.

Well, if you aren't doing anything or going anywhere that day, then what's the problem?

Frankly speaking, folks who work for the government need jobs too, so why fight the system? Go with it, I say. Let's all put our differences aside and work towards making what we have work, rather than complaining all the time, like some "Austrian grandmothers" who will remain nameless at this time. I think folks who have to dig through our garbage to make a living need all the help they can get.

Believe me, looking through someone's garbage is no easy chore, so make it fun for the folks who do. How? This is really simple, and your imagination is the limit.

Start, for example, by doing simple things. Always tear up any paper that you throw away into thousands of little pieces, remembering to only throw away half the torn paper at a time. FBI people just love puzzles. Do you eat eggs? Of course you do. Whenever disposing of eggshells, make sure that you only throw away 1/2 an eggshell at any given time! Imagine the fun and excitement the FBI guys will have when they find only 1/2 an eggshell in your trash! "What happened to the other half?" Or, "Could this be a sign of some kind of satanic worship going on at the breakfast table?" They'll have hours of enjoyment trying to figure out what happened to the other 1/2 of the shell. I know I would.

Magazine subscriptions? Sure. Sign up for all the magazines you possibly can, making sure you send out cancellation notices the next day!

In Summation

Now, there are a few too many folks who think that the government has gotten too large for our own good. There seem to be a lot of folks who have some idea that the government is some over-bloated Titanic, just sucking up people's tax money in bureaucratic nonsense. I just have to ask those folks, "So what's your point?"

Have you ever worked for the government? If the answer is "No," then perhaps one of us is talking out of their hat. Good folks who work for the government need our support, not our incessant complaining.

So that's why I am asking you to join with me in making our government, as well as the Patriot Act a successful—and fun—venture for all of us in the coming year. So join the crowd! Shout it out loud!

After all, it is your duty as a freedom-loving American to cooperate! God bless America! And God bless the American way! If you use your imagination to help them to help you, then we can all enjoy a safe, humorous, and terrorist-free nation in the coming years. You'll be glad you did.

Porky Pig Goes to Japan: 103 Years of American Pork

Wow, kids! It's Porky Pig! Porky's famous all over the world and has been on TV in Japan for years! Kids, adults, and especially politicians just love Porky. Hey, Porky! Will you tell us about your ex-pat American pig experiences in Japan?

"Why sure, Mike. I remember it well. Like it was just l-l-l-l-last...the other day. Commodore Perry was sailing into...Yokohama b-b-b-ba Port, was it? With his Black Ships. Forcing the Japanese to open their market to American goods..."

Uh, thanks Porky. That's enough.

Well, you heard it from the pig's mouth. Of course Porky is going to say that: He is a lackey for the government; they pay him. Forget about the Black Ships. It never happened, at least not the way we are taught it did in government-run schools. Porky is just a lying pig. Events over these last 25 years have led me to conclude that this "Perry story" was probably just some made-in-Wall-Street promotional scam. Let me explain:

It was 1979 and I had some extra cash lying around from a student grant, so I decided that instead of spending it on school, I'd spend it on a vacation to Japan, screwing around with my crazy friends. You may remember that back in those days, Japan and America were having a row over trade relations. More exactly, Japan had a burgeoning trade surplus with the United States because Japan was making high quality products for a good price and United States products were expensive junk.

The US government, doing what governments are supposed to do, strong-armed the Japanese into buying more crap from the States.

I can't really remember how this all turned out, but it seems to me that Japan's economy got just as screwed up as America's.

Back then, I remember riding in taxis all around Tokyo and seeing red, white and blue stickers that said "Import Now!"

I thought that this campaign was a tad bit ridiculous for a few reasons. Well, first off, the entire promotional campaign's posters, stickers, etc. were all written in English. This being Japan, lots of people—especially older people—couldn't read or understand what the signs said. Second, even if the average Japanese could understand what they meant, it wouldn't matter. I mean, Joe Japanese living next door doesn't usually run an import/export company.

Funny that.

So, the other day my wife and I were riding the subway and there on the roof was a poster that said (in Japanese), "American Pork." It had this really keen-o red, white, and blue pig logo that made me proud to be an American. Next to the logo was some great catch copy about how delicious and soft American pork is, and how all the Japanese people and all the American people everywhere are "Celebrating 103 years of American Pork."

What a great promotional event! I'm sure these posters will just help sales of American pork skyrocket in the Japanese market. How will it help American pork sales in Japan? I'm not exactly sure, but you can bet that if the US and Japanese governments are in a *pork project* together, it's just gotta be money well spent.

Of course being just an ignorant foreigner, I would think that if the poster said something like, "Fuji Supermarket has American pork on sale for half price through July" or something like that, it would be more effective to the average Japanese housewife. But hey, what do I know? I don't even eat pork.

Of course I wasn't there at this particular planning meeting, but I have been to many just like it. Let me tell you how these types of promotional events happen. Imagine that we're in a cigar smoke-filled room in New York. No! Make that Wisconsin. There are several fat American bureaucrats standing around a table. The boss guy looks like Edward G. Robinson. He says, "Look, guys, this Mad-cow scare has really hurt our beef sales in Japan, see? Now, I don't want this to affect our pork sales, see? We need a plan. We need to make sure those Japs buy our pork products. We need to show them we mean business. Now we got all this money from the government and we gotta use it, see? Any ideas? How about you, Smith? What do you think?"

"I think we should all go to Japan and wine and dine the Japanese and convince them to buy more pork."

"Good idea. But besides that, we need something else to show the boys back in Washington, see? We need something to show them for all of our efforts. How about you, Wilson, got any bright ideas?"

"We'll talk them into paying for another promotional campaign, just like our successful, 'Import Now' plan."

"Great. But Japan's economy has gone to hell. I hear that people don't ride taxis like they used to. And besides, the 'Import Now" campaign was all in English. I hear that most Japanese didn't understand it."

"We'll convince the Japanese to put up Japanese language posters in all the trains and subways instead."

Edward G. replies, "Good job, Wilson. Someday you are gonna be the boss around here. Get on it, boys. And I'll want some of those posters to show the boys back in Washington. They'll want some proof that we're doing a good job."

Now, cross-fade about 8000 kilometers over to the other side of the world. Imagine that we're in a cigarette smoke-filled room in Tokyo. No! Make that *Gumma*. There are several skinny Japanese bureaucrats sitting around a table. The boss guy looks like, er, well—he looks like Odd Job. He says, *Komatta, ne? Kono kyou-gyu byoo no mondai.*

All right, since this is a movie, I'll put up sub-titles for you:

"This is very worrisome. The Mad-cow disease scare is hurting our domestic beef sales. Even with that, the Americans are insistent that we buy their beef. What shall we do? We need a plan. Now we have graciously received this honorable money from our government. We must use it wisely to block American meat sales in Japan. Any ideas? Sasaki-San, would you care to enlighten us with your wisdom?"

"Perhaps we should invite the Americans to come to Japan and wine and dine them."

"Excellent idea. But besides that, we will need something else for them to take as a gift back to Washington. We need something to show them that we appreciate their honorable intentions. Tanaka?"

"We'll talk them into paying for another promotional campaign, just like our successful 'Import Now' plan."

"Wise. But our economy is not so strong. The public does not ride taxis like they used to, and I believe that the Americans may have become suspicious of English advertising in Japan."

"We'll convince the Americans that posters in all the trains and subways are better. We'll write them in Japanese! That way the Americans won't be able to read what they say, so we can tell them whatever we decide later."

Odd Job replies, "Excellent work Sasaki-San. Someday may you be promoted to section chief. Let us begin immediately. Press up some extra posters; we will want them to take some back to Washington. We'll want some proof that we're doing a good job."

And the posters go up. The American guys come over to Japan. They wine and dine and get drunk every night. After that, they go to Karaoke with some Japanese bureaucrats and their paid girlfriends. Who knows what kind of hi-jinks goes on!

And this cycle goes on and on—every night, with a different set of American and Japanese bureaucrats. Day in and day out. Week after week. Year after year.

And this is why I believe what I believe today. There never was a Commodore Perry. It's all just a myth. The whole thing—Perry, the Black Ships, some samurai dude—it's all just make-believe. It never happened. It's all just some promotional scam to waste our tax money and sell us stuff we don't want.

Okay, well, there *might* have been a Commodore Perry. I'll give you that much. But I know, even with Perry, there *definitely* had to be lots of wining and dining*and* paid girlfriends. The only part of all these stories that you know has got to be 100 percent true is the part about the pork.

The more things change, the more they remain the same.

Japan-US Relations: Celebrating 103 years of Pork.

Revenge of 9-Foot Killer Chinese

The United States government runs a huge world—wide empire. This empire is going to bankrupt the United States some day real soon. Not only does the empire suck your tax dollars down a bottomless pit, it makes people around the world despise Americans.

What really makes people angry is when the US Empire starts interfering in what folks in other countries see as their own domestic affairs. Japan learned this lesson in World War II. When will Americans ever learn that this kind of interference is a no-win situation for the United States?

When it comes to China, all I can say is "Watch out America! You're in big trouble. While you weren't looking they came…and no one and nothing can stop them! They are 'The 9-Foot Killer Chinese!'"

You've seen that seven-foot six-inch tall Chinese guy named Yao Ming who plays NBA basketball for the Houston Rockets, right? The guy is a giant. Well, I know for a fact that there is a covert Chinese government plan to take over the world using "clones" of this man, and there are 10,000 guys just like him in China right at this very moment. What's even scarier is that no one has had the guts to bring this information out into the open until now.

I turn on the TV and watch the BBC and Japanese news, as well as news from Germany and France. The big story? The US dollar is taking a severe beating—*again*; it looks like it might lose 5 percent of its value this week alone. In the last four years, the US dollar has lost somewhere near 40 percent of its value versus the Euro; people have begun to say their final words of parting. It's just a matter of time before the US dollar becomes a junk currency and the United States winds up like Argentina.

I switch the TV to CNN. The big story in America? US forces alongside a couple of unemployed Iraqis are blasting some dumpy city in Iraq for some reason. Shoot. Shoot. Shoot. Spend. Spend. Spend. And for what? Perhaps they are trying to "even the playing field" by making you folks in America just as broke as the Iraqis.

Any stories on CNN about the US dollar in danger of becoming a junk currency? Nope.

Many years ago the world economy was pegged to the British Pound Sterling, but after the "fall" of the British Empire, the economic factoring switched to the US dollar as a tool for measurement. Now, with the US dollar heading for the garbage bin, some people think that the Euro will take over, but according to several presidents of investment firms who were speaking on the BBC, that's not going to happen. Why? Because they said that the Euro is a "political currency." What *is* going to happen, according to these folks, is that the world's economy is soon to be pegged to the Chinese Yuan, which is an "economic currency."

Now, I am no economics expert, but I do have enough sense to allow my wife to handle all of our finances, so I'm trying to spell it out very simply for you folks here. I have read several articles on Lewrockwell.com recently, dealing either directly or indirectly with this matter that I can recommend to you if you want to read what others who undoubtedly know a whole lot more on this subject than I do have written—articles by Gary North, Paul Craig Roberts, and also Charlie Reese. Read them all; they make frightening common sense.

Anyway, due to the drop in the dollar, the Chinese Yuan has also dropped 40 percent because it is pegged to the dollar, but that's all going to change. And that's not conjecture on my part; that's a fact. China wants to join the World Trade Organization (WTO) in 2007, and one of the rules of the WTO is that the currency of all member countries must be floating. Give you one guess what's going to happen to the dollar by the year 2007 when China floats the Yuan. That's right…Did I already mention the high possibility of the US dollar becoming junk currency? I did? Fine. Also, 2007 sounds like a long way off, but it's not; it's just around the corner.

Also, don't forget that this *will* happen, as China will join the WTO and will also host the Summer Olympics in 2008.

I've been to China three times. I love the place. Kinda crowded, but what a bustling buzz of excitement! Imagine the high-tension wire of the New York Stock Exchange that you see on TV on any given day on any given street in any of China's big cities; that's what China is like.

Not only that, but the Chinese are quite excellent at foreign languages, and the Chinese are all around the world. They have great business sense and connections. Everywhere they have gone that I have seen them, they have been successful; be it America, Japan, Thailand, or England: The Chinese have done quite well, thank you.

I have even been to Hong Kong and Macao before those two reverted back to mainland rule. Before they changed hands back to "the communists," people were freaking out that all hell was going to break loose. But you know what? Not much has changed. So much for "Red China."

I have some friendly advice for my brothers and sisters in the USA: When it comes to China and Taiwan, do yourselves a big favor and don't touch. Be smart, like the Japanese are. When it comes to Chinese and Taiwanese relations, just say that you are against violence. Period. End of story. There will never be any way that America can make any difference when it comes to China's "run-away province." Don't forget that we are talking about a country that is well over 5,000 years old, and the Chinese can wait us out. The USA will never benefit from any sort of military confrontation with China. I think the Chinese know this. The Japanese know this, and they know better than to get involved or take sides.

Also, know that the world is passing you by, America. Japanese and Chinese banks are floating the US dollar, but they are about to pull the plug on your red ink and your diving currency. When that happens, you are a not a sinking ship; you are already sunk.

Lots of Americans seem to have some idea that when America's economy goes down it'll take the rest of the world with it. I am beginning to seriously doubt this. Sure, it will hurt, but Asians save money. Credit cards were virtually unused in Japan until 1990. We still do not use checking accounts to pay bills. Bills for utilities, etc, are paid at any bank, post office, or convenience store. And the Japanese people have huge personal savings up to their rear-ends. Americans are in debt way over their heads, and it's just getting worse. Oh, but sure, you are different. This bad news won't happen to you.

It's just like the Chinese basketball player, Ying Mao. I know people will say, "If there were more guys like him, they'd be coming over to America to play ball." Well, yes and no. I also know of an old "pick-up" line I've heard in American movies, "You are a one-in-a-million girl/guy."

Well, that's all well and good, but when it comes to China, they have a saying that goes, "One in a million in America means that there's 10,000 other people just like you in China." Think about it.

So look out America! It's lurking there just in the shadows. It's already here; it's The Revenge of 9-Foot Killer Chinese. Just make sure you are not on the receiving end.

—*Coming soon to a neighborhood near you.*

The Japanese TV Police: PBS With Teeth!

Some people I have met have told me that Japan is not a free country. Some others have told me that it is. Some have told me that this is a Socialist nation.

In some ways I think this is a much freer nation than America (and I thought that well before Bush ever became president), and in some ways I think this is not such a free nation at all. Confused? Yeah, me too.

One of the ways Japan seems to me to be a very free country is that there is still very little crime. When I lived in America, I always worried about my parents or my wife being a victim of crime whenever they stayed out after dark. Heck, I was afraid to be out in downtown Los Angeles by myself after dark! Maybe I was made so afraid because of sensationalist TV news in America. I don't know. I don't think I can make an objective judgement about that anymore. But I think fearing for your own personal safety in your own neighborhood is a kind of "oppression."

I have never felt this fear in Japan. Okay, well I did—once. I was walking down the street, late at night by myself, after drinking with some friends. It was probably about 1:30 in the morning. I had just gotten to Japan and still didn't really know what was going on here. Anyhow, I was walking down this dark street, and out from behind me pop two guys from a dark alley. I got real scared! I thought these two guys were going to "roll" me. I started walking a bit faster, but they were gaining on me! Then I remembered I wasn't in downtown Los Angeles; I was in downtown Tokyo. Maybe living in L.A. so long had made me a bit "jumpy." (L.A. has a funny way to make anyone "jumpy" for that matter.) I thought, *These guys aren't dangerous. Hell, I'm probably the most dangerous person around here!* I stopped, and the two guys walked by me. I overheard them talking about some girl at work that they thought was "hot."

A few of the ways that Japan is not as free as America seem sometimes to really have nothing to do with what the government does or decides. This is an extremely crowded place. Imagine your worst last minute Christmas shopping at the mall nightmare and multiply that by 20. Yeah, that's about right. That's what any train station around Tokyo is like on any given work day at eight in the morning.

Some comments I've heard from people here are, "It's so crowded here that you don't have room to change your mind." Or "My apartment is so small, I put the key into the front door lock, and poked a hole in the back door screen." Being so crowded, Japan is a great place to learn patience. There's no point in getting mad or really being in so much of a rush. You aren't going anywhere!

And if you got mad here, lost your temper and started screaming, well that's the worst thing you could do. Japanese people don't really raise their voices (unless they're drunk), and if you raise your voice and start screaming, the only thing they will understand is that you are mad. You could be shouting the most logical, rational sentence in the entire world and all they will do is give you a blank look and think *What's this guy shouting about?* So it does you absolutely no good to start shouting here. You'll be "turned off" by everyone around. You'll be ignored, and you'll realize a few moments later that you are standing there shouting by yourself, and everyone is staring at you with little question marks floating over their heads.

But there are times when the Japanese government makes rules about this or that. Well, I guess so. Isn't that what governments do? Sure the US government screws things up and very often makes rules that are just ridiculous. They all do!

I am reminded of the warning label on a package of drain cleaner I saw in the United States that said something like, "If you are unclear about the proper usage of this product or you are unable to understand or *unable to read these instructions*, do not use this product!" (I'm not making that up either!)

But the Japanese government has their own unique, well—let me say "cute" way of screwing things up. One great example is what I call the "TV Police."

I'm sure if I say "TV Police," it conjures up images in your mind about jack-booted cops bursting into your house and clubbing you over the head for watching some anti-government propaganda programs. Or like the RIAA Nazis you have in America who want all 12-year-olds arrested for downloading music off the Internet.

No, no! That's not it. It's even more ridiculous, simple, and devious than that!

The doorbell rings one day. I answer it. The guy says he's from NHK. NHK is the nationally-run broadcasting station here in Japan. It's kind of like PBS, except they have interesting programs—sometimes. I open the door and talk to the guy. He tells me I have to pay some money.

"Money? For what?"

"For your TV."

"For my TV? Why?"

"Because it's the law."

"What?"

"It's the law in Japan that all people who own a TV must pay a monthly fee."

It *is* the law. NHK is the government-run broadcasting network here, but they don't take money out of your taxes to pay for it. No! They have a much more efficient system of running it here! They have some guy who comes around to every house in the neighborhood, kind of like the newspaper boy, to make "collections."

"I'm not going to pay you any money!"

"You must! It's the law!" I can tell that this guy isn't going to go away easily. I realize that I had already blown it by speaking Japanese to him in the first place.

"I don't watch NHK," I counter.

"It doesn't matter. Everyone who owns a TV must pay!" he demands. This does not register in my brain. It's like I'm having some sort of short-circuit. Sparks are flying out of my ears, and my eyes are twitching. I can't think straight. I repeat, "But I don't watch NHK!"

"It's the law. Everyone who owns a TV must pay for NHK, regardless of whether they watch it or not!" He hands me an explanation paper. It's written in crappy English. The guy is maneuvering me into a corner.

I come up with my next snappy line of reasoning. "I'm not paying!"

"You must pay. NHK does not have commercials, so everyone must pay!"

"What? Look, this isn't the Soviet Union!" I say. "If you guys don't want to have commercials, that's your choice. I didn't decide that! No one asked me!"

"It's the law that NHK has no commercials!"

"Look," I say, "I'll write you a note giving you my permission to air commercials. Okay?"

"No! You must pay!"

I act like I'm going to step out of my apartment, so he steps back. That was my chance! As soon as he stepped back, I slammed the door shut and locked it!

"Whew!" I thought. But damn if this guy wasn't persistent! He must have kept knocking on my door for two minutes after that, until he realized I wasn't going to answer it so he gave up and left.

"What a bunch of crap! I don't even watch NHK!" I thought as I turned on the TV and watched Sesame Street with my kid. Okay, well, I do watch NHK. They show Sesame Street! That "Cookie Monster" and "The Count" just crack me up!

The next day the doorbell rang, and it was the same guy. I couldn't believe it! And this time he showed up with his boss! My kid answered the door, so it was already open. I couldn't act like I wasn't home.

The boss was even pushier than the other guy. We go around through the same conversation that we did the day before. The boss is not going to give up as easily as the other guy did. He's got his foot in the door. He's not going to leave until I give him the money. What am I going to do? Well, what would any self-respecting husband in Japan do? I blame my wife! Yeah. I tell them that I don't have any money, anyway, and that my wife controls all the money, so talking to me is just a big waste of time.

That kind of logic works well in this country. People in the West think Japanese women are treated as second-class citizens. In some ways, yes; in some ways, no. But in a very large percentage of households in Japan, the wife has complete control of the family "purse-strings." So you tell me, if the women have all the money here, who really holds the keys to power in Japan?

So the NHK guys ask me when my wife will be back. I tell them "tomorrow."

The next morning I'm at work, talking with an old-timer in the broadcasting business here in Tokyo. This guy had worked in the broadcasting business for almost 40 years at the time. I'm sure he is retired by now. I tell him about my little escapades with the NHK guys. I ask him what I should do. He says, "Don't pay."

I am quite surprised at what he tells me. I mean, here is a Japanese guy, working in this broadcasting business, and he's telling me not to pay!

"No one in this business ever pays, Mike," he says.

"But what about the law? If I don't pay, they said they'd penalize me!"

"Yeah," he says, "in the law it is written that if you don't pay NHK, you will be given a penalty. But the law doesn't state what the penalty is!"

"Just like Japan!" I think. I say, "So if I don't pay, there's nothing they can do about it?"

"No," he says, "they are just worried that if the neighbors find out that you didn't pay, the neighbors will stop paying too. That's all. I had the same experience, and after several times that NHK came over, finally they sent a very high-ranking official to my house. He told me, 'Okay. You don't have to pay. Just don't tell the neighbors that you don't pay and we won't bother you anymore.' So we agreed."

Unbelievable! Well, actually very believable, if you've ever been here before.

So, that was about 15 years or so ago. I have seen the NHK guys many times since. I've tried everything to get rid of them! I acted like I couldn't speak Japanese; that didn't work. I've acted like I wasn't home; they waited for me. I've even tried to act like I was just the house—keeper; no dice! I guess I'm a bad liar. It must show on my face. They keep coming back.

The other day I woke up in the morning and saw my 15-year-old daughter standing at the door, talking to a different NHK guy, and he was having her sign a form for an automatic bank withdrawal for the fees! A 15-year-old kid! I grabbed the form from her and told her I'd take care of it. The form was in Japanese, so I acted like I couldn't read it. I pointed at a line on the form and said to him, "What does this say here?" He adjusted his glasses and took the form from me so he could explain what was to be written in each space. As soon as he did, I slammed the door shut and locked it.

Of course he stood outside and knocked on my door for a while until he gave up. God! Do I hate these control freaks! So I goose-stepped into the living room and told my kids that if it's the NHK guy at the door, they are *absolutely verboten* to answer the door under any circumstances.

So now I am trapped in my apartment—living in fear. I'm afraid to go outside and be accosted by the TV Police. Yes. NHK in Japan: PBS with teeth! Well, maybe not teeth—more like dentures.

There Ought To Be a Law: Buckle Up or Go to Prison!

There are some things in Japan and America that are the same: The government intrudes on our daily affairs to the point of absurdity, and it's getting worse every day. Japan is still behind the States, but they just passed a seatbelt law a few years ago. What's next?

Do you fasten your seatbelt when you drive? You *know* you should, but a lot of people don't. What are *we* going to do about all these people who drive without their seatbelts fastened? I have a solution! I think it's about time the government made a law that makes an unfastened seatbelt a serious crime! None of this "paying a fine" nonsense for me! How about a "three strikes and you're out" type of law? Hell, let's not stop there! An unfastened seatbelt should be a capital crime!

About a month ago, I found a cell phone that someone dropped on the street. Being a good guy, I knew it was my civic duty to turn the phone in to the police lost-and-found. When I got to the police station there was an old Japanese guy—I'd say he was at least in his late-mid-seventies—demanding that the police arrest him. This old guy was furious!

I started to eavesdrop on the conversation the old guy was having with the cops, and I realized that I was hearing some really interesting interpretations of the law. I figured I should pay attention to this lesson in legal maneuvering in case I should ever find myself in the same position. And let me tell you, this old guy would have been a great defense attorney! He ran circles around those hapless cops.

It is illegal to drive a car without your seatbelt on. I guess this old guy was driving down the street without his seatbelt fastened, and there was a policeman standing at the intersection. When the man saw the policeman, he quickly fastened his seatbelt. Too late! The policeman saw him first.

The policeman, who looked to be about thirty, waved at the old man to pull over, and the argument began. The cop wanted to give the guy a traffic citation for not wearing a seatbelt, but the old guy would have none of it. He stated, "But I had my seatbelt on!"

"No you didn't! You put it on after you saw me!" said the policeman.

"I didn't see you!" the man insisted.

"Yes you did!"

"No I didn't! Do you have any proof that I saw you?" the old man shouted.

Whoa! I thought, *This guy's got some real talent for the legal wrangle-dangle!*

The policeman retorted, "You saw me! And besides, you didn't have your seat-belt on!" By this time there were three policemen dealing with this old guy. The first policeman wrote out a citation and told the man to sign it. He refused.

"I had my seat belt fastened!" the old man said.

"Yes, but you fastened it only after you saw me!" replied the policeman, getting visibly rattled by the old guy.

"No I didn't! I was in the action of fastening it anyway!" the old guy said. He added, "It was fastened when you stopped me!"

The old guy was right. When the cop stopped him, the seatbelt was fastened. A higher-ranking policeman interrupted. "Well, just sign the citation and you can talk to the judge about it."

"No! I will not sign this citation!" the old man shouted. "My seatbelt was fastened when the policeman stopped me!"

The policemen and the old guy argued back and forth, the old man insisting that he was within the law and the police insisting that he broke the law and that he sign the citation. Neither side was getting anywhere.

Then the old guy decided to change his defensive tactics. "If I sign this citation, then that means I acknowledge to you that my actions were illegal, which means that I acknowledge to you that I am a criminal. I am not a criminal, so I cannot sign!"

The cops looked like they were lost. "You didn't have your seatbelt fastened when I first saw you!"

"So I am a criminal because you claim to have seen me before I saw you? This is ridiculous!"

He's right, I thought. This was completely ridiculous. It got even more ridiculous when the Japanese cops kept following his line of logic and arguing each point with him.

The old suspect added, "In Japan, crime is getting out of control! If you guys were doing your job, you wouldn't have time to just be standing around on street corners!" An excellent point that had the cops at a loss for words.

I was wondering why they just didn't whack him over the head with a billy club and arrest him for resisting arrest or assaulting a police officer, like they would in America.

The old guy was at the police box for at least 45 minutes, arguing about whether or not he had his seatbelt on—which he did when the cop stopped him. He refused to sign the citation and placed his wrists on the counter and spread his legs out as if to be body searched. I almost burst out laughing, but I kept my cool.

"If you are going to treat me like a criminal, I demand my right to be arrested!" he shouted. Man! I thought this guy was going to burst a vein in his neck or something. That's how pissed off he was!

Finally, the old guy's wife walked in. She must have been shocked to see her husband stretched out on the counter, demanding to be arrested. She shouted at him like he was a little kid. "What are you doing? Just sign the citation and let's go! I have to get to the post office!"

"I will not sign!"

The wife then grabbed the citation, signed it, and slapped it onto the counter. She began scolding her husband. After that, she started apologizing to the policemen. She grabbed the husband's arm and dragged him out of the police box. He was fighting and shouting the whole way.

When she finally yanked him out of the door, he looked back to the police, and in one last moment of defiance he shouted, "As soon as I get to where you guys can't see me, I'm going to unfasten my seatbelt. What do you think about that, smartguys?"

You know, he does have a point there. The law says it is illegal to drive without your seatbelt fastened. But doesn't that law allow for a loophole large enough to drive a truck through? The guy did have his seatbelt on when the cop stopped him. That cannot be denied.

The three policemen looked at the citation that the wife signed. They looked like they had just been through a thorough beating, which they had.

The older cop said to the younger guys about the citation, "Just send it in."

"But he didn't sign it!" said one of the junior policemen.

"Just send it in," and they all slumped into the back room.

The older policeman knows that the government will just send a bill to the old guy's house. The husband will order his wife that if a bill to pay a fine comes in the mail, she is to ignore it. She says, "Okay," and then ignores the husband. The wife will probably just pay the fine instead of wasting time on it. He doesn't remember anything about it. She forgets the whole thing. And everyone is happy—well, sorta. The entire situation is preposterous.

And why are the police screwing around with this old guy? Three cops, an hour of wasted time. Forms to be filled. Fines to be paid. Mail to be sent back and forth. Staff to process paperwork. My tax money down the toilet. And for what? I mean, if a 70-some-year-old man wants to drive his car without a seatbelt on, then who cares?

When you stop and think about it, this is completely asinine. Here's a 70-plus-year-old guy driving without his seatbelt on, and some 30-year-old policeman is going to write this guy a citation. And he's spending my tax yen (dollars) on this crap!

I mean, if the government is going to pass laws telling people what to do, especially old people who have lived through life's little pleasures like the bombing of Tokyo—you know, silly stuff like incendiary bombs landing on their houses—the Great Depression, military occupation by a foreign power, then I think we shouldn't stop there!

It should be against the law to have a policeman *see you* before you *see him!*

The law should read, "It is illegal for you to have a police-person see you operating or driving any sort of vehicle without your seatbelt fastened before you see him/her/it, or before that police-person sees you driving said vehicle without your seatbelt fastened." That would alleviate any misunderstanding in this type of case.

The penalty should be 25 years to life. There ought to be a law for such a particularly heinous crime.

I Found Some Marijuana in My Apartment!—Hints on How to Live Right

Despite what you may have heard, *smoking marijuana in Japan is not illegal*. The law is quite clear on this: *possession of marijuana is illegal*. Possession precedes usage. So the law is written with the understanding that if you don't have marijuana, you can't smoke it. Makes sense. That's not to say that if the Japanese police thought you were smoking marijuana that you wouldn't be "detained"; you most certainly would. But even if they gave you a blood test and marijuana showed up in your blood, unless they found actual marijuana, they could do nothing to you (except try to make your life miserable).

Two decades or so ago, former Beatle Paul McCartney showed up for his Japan tour with a bag of marijuana handsomely displayed on the top of his clothing for the customs agents to see when they opened his luggage. Sure enough, they threw him in jail. Of course, because Paul is rich and famous, they let him go after a few days. Had that been you or me, we probably would have gone to jail for at least three years, maybe ten; we would have definitely been deported. They don't mess around with marijuana in this country.

I was so bored at home today that I wanted to scream! I actually watched TV! Did you know that "Colombo" was a huge hit TV show here in Japan way back when? Yep! Re-runs are going on, even now! So I decided to watch Colombo. It's a story I had already seen a long time ago, but I watched it again. Like I said, I was bored. Anyhow, this particular Colombo episode is one where Colombo catches a wife and her lover trying to "set up" the husband for a murder. Things don't fit right, and Colombo catches their butts and they go to jail. "Ha!" I think. "My wife wouldn't dare to try to kill me for my money. I don't have any." (Hint: Guys always give your wife all your money. That way she won't try to kill you, at least not as often.)

My wife told me she saw this huge cockroach in the kitchen last night. She's freaking out. You guys don't have big cockroaches in America. I have seen cockroaches in Japan that were about four inches long and they can fly! (Maybe that's where the Japanese got the idea for these B-grade monster movies?) So, being the good house husband that I am, I decide that I will clean the entire kitchen. What the heck, eh? I have nothing else to do! You name it, I cleaned it: the dishes, the floor, the sink. And to top it all off, I actually cleaned the gas range. I replaced the foil covering the entire thing, cleaned the grease off the grill, everything!

Then I set a trap out for the cockroach. As of this moment, I haven't caught him, but he's as good as dead. (Hint: Don't buy cockroach traps at the store. If you have lots of free time and you have a scientific mind—like me—make your own!)

Then, after cleaning the kitchen, I got really industrious and decided to vacuum the entire house! So I was vacuuming and I looked under the table in the living room and I see this little green flowery thing. "What is that?" I think. I picked it up and tried to get a closer look.

It looks like marijuana, actually. But, as you get older you will see that—well actually, you probably *won't* see that because your eyes are getting bad. I stare and stare at the green leafy thing, but it is so small that I can't see it well. "It looks like marijuana!"

I smell it. "Hmmm, It smells like marijuana…"

I got suspicious. Just a few days before, my wife and I went to visit her parents' home. It is far away so whenever we go there we always stay for a few days. And, since I have daughters who are high school age, they have parties at the house when we are away. I am not mad that they have parties; I just hope that the neighbors don't complain and my kids don't destroy the apartment while I am gone. I mean, how could I get mad at kids who have parties when their parents are gone? Don't all kids do that? I did. Heck, when I was about 12 years old I would steal my dad's whiskey and drink it when he wasn't around. (Hint: So dad won't know you drank his whiskey, always replace the amount you drank with water—and add soy sauce to keep the color correct!)

We live on the 5th floor of an apartment building. The wife and one of the kids have allergies, so we don't have any plants in the apartment. Zero. None. No plants, no flowers. My wife gets allergies by just looking at a picture of cherry blossoms! I think it is all psychological, but if I tell her that, she gets mad. (Hint: When your wife feels sick, don't tell her that she is imagining things. That way, while she is sick in bed, she'll give you money to go drinking or gambling!)

So I peer closely at the little green "flower" I found. This plant looks familiar. I was sure, right then and there, that I had found some marijuana on the floor of my apartment.

Since my kids have no money, they couldn't have been the ones who bought this marijuana. I figured out that when my wife and I went to her parents' house the kids had a party and one of their friends came over and they all smoked marijuana. I was furious! Why? Well, smoking marijuana is illegal for one. And two, I am sure that the Japanese Gestapo would love to come over to my apartment in the middle of the night and bash me over the head with a bat and arrest me and try to have me deported.

But I wasn't absolutely 100 percent sure if this was marijuana or not. Sure looked like it. I didn't know what to do. If I yelled at my kids about it and it wasn't marijuana, then they would yell back at me, "Why don't you trust us, Daddy?" (Hint: Don't yell at your kids for something they didn't do. That way you won't look so stupid later.)

I had to find out if this was really marijuana or not. But how? I couldn't smoke some of it; that would be illegal. And, if it was marijuana and I did smoke it, I might get "high." And if you have ever smoked marijuana, you'll know that it makes you forget what you were doing. So I…uh…uh…oh yeah! Now I remember! So if I smoked the marijuana, I'd forget what I was mad about. No! I decided that I had to go to the police station and give the marijuana to them and tell them the whole story. So I put the little marijuana flower into a small vinyl bag and went down to the local police box.

So I get the police box and sit down. I try to act like a calm, responsible parent and explain the entire situation to the policeman. Next thing I know, I have to explain the same thing to another policeman. Then another. Finally, I have to tell the whole story to six different policemen. Each time I have to tell the story to a higher-ranking policeman than the one I just talked to before. It becomes a big "production." I guess I must have spoken to every policeman that worked at that particular *Koban* (police box).

None of us can tell for sure if this green flowery thing is marijuana or not. I tell the police that I think it is marijuana, because I smoked it a lot when I was a university student in America (all American university students do, don't they?) So I tell the policemen that I think I know what marijuana looks like. The policemen start looking at me funny. "Are you sure you didn't smoke marijuana in Japan?" they asked me.

"No! Never! Absolutely not!" I say as some cold sweat starts to come down my forehead. (Hint: Don't act paranoid around policemen!)

Then the top police guy tells one of the other guys to call the big police station head office and have some people from the "drug squad" come over. He calls, and then he says, "The detectives will be over in about 30 minutes. Can you wait here?"

I began to get really nervous. I mean, all I wanted to do was find out if this little flowery thing was marijuana or not. If it was, then I was going to take care of it myself and yell at my kids. But no! The police had become involved, and this was turning into probably one of the most exciting drug busts for the local police for the entire year!

When the policeman asked me, "Can you wait here?" he said it nicely, but I got the impression that what he really meant to say was "You stay here. You are not going anywhere." So, like I said, I began to get nervous.

Time went by and they let me step outside for a few moments to have a cigarette. I thought about running away and escaping, but I couldn't; the police knew my name. They had my address and phone number, and worst of all they had the piece of marijuana with them as evidence against me if they wanted to arrest me!

"What an idiot I am!" I thought. "Why didn't I just flush the marijuana down the toilet and forget about the whole thing?" I knew it. It was my wife's fault! She asked me to clean the house! She says she saw a cockroach. But did she? I didn't see any cockroach! Maybe this was an even more devious plan than the one I saw on the Colombo TV show! That had to be it! My wife planted the drugs there and knew I would find them. Then she would have me arrested and deported! That way she could have all my money!

Wait! No! I don't have any money! I threw the cigarette down and walked back inside the police box. After awhile, the police detectives from the drug squad showed up. There were six of them! Two looked like doctors or something. Two looked like undercover policemen—CIA or something. And two others looked like high-ranking police chiefs.

They took me into another room and began asking me a whole bunch of questions—the same questions the other policemen asked me—so I went over the entire story again. I was vacuuming, found the marijuana, came down to the *Koban*, blah, blah, blah…

They set me down and began taking instant photographs of the marijuana. One of the "doctors" put on white gloves and slowly pulled the marijuana out of the little bag. The other police "doctor" took instant photographs of the entire process. Every step of the way, they took photographs. *What a waste of film!* I thought. Instant photo film is really expensive, and this little piece of marijuana was about the size of a half of a corn kernel!

Then the doctor took a tweezers and slowly pulled off a small piece of the marijuana and put it into a small vial. Once again, photos were taken. The two "detective" policemen didn't really say anything, but I could tell that they were really excited. They whispered to each other and paced up and down the room. One of the older police "boss" guys was sitting next to me, asking me more of the same kind of questions: "Who are your kids' friends? What are their names? Do your kids do speed? Do your kids drink alcohol when they are with their friends? Do they smoke cigarettes?" How the hell am I supposed to know this stuff? Of course my kids probably drink alcohol and smoke cigarettes with their friends! Don't all high school kids do that? But of course I had to say, "No!"

Then the doctor pulled a chemistry set out of his bag. It had five or six different chemical tubes in it. "Wow!" I said, "I have never seen one of these. These must be expensive!" The older policeman told me that one chemistry set for testing drugs costs about $220—at government prices (probably $3 at the drug store for you or me). There are different kits for different drugs. This kit was especially made for testing marijuana.

The doctor kept mixing the marijuana and the different chemicals together. The entire process took about 15 minutes. Finally, he put the marijuana into the last vial and sighed, "Okay, in about three minutes we will get the results. When the chemical turns purple, then we will know for sure it is marijuana."

The entire room began to feel electric. Everyone was staring at the chemical vial, waiting for it to turn purple. *Wow! These guys are really excited about this!* I thought. I stared intently at the little glass vial. Then I had a strange thought. *Oh, oh…What if this isn't marijuana? What if this is just some plant? What if I had come down to the police box and wasted 2 hours of 10 policemen, 2 detectives, and 2 police chemist's time? How much money in taxes have these guys spent doing this? They came by car…It was far away…The chemical set costs $220, plus about a dozen instant photos. Plus these policemen's time, they'd have to fill out reports, etc. Uh, oh…*

The time went by slowly. The CIA dudes kept whispering to each other. They were probably planning to raid my apartment—or worse, arrest my kids! The tension was about to make me explode! And then the vial…the color turned…it turned…well, actually, it didn't turn any color. It stayed clear. It wasn't marijuana. It was just a piece of some flower. The police chemists and detectives looked like they were so disappointed. Actually, they looked shocked—and really sad.

Talk about anti-climatic! It was kind of like a baseball game! Two outs, bottom of the ninth, full count. Bases loaded and down by one run, and up to bat comes the homerun hitter! He hits the ball long! It looks like a bases-loaded home run! It's going! It's going! It's—a foul ball! Next pitch…. He strikes out!

"It's not marijuana? Oh, no!" I felt my entire face turn red. The policemen were all bummed out. I stood up and said, "Hey guys, I'm really sorry about all this. Really! I'm sorry…Better luck next time, eh?" And I was bowing to the cops. They seemed like little 10-year-old boys about to cry. "It's okay," the one policeman said. "It's our job." He heaved a deep sigh.

I got up and started walking out of the police box. I was bowing and saying sorry the entire time to all the policemen. One of the regular cops said to me, "It's all right. It's good that it wasn't marijuana." But I could tell they were quite disappointed.

Why were they disappointed? Well, for one, they were disappointed because it wasn't marijuana, and they were probably all excited because they finally found something to do that day. Second, they were probably disappointed because they missed watching the ending of the Colombo TV show down at the police station. (Hint: If you find something that looks like drugs in your apartment, flush them down the toilet and watch reruns on TV.)

The Trashman Cometh

Throw your money in the garbage! Or perhaps I should say, "Wrap your garbage with your money, and then throw it in the garbage," because that's what's going on here in Tokyo.

Depending on the year, Tokyo is rated as the number one most-crowded city in the world. I have heard that 33 million people live in the entire Tokyo metropolitan area. That's a lot of trash—garbage, I mean, not "low-life."

The disposal of garbage in Japan is one of the most talked about and controversial subjects among all Japanese people. It doesn't matter whether you are in Tokyo or climbing Mount Fuji, trash is a problem for everyone here.

Japan is divided up into prefectures. What is a "prefecture"? Good question. I looked it up in a dictionary and found that a prefecture is an area governed by a prefect. Next question, what's a "prefect"? Prefect comes from Middle English or Middle French, from Latin*praefectus*, from past participle of *praeficere* to place at the head of, from prae-+ facere to make. 1: any of various high officials or magistrates of differing functions and ranks in ancient Rome.

Does that answer the question? No? That's fine, because I still don't know what a prefecture is. I guess it's somewhat like a state or a county, only more so.

Anyhow, various prefectures around Japan are experimenting with different ways of disposing of their trash. Of course anywhere you go here, you must divide up your garbage into combustibles, non-combustibles, cans, plastic bottles, paper, cardboard, large items, and even batteries.

In Tokyo the different kinds of trash are collected by the nice men in gray uniforms on various days of the week. In the neighboring prefecture of Kawasaki, you can throw out your trash any day you wish, as they will pick it up daily. But not in Tokyo! No! Mondays, Wednesdays, and Saturdays are burnable trash day. Tuesday and Thursday are non-combustibles. And cans, plastic bottles, etc. are all once a month (I don't know what day). The local newspapers all handle the pick up of old issues once a month.

The newspaper pick-up days are the best, because you'll receive one roll of toilet paper for free for every large bag of newspapers you fill up and throw out.

About eight years ago, the Tokyo Metropolitan government was wrestling with the problem of an ever-mounting burden of trash. Until that time, and even now, the government tried all sorts of measures to deal with the trash. They cut down on collection days, they reclaimed land from the ocean and built huge garbage landfills upon which, now, giant vacant skyscrapers stand (all well and good until a big earthquake comes along and liquefies the landfill). They even tried selling garbage to other countries!

Nothing seemed to work. They even built large incinerators at the cost of hundreds of billions of yen that can only cleanly incinerate a few tons of garbage per day. When you are dealing with tens of thousands of tons of garbage, those incinerators don't really do the job. Yes, I know what you are thinking: "What a bargain for the price!"

It got even better when in 1998 (just seven years after building the previous generation of incinerators) the local government decided that it would be better to build newer, more expensive incinerators that not only burnt trash cleanly, but also produced energy! So they built the new fangled incinerators, and now those incinerators can produce 0.0002 percent of Tokyo's daily electrical needs at merely 125 times the cost. Ah, government bureaucracy! Ya gotta just love them.

You know the old saying, "One man's trash is another man's treasure." Nowhere in the world does this hold truer than in good old Japan.

There's no doubt that Japan is leading the world in the fight against garbage. I'm now going to introduce to you some of the really fantastic ideas on how the Tokyo Municipal government has decided to deal with the trash.

The Tokyo government, after spending hundreds of gazillions of tax dollars on building brand new government offices in downtown Shinjuku (so that all Tokyoites can look up at those gleaming spires and proudly say "This is my city hall") decided, after furnishing their new offices with tax-payer financed Renoir and Van Gogh paintings, that something had to be done about the "trash problem."

I mean, come on, what's the point of having a shiny new castle to live in if there are cigarette butts and empty cans on the street, ruining the view from your 65th story office?

Your tax (Yen) dollars at work! The black arrow at the top right shows to Tokyo Metropolitan Government building—one of the finest (and tallest) pieces of architecture in all of Asia.

So the Tokyo government came up with a really good time-and-money-consuming plan. First off, they spent millions of yen and hours at meetings talking about a revolutionary new idea—digging a big hole in the ground and dumping the trash down in it. This is an excellent idea. Not only does the government get to spend billions of dollars of our tax money on digging a hole; they'll get to spend billions more filling it up.

No doubt about it! "Creating jobs for a better future!" That's my motto.

And for all the nature lovers in Japan, several large oil companies have started their "Green Campaigns," where they show lots of TV commercials telling you how much they care about clean energy and other neat-o phrases like that. What these commercials do to protect the environment I haven't been able to figure out yet, but you can bet that people at least feel better when they are paying for gasoline.

The Japanese government has also made *posturing* like they care about the environment a *top priority!*

In fact, I went fishing at Lake *Yamanaka-ko* near Mount Fuji the other day, and it was beautiful! The water was deep blue, and the forest green. I'm sure it's kept that way by the loudspeakers installed all around the lake, blasting out the message, "Take your trash home with you! People throwing out litter will be fined!"

Conservation is everyone's business! Don't throw your empty beer cans over the side of the fishing boat. Fill them up with water so they sink to the bottom!

A few years ago, the government started collecting plastic "Pet bottles." I've been checking it out and have found out that the manufacturers don't want to recycle the Pet bottles because of the cost, so it is unclear what happens to these bottles once they are picked up.

But hey! At least they have a system to pick up the Pet bottles! They're working on a system on how to deal with them once they are picked up right now. It's kind of like that Beatles song, "Drive My Car."

> *Baby you can drive my car...*
> *Baby you can drive my car...*
> *Baby you can drive my car...*
> *Blah, blah, blah,*
> *I got no car and it's breaking my heart...*
> *But I've got a driver and that's a start.*

The garbage dam is about to burst. Everyone here knows it, so let's stick another finger in the dam.

Now the Tokyo government has launched a trash plan that is not like any other trash plan I have ever heard of in my life. They decided that they were going to gather money for not only the trash collection, but they were going to tax people for the *trash bags!* Genius!

Now I'm not talking about any old "thingy" tax; I'm talking about an absurdly brilliant taxation system that was touted as a way to "cut down on the trash amount" by the local government.

You see, the government already taxes people for garbage pick-up, so some smart bureaucrat (I guess there might be a few) decided to make a law that stated that "garbage must be placed in government-certified garbage bags."

And it gets even better! Not only do you *get taxed* for the bags; you have to *buy* the bags at the store yourself! And they heap on a *5 percent sales tax.*

That's right! Think about it:

The Japanese government charges you income tax. The local government heaps on more tax for your garbage collection services. The after-tax money is spent by the government producing government-certified garbage bags. And as an added bonus, you get to pay sales tax to the government when you buy the government-certified garbage bags—because your garbage *must* be placed in government-certified garbage bags or they won't pick up your garbage! What a deal!

I wonder if any bribes changed hands between some bureaucrat and some printing company for the contract to print the government-approved garbage bags. Nah! The government would never cheat the taxpayers!

I also asked many government officials to explain to me just how it is that having an *extra* government-approved garbage bag was going to cut down on the garbage. It's just an extra bag right? The best answer I got was from a lady at the local government office. She just gave me a blank look and said, "They'll cut down on garbage because they are biodegradable." So they are biodegradable. So what? It is still an extra trash bag.

This insane garbage tax on tax on tax system has led to all sorts of problems that will lead to all sorts of discussions and meetings that will lead to all sorts of tax money being spent on more meetings to discuss these problems.

Now that we get to be quadruple taxed for our garbage in Tokyo, many people have started illegal dumping. Hey! No honor among thieves.

And it's not just fly-by-night shady types who are doing this illegal dumping, but it's the average citizens.

Some people have resorted to taking their trash to the local convenience stores at night and dumping it into the bins in front of the convenience stores! So now just about all the stores in Tokyo have a "No dumping" sign in front of them. I've heard that the problem is so bad that at some convenience stores they are planning on putting up surveillance cameras to stop people from dumping their trash!

I guess it's kind of like the cameras inside a store that are used to stop shoplifters, except these cameras are in reverse—sideways, sort of.

The government here is making so many rules about trash that it is mind-boggling.

In Kyoto, the Environmental Chief and an "accomplice" were busted for bid—rigging of the local garbage collection contract. The accomplice apparently paid off the Chief about $5,000 per month for the "privilege" of collecting the garbage. I'm not sure, but I think the accomplice also had his hand in the printing of the government-approved garbage bags. Of course, after this all came to light and these guys got arrested, the mayor and other officials were completely indignant about how their garbage had been molested by the "underworld," and they all claimed ignorance.

"Ignorance?" Well, at least there is one honest politician running around.

Since these sorts of hi-jinks are going on with our garbage, many Japanese people have called for even more stringent controls on how our treasured junk is disposed of.

I will say one thing about this new trash system. Many foreigners who come here don't have a problem furnishing their apartments. Really! Because you can just go out to a trash collection zone and load up on goodies.

Several years ago my friend Jeff picked up a good working refrigerator, color TV, Persian carpet, chest of drawers, etc. etc. He furnished his entire apartment for free with good stuff he collected off the street.

Jeff didn't want to take the Persian carpet, though. I had to talk him into it. He thought it would be dirty. Heaven forbid! Japanese always clean their garbage before they throw it out. The Persian carpet was beautiful, and worth probably quite a lot of money.

The other day, in fact, I picked up an original painting that was in the trash. The artist, *Kaoru Kawano*, is quite famous in Japan, and her art sells for anywhere between $10,000 and $50,000. I picked up the picture because I know what an expensive frame looks like. When I got home I checked it out and sure enough, it was an original 1963.

I can't believe the stuff people throw away here.

Can you imagine walking along the street in New York and finding an Andy Warhol print in the trash? No way!

But I digress. The trash problem here is seeping into every fabric of life in Japan, and the government is sure to keep wasting our money on talking a lot and doing nothing about it.

Do you folks in America divide up your trash also so that it can all be dumped or burned in the same place at the same time? We do. But there is one place where Japan has America beat hands down: zero emissions. That's right. Japan has signed the Kyoto Protocol.

And Japan is not only worried about zero emission fossil fuel alternatives and such. Japan leads the world in zero emission beer!

No, this is not what you think (all beer makes you belch). Most beer manufacturers here have managed to bring waste emissions down almost 20 percent.

The materials used for beer, like glass, have been recycled for a long time now. In fact, many manufacturers in Japan use other manufacturers' bottles and vice versa. Now beer companies are recycling the paper from labels, screens, plastics, etc. They separate waste into 34 different categories! Apparently Kirin Beer leads the pack with a remarkable 99 percent average of recycling of its beer products!

And, guess what? These beer manufacturers have organized all this recycling by their little old selves. No government interference!

From now on I will salute the garbage man, the Japanese beer manufacturers, and I will drink Kirin beer as I dig through my neighbors trash…er, I mean treasure. Heck, I need a new Persian carpet. The one I got from Jeff is dirty.

Disappearing Kamikaze Taxi Drivers

Owning your own car in Tokyo is insane. There are so many rules and regulations about car ownership in Tokyo that I have come to the seemingly obvious conclusion that it is far cheaper, faster, and much safer to take a taxi wherever you want to go.

Since Japan is such a crowded country, the law requires that if you own a car not only must you show proof of insurance, own a license (of course), but you must have proof of ownership or a lease on a parking space for each vehicle that you own.

Before I moved to Tokyo I did own a car. I lived in Yokohama then, which is not nearly as crowded as Tokyo, and I could park for free. It seemed feasible to own a car at that time.

In front of my current apartment there is a large parking lot. The lot is used by people around here for their permanent parking. I checked into it and found out that in order to reserve a parking spot in that lot it costs 44,000 yen per month! That's somewhere around $420 dollars per month, just for car parking!

On top of that, throw in car payments, insurance, maintenance, gasoline and oil, a bitchin' stereo with awesome speakers (gotta have that), and you are talking somewhere in the neighborhood of about $1100 per month (or more), just so you can have your own wheels. Are you out of your mind?

Never mind the air compression shocks and the dingo balls that are necessary for having a really "cherry" low-rider. No, thanks. Not me!

Absolutely, in Tokyo taxis, trains, and the subways are the way to go.

I'd like to point out a small item here before many readers think *What? Trains and subways are public transportation, and therefore a government money drain!* Well, in Japan, that's not always true.

Many of the trains are run by private companies. For example, the *Toyoko* Line, which runs from Tokyo to Yokohama (hence the name *To-yoko*), is owned and operated by the Tokyu Department store chain. The trains are clean, safe, fast, and very efficient.

189

How could a department store run a train system and make money? Easy. The train runs from underneath its Shibuya store (in Tokyo) to directly under its Yokohama store. It stops at 35 or so stations along the way. That makes it easy for people living in the outlying areas to go straight to the department stores and spend money, and it doesn't cost the taxpayer anything. In fact, the train fare for the Toyoko Line is cheaper than the government-run train lines—and the trains are nicer. But that's no surprise there, is it?

Anyhow, this article is about Tokyo taxis.

Tokyo taxis are the best. Just about all the drivers are courteous, they know the roads, and these guys are great drivers.

Mr. Kobayashi, who is a professional taxi driver and became a good friend, has been driving taxis in Tokyo for nearly 40 years. When I say he is a "professional" taxi driver, I don't want you to misunderstand; I believe that *all* taxi drivers in Japan are professional drivers. It takes ten years of driving experience and a very strict licensing procedure to become a taxi driver in this country. One car accident—even a little fender bender—and you lose your license!

Not only do the taxi drivers have to have a solid knowledge of the roads, rules and regulations, they have to be of a certain "mind set" to become a professional.

I have been in taxis many times when the driver in another car "cut" in front of us. Being an American and used to the ways Americans drive, that would anger me for a moment, but I have been very surprised at the reaction of the Japanese taxi drivers. The other driver would cut us off and I'd think, "Jerk! Speed up and get in front of him and cut him off!" But the Japanese taxi driver would just chuckle and say something like "Oh! He must be in a hurry!" And that would be the end of that.

I guess that kind of attitude is necessary for anyone to be a professional car driver in the most crowded city in the world. Kind of like a "Zen Buddhist" taxi driver attitude.

For about eight years I used to come home from work very late at night, and in all that time I never saw a car accident involving two taxis. I saw many involving "regular" drivers, a few with a regular driver and a taxi, but never have I seen a two-taxi car accident in the entire time I have lived in Japan. And you have to realize that after 11 PM, about 70–80 percent of the cars on the road are taxis.

Taxi drivers here are a different breed. The typical taxi driver works once every two days, and I'm not talking about an eight-hour shift. No, they work from 5 a.m. until 5 a.m. the next day. Then they have a day off and go do it all over again.

That's why you will often see taxi drivers sleeping in their cars on quiet Tokyo streets in the daytime. There are fewer customers then, so they can get some shut-eye. At night is when they can get lots of customers.

That's also why it seems rare to me to meet a taxi driver who isn't divorced. How could any family put up with a guy who is gone all day one day and in bed all day the next?

Taxi drivers in Japan usually work on a quota-and-commission system. They have to carry a certain number of fares, then they get a commission for any amount over their quotas.

That's why it is advantageous for the taxi drivers to know all the back roads around Tokyo and to know the areas they work well. They know when certain popular pubs have their closing times; they know when and what time events like concerts, baseball games, etc. are being held and when they finish.

Heck, Mr. Kobayashi even told me once that he knew where to go at certain times of the night to pick up famous people and politicians who have been out in places where they are "not supposed" to be.

The drivers know which roads are under construction and at what times...These Tokyo taxi drivers know everything.

I guess, depending on your circumstances, you could say that they know too much.

Since they get commissions over their quota amount, that's when you can ride in the infamous *Kamikaze taxi*. These guys have made their quota for the month already, and everything after that is gravy for them. They get about a 50 percent commission, so if you hop into one of those, hold onto your hat! It's the white-knuckle ride!

Sadly, since the Japanese economy has been in the doldrums over these last 15 years, the *Kamikaze taxi driver* is rare. I hear that it is unusual for drivers to break quota anymore.

It used to be, during the late 1980s "Economic Bubble" at Shibuya station in Tokyo, you would have to stand in line for at least 2 hours to get a taxi after 11 p.m., but not any more. Nowadays, if you have to wait 6 minutes, that's a long time.

Tokyo taxis are one of the simple pleasures of living in this country. You know that when you and your family ride in one you are being driven by a person who is truly a professional and who takes pride in their work.

The cars are spotlessly clean. The drivers all wear white gloves, and they are very polite. Many of them will give you the weather report, sports scores, and all sorts of information, if you ask.

I have never felt safer riding in a car than when I was riding in a Tokyo taxi.

Minamata: Real-Life Horror Show

The federal government always claims to be doing things in the best interests of the public, but we know that this is not always true. Whether it is the Soviet government covering up the disaster at Chernobyl or the US government covering up the disaster at Three Mile Island, we can always know that the government will always protect itself and its position before that of the public. Japan's government is no different.

Minamata is a very small fishing and farming town in *Kumamoto*, on Kyushu Island in southern Japan. A beautiful place, graced by a gem-like harbor and a rushing river, Minamata does not seem to be the scene of a tragedy. Today, most young Japanese people are unfamiliar with what happened here so many years ago, but just like Hiroshima or Nagasaki, Minamata is world-famous for a different kind of manmade catastrophe.

About fifty years ago, strange things began to happen in Minamata. At first, unable to understand what was happening to them, the local people were afraid to talk.

Some of the townspeople began experiencing delirium, blackouts, and numbness of their arms and legs. Soon some of them became partially or completely blind, while others experienced slurred speech. Others were thought to have become insane when, unable to control the movements of their appendages, they shouted at random. Those afflicted were rumored to be possessed by the devil when they could not control their facial muscles, and their contorted expression made them look like "monsters." Local doctors were dumb-founded by the epidemic outbreak.

The sinister symptoms began to afflict the animals of Minamata. Cats and dogs began to exhibit inexplicable behavior. Townspeople reported that cats were "committing suicide." Some cats chased their tails for days on end until they dropped from exhaustion. Dogs disappeared and were found dead days later. Even more shocking, afflicted birds began falling from the skies.

In 1932 the small town of Minamata boasted only one large factory, which was owned by a company called the Chisso Corporation. In Japanese, the word *chisso* means nitrogen. The Chisso Corporation was in the fertilizer business.

For hundreds of years, the townspeople of Minamata had lived primitive lives as fishermen and farmers. Minamatans were glad when in 1901 the Chisso Corporation set up a plant. Employment became abundant. By 1932 the Chisso plant had become very large. Since the Chisso Corporation was not involved with munitions manufacturing, they were spared bombing during the war and confiscation by the allies after the end of World War Two. By 1950 Chisso had become one of the leading businesses in Japan. Hand-in-hand, the Japanese government worked with companies like the Chisso Corporation in order to provide much-needed jobs to a post-war Japan. Chisso became so successful that it expanded into other chemical manufacturing.

By 1953, the strange plague had directly affected almost one-half of all the people in the small town of Minamata. People who came down with this bizarre disease were treated like lepers. Because no one knew if the disease was contagious, society shunned the sufferers.

Minamata babies began to be born with grotesque deformities and massive brain damage. Minamata fishermen began to catch two and three-headed fish. At this point, the government and the Chisso Corporation became alarmed.

The Agricultural Ministry of Japan—financed by the Chisso Corporation—ordered research into the causes of the freakish sickness that was attacking the people and killing the wildlife.

In 1956, Dr. Hajime Hosokawa was assigned to study the case. Dr. Hosokawa was an honest man, and even though he was paid by and worked at the Chisso Corporation Hospital, he reported "an un-clarified disease of the central nervous system has broken out in Minamata." Hosokawa's report pointed to chemical dumping by Chisso. The Chisso Corporation didn't like this news at all and "removed" Dr. Hosokawa. In order to not alarm the populace, Chisso and the Japanese government covered up Dr. Hosokawa's findings. Chisso continued with their business in Minamata Bay.

By 1958, the cover-up was well underway, while the disease gained momentum. At this time, the Chisso Corporation tried to hide the problems by moving their business to nearby Minamata River, but after a few months, people near the river began to experience the symptoms of the strange disease.

By now people were beginning to panic. The government of Kumamoto decided that they had to act, but instead of forcing the Chisso Corporation to suspend operations, the Kumamoto government made it illegal for the Minamata fishermen to sell locally caught fish. You read right. *The Kumamoto authorities did not make it illegal for people to catch and eat local fish; they made it illegal for the local fishermen to sell their catch on the open market.* The new law caused the Minamata area economy to suffer anew. Since Minamatans no longer had the money to purchase foodstuffs, they were forced to eat more locally caught fish.

By 1968, the problem had grown to crisis proportions. The Chisso Corporation began acting like the Mafia by forcing people to accept hush money in return for signing contracts that absolved the Chisso Corporation from liability for damages. The Minamatans were ignorant of the law. Their livelihood and their families were destroyed. What else could they do but accept Chisso's "hush money" and keep their mouths shut?

In 1969, a voluntary general citizens' group was formed to support the victims of the disease. The People's Congress for the Minamata Disease joined with a group of lawyers, and using the testimony of Dr. Hosokawa from his death bed, sued the Japanese government and the Chisso Corporation for damages related to what the lawyers termed Minamata Disease. It will never be fully known how many people actually suffered from this disease. Some estimates have the number in the tens of thousands, but as of today only 3,000 people have been compensated.

Consider the babies that were born deformed or brain-damaged. Imagine the people who died or whose lives were ruined by an unknown disease. Minamata disease is one from which there is no possibility of recovery. It is a disease for which there is no cure. Today that disease is known as Methyl Mercury poisoning.

For mankind, there would be more cases to follow: Three Mile Island, Love Canal, Chernobyl, and Bhopal to name a few. But people should not forget that the world's very first large-scale man-made environmental disaster was covered up by the government that was elected to protect its citizens—a disaster called Minamata.

Japan's Public Pension System: The Sex Star Scandal

Whether it is Japan or the United States, government-run pension systems are all a disaster and in danger of becoming insolvent. A theme you'll find running through this book is proof that the more the government controls of our lives (and our money), the more screwed up things will be. When it comes to Social Security, the governments of both countries are continually coming up with schemes to fund or refinance what is ultimately a losing battle. As the population ages, the numbers of recipients for Social Security rises. As the birthrates in Japan and the United States decline, that puts fewer and fewer new people into the workforce to fund this system. This retirement pension system is the closest that either the USA or Japan has ever come to out-and-out communism. This cycle cannot continue indefinitely.

As many of you who keep up on current Japanese affairs might know, Japan's aging of the population problem has risen to crisis proportions.

I live in an area called *Setagaya* ward in Tokyo. Setagaya ward is a nice upper-middle class place. There are many famous actors, actresses, politicians, company presidents and the like living around here. Lots of rich people.

And then there's my family. We are kind of like a barren desert island in a sea of opulence. While the neighbors are all driving their BMW's and Porsche's, I'm riding my 15-year-old daughter's junky bicycle that I won playing Pachinko a few years back.

This bike is such a piece of trash that I have not locked it in almost 4 years and no one has ever stolen it. Actually, I wish someone would steal it for me, that way I won't have to pay money for someone to take it to the trash dump.

I also like to sit in front of the apartment and smoke cigarettes and think profound thoughts. I can tell when the neighbors walk by that they all wonder: *Just what does that foreigner do for work?*

But don't think that I am looked down upon by my neighbors. Oh no! I think they just can't figure out exactly what it is that I do all day. They never see me wearing a suit and necktie, and I'm always hanging around at home. I also quite often sport my very suave Yasser Arafat "unshaven and disheveled" look.

The old-timers in the neighborhood all call me "Mister Mike." I usually meet them at the local bar and the Pachinko parlors and have drinks with them and enjoy small talk.

In Setagaya ward, and throughout all of Japan, we are heading for an aging population crisis that is really worrying a lot of people. The reason for the worry is another government-run screwed up system: National Public Pension Welfare.

The system (in theory) works like this: people pay a small portion of their monthly pay into a government-run pension system. Once they reach 65 years old, they are entitled to a monthly annuity. This payment is much like the extremely successful Social Security system that you Americans so much enjoy to this day.

Well, like I said, Japan's population is graying rapidly. According to my local government office, Setagaya ward will have more than 55 percent of its population over 60 years old in 2005.

Now it doesn't take much of a math whiz to figure out that if such a large percentage of the population is to receive this payment, then someone has to pay the money into the system, and that has to be the remaining 45 percent (or less) of the population.

That's where the problem comes in. The economy, in spite of what the Japanese government has been saying for the last 15 years, is still in a deflationary spiral, and many young people have no desire to take on full-time employment. And why should they, actually? Their parents lived through Japan's boom years, and the middle class of Japan seems to be much wealthier than the middle-class of America. I suppose that's because Japanese people have the highest savings rate in the world, and that plays a big part in it.

I have met many 25- or 30-year-old young Japanese people who were worried about their futures because they told me that they "Had only $60,000 or $80,000 saved in the bank!"

$60,000 dollars? When I was 30, I don't think I had $20 dollars saved.

Anyhow, many young people have now come to believe that if they pay money into the National Pension system that in 10 or 20 years, it will be bankrupt anyway and they will never get their retirement money. An understandable concern.

So this bad reputation about the pension system has snowballed into a crisis. Young people are refusing to pay, and elders are getting mad about how irresponsible young people are today.

Me, too! Hell, I'd be happy if my 20-year-old daughter could hold down a part time job for more than 2 weeks! She always gets bored and quits!

I'm not exactly clear on this point, but (and it wouldn't surprise me) it seems that the Japanese government has yet to establish a system to force people to pay, so they don't. It's kind of like the Japanese TV police system. You must pay, but they haven't specified what the penalty is if you don't pay.

Ah, Japan! You just gotta love it.

So what's a completely inefficient and top-heavy bureaucratic socialist government to do to get people to voluntarily pay into the pension plan? Well, they came up with a great idea!

All Japanese like famous stars, even though it seems to me from watching Japanese TV, that there are only a total of 12 or so famous actresses and actors in this entire country!. Okay, I admit it; I'm exaggerating. There are probably only 6 or so. So the Japanese government decided to launch an all-out campaign to convince people that paying into the pension plan was not only good for the country, it's good for your family. It's good for you. And, it's cool, too!

So they launched a huge advertising campaign, using the top actress in Japan as their "poster/image girl" for this media blitz. Her name is Makiko Esumi. And is she ever hot!

You put her face on something here in Japan and it sells. So the government took $3.6 million dollars out of the pension fund—the people's pension fund—and re-allocated that money for a nationwide mass media blitz.

The campaign was a smash success. I read where during the campaign, contributions to the pension plan had risen almost 20 percent!

Sure enough, Makiko Esumi may have single-handedly saved the Japanese National Pension system. Hurray!

The girl is fine, but $3.6 million dollars for this crappy design?

The TV and poster for the campaign had Makiko, with her trademark stare (looking babe-e-licious saying), "If you pay now, you'll be paid later. Do you want to end up crying in the future?"

Well, that did it for most people—even me. Heck, I was throwing my money at the TV!

Makiko Esumi is her own woman. Young people could look up to her. I've even read on some Blogs where young Japanese girls want to be just like her. She's a super-star!

What a fantastic, well-planned promotional campaign. A smash success! Except for one tiny little detail...It came out in the news that Makiko Esumi—the girl who was paid millions for this advertising campaign—hasn't been paying into the pension plan herself either.

Great planning by the government, eh? Now we can expect all these young people to be just like her. I know I'm going to be.

Dumb Foreigners and Gift-Giving in Japan

Westerners who live in Japan often commit gross faux pas when giving gifts in Japan. This is an ancient country, and since it is so, there are many rules on what types of presents can and cannot be given on certain occasions. I'm sure it is this way in all "old countries."

For example, you may have seen on TV a reporter talking about melons that cost $300 in Japan. Well, it is true; there are melons for sale that cost this much—maybe more—but you have to realize that these are not melons that the typical housewife would buy to take home for her family. These types of fruits and gifts are for *Omimai*.

Omimai are gifts reserved for taking to people convalescing in the hospital or as seasonal gifts to someone who has really taken care of you over the years. Just as in the West, people may spend $250 to $300 for a beautiful bouquet of flowers or roses on such an occasion, the Japanese generally will buy fruit or very high quality tea or seaweed. So to consider a melon that sells for $300 as a typical grocery store price for such an item is to not look at the whole story. In 2005, a melon for taking to one's own home and sharing with the family is probably about $15 to $20.

One of my best, and more unusual friends Seth, just had a baby. Well, I mean his wife just had a baby. Seth is a famous cartoonist and he mainly draws "Green Lantern" comics for D.C., back in the States. Even though D.C. comics are located in New York, I think, Seth travels around the world and draws his comics from wherever he happens to be. Pretty cool job for a total geek, eh?

Seth has lived in Japan for these last few years and married a while back and then decided to become a daddy (not necessarily in that order). Seth's wife is Japanese, as is mine.

Now this is where the problem begins. In Japan, there is a custom (notice I did not say "silly") called *Okaeshi*. *Okaeshi*, like most Japanese words, has dozens of meanings. In this case, *Okaeshi* would mean, "to honorably give back (something)."

So Seth, being my buddy, and having his first kid—well, this is Japan. I have to send him a present for his son. In all actuality, I have to ask my wife to send a present to his wife and son, as I have no money.

Oh! Will Japan ever teach you patience! So I ask Seth for his mailing address. He sends it to me. But Seth, also being a dumb foreigner like myself, sends me the mailing address sans postal code. Well, that's no good. My wife gets mad at me.

"Of course I need the postal code to send a present. What are you thinking about?"

So I e-mail him again and ask for the postal code. He sends it to me. My wife goes out and buys one of these little kid's cell-phones that are so popular with the little tykes. Then she asks me for the paper with the address, etc. on it.

"Doh!" I think I erased it. So I write back to Seth again, telling him to send the info one more time. He does. I give it to my wife. Then my wife gets mad at me cause I don't have Seth's phone number; I don't have the Chinese Kanji for how to write his sons name; I can't remember Seth's wife's name. My wife gets a bit perturbed at me:

"You've lived in Japan for over twenty years and you still don't know the rules of such a basic custom? Why don't you try to make a bit more of an effort to assimilate into Japanese society?" she snorts as her back curls like the ancient dragon rising from the lake.

"You mean I should start when? After I finish vacuuming the house, washing the dishes, scrubbing the bathroom, grocery shopping, and cooking dinner?" I mumble.

"What?"

"Oh, nothing, my little piranha fish." I smile.

So I write another e-mail to Seth. It says "Come on, dude! How long have you lived in Japan? You should know by now that I also need your telephone number, son's Kanji, and wife's name to send a present. Have a clue! Certainly you have lived in Japan long enough to know at least that much about basic Japanese customs. Get with the program, you dumb *Gaijin* (foreigner). That's basic! God! I mean, come on!"

Seth, being the polite gentleman that he always is, sends me the information with a note that says "Gee, your wife is thorough!"

I tell my wife what Seth wrote and she says, "That's not being thorough; that's just having a little common sense!"

So the present is sent. Seth and his wife and kid seem happy. Seth writes to me that now his wife (who I am assuming has common sense) will send an *Okaeshi* present. I think to myself, *No. It's not necessary*, and I want to write that to Seth. But my experiences in Japan have taught me better. I say nothing.

So now the cycle begins. My wife sends a present to Seth's wife. Seth's wife sends a "thank you" present for the present. My wife sends a "thank you" present for the "thank you" present. Seth's wife sends a "thank you" present for the "thank you" present for the "thank you" present.

And we're off to the races. This cycle (notice I did not say "absurd") will go on until who knows when. I'm embarrassed that I am unable to tell you when this cycle will end. I'd have to ask my wife about it, and I don't want another lecture about the culture of Japanese gift-giving.

I can tell you when these cycles won't end, though. It's when Seth and his wife have their second child, and the one after that, and the one after that. The cycles of having our Japanese wives lecture us about the intricate ways of Japanese culture also won't end until Seth and I stop being dumb foreigners—which means never. This is, after all, Japan.

Check out Seth's very cool and strange art here:
http://www.floweringnose.com/

Let's Go Department-Store Shopping in Japan

Shopping in Japan is definitely a unique experience. I used to hate going shopping in the United States before I moved to this country. Why? I used to get so frustrated when I went a store and couldn't find a single store employee to answer my questions or to pull down that barbecue I wanted from the top of a very high shelf. Or when I finally did manage to find an employee, they'd say, "I don't work in this department. Let me find someone for you who does." And with that, they'd disappear. I'm sure we all have shared this experience.

Service in Japan is world-renowned. Even now, after being here all these years, I am sometimes dumbfounded at the lengths stores in this country will go to offer the best service, and therefore get you as a satisfied return customer.

So, this chapter is for the ladies. Or, if you are a guy, then you may tag along with us while we shop, or you can just stay home and watch TV. But I guarantee you that going to a department store in Japan, at least once in your life, is an experience you will enjoy.

In the West, when business is bad, stores will cut back on employees or employee hours in an effort to cut costs. In Japan, the thinking is the opposite. The stores will increase service and increase staff in order to give better service, and therefore make those sales that might have been lost without a little knowledgeable "sales talk" from an employee to a prospective customer.

Today I have to buy a wedding present for my friend in the States. It's the second marriage for both of them. They are both well off; so what shall I buy?

There are lots of rules on etiquette and customs on what can and cannot be given as a wedding present. Of course this is probably true anywhere in any country, but particularly so in old ones.

For example, the number thirteen is an unlucky number in America. In Japan, the unluckiest number is four. Four in Japanese is *shi*. *Shi* has many meanings, but the one meaning that makes it so unlucky is that *shi* also means "death," so we won't be giving any wedding presents in groups of four. Not today, at least.

The other unlucky numbers are two, six, and eight. That's a lot of unlucky numbers, when you think about it, so there are many concerns about symbolism when buying wedding presents in Japan.

If people are getting married for the first time in Japan, and in most Asian countries, too, money is usually given. I know that in the Philippines, money is pinned to the bride's gown as she dances with the groom at the reception party. I'd sure like to be the cleaning lady after a wedding in Manila! Not only would I be able to sweep up all that extra money that fell between the tables, but I could fulfill one of my life's dreams of wearing a dress. But more about that later in the book. (Of course, I'm only joking.)

In Japan, a wedding gift of money must be in an "odd" numbered amount. For example, 30,000 yen or 50,000 yen are the usual amounts.

Now, I know you are saying, "But 30,000 or 50,000 yen is an even number!" Yes, but in this case, they are not. Confused? Yeah, it used to confuse me, too. But my wife Yuka, who is an expert shopper will explain it to you:

"The reason that any amount starting with a 3 or 5 is considered odd numbers, and therefore acceptable, is that in case of a divorce, the money cannot be split without a fraction. To give an amount that starts with a 2, 4, 6, or 8 would be a bad omen, as it is easily divided."

Got that, ladies? Two people are getting married. So we cannot give them anything that can be easily divided.

Now that we have our rules, let's go to the department store.

Probably one of the first things you will notice about a department store in Japan is that they are immaculate. There is no dust and dirt on the floors or the shelves. I don't know how they do it, but there are no scuffs and scrapes on the floors; of course there is no leftover chewing gum to ruin your shoes, either.

Also, inside Japanese department stores, you are kindly asked to refrain from smoking.

The second thing you will notice is the care taken in the display of products for sale. You will rarely ever see a large basket with clothes or items haphazardly thrown in. The products on the shelves are lovingly lined up to be easy to find and beautiful to look at. Thought is given to color, presentation, and display.

Besides this, just about every store will have an employee at the store's front entrance. The employee will bow towards you and say, *Irrashai mase*! (Welcome!) whenever you enter the store and "Thank you. Please come again" when you leave, even if you haven't bought anything.

In the West we used to say, "The customer is always right." But in Japan, the saying goes *Ogyaku-sama wa kami-sama.* (The customer is God.)

On the basement floor of all Japanese department stores are the "food floors." These are different than a grocery store; the department store food floor shops all sell prepared food for the housewife or house—husband to help them with their busy schedules and allow them to buy a ready-to-serve gourmet meal and just take it home and serve.

Here, on the food floor, you may come at any time of the day and see fresh food being prepared in *incredibly* spotless kitchens, and all the staff dressed in uniforms that would be clean enough for a hospital.

I'm sure that there must be some rules and regulations concerning the handling of food. In Japan the stores will go over and above the rules in extremely stiff competition to get new customers and keep the old ones coming back every time. You will never see a food-floor employee without a hat and clean uniform, and you will never see a food-floor employee that is not wearing latex gloves when he handles food.

The part about the "food floors" that you will just love is that you may walk around, any time of the day, and sample all the various taste delights on offer. When I used to work at a day job, I would often go to the food floor of the nearest department store and eat to my heart's delight. (Well, yes, I am a cheapskate.)

In Japan, an aesthetically pleasing design and display are critical to a fine dining experience. This is why, for example, a plate of sushi will always offer a colorful treat for the eyes, as well as a delicious taste for the palate. In the department stores it is the same; you may see what's on the menu and be able to imagine how this food can be served to your loved ones at home as something that you would be proud to serve from your own kitchen. This food tasting is a definite "must experience" when visiting any department store in Japan.

On the other floors, just like anywhere else in the world, are the children's clothes, ladies' and men's fashions, furniture, household goods, shoes, and baby clothes. Also, besides the "anchor store" there are always many individual boutiques, famous fashion designer stores, various accessory shops, and a wide variety of independent shops, all under one roof.

Of course since service is a priority, all department stores offer baby-changing rooms, rooms for mother to give milk to her baby, and a designated place for the rest of us to sit and wait while smoking a cigarette or having something to drink.

Now that baby is done drinking his milk, we'll head up to the fifth floor, where "Japanese things" are sold. I know you want to look around at the other shops, but since I'm with the wife and baby, we don't have so much time to window-shop, so I'll take you to the fashion and accessory shops in a future book.

Okay. We need something small. Something Japanese. Something that we can send in the mail easily, and it can't be so expensive. That leaves out just about everything. How about teacups? In fact, they are on sale! And look at them all! Teacup city!

Nah! Teacups might break in the mail, regardless of how well they are packed.

So I walk around, looking at various things. There's beautiful china—various hand-made drinking glasses, cups, plates, dishes, and serving trays. While these are all very beautiful and would make great presents, they are not so suitable for my purposes, as just like with the teacups, they might break in the mail.

For marriages, items relating to food are always a good choice in Japan. The thinking goes that a couple who will spend a quiet, delightful time eating together and talking with each other every night will have a happy marriage. Since this is their second marriage, my wife suggests very high-quality chopsticks.

"Chopsticks?"

But then she explains to me that "chopsticks" in Japanese is *Hashi*. Besides meaning those long wooden eating utensils, *hashi* also means "bridge."

"Ah! I get it!" The symbolism is great. Besides being able to eat together with a high quality his and hers chopsticks set; the chopsticks will also symbolize "a bridge between each other," and "a bridge into their future together."

Isn't that type of thinking so very Japanese? So we go look at the chopsticks. And my jaw drops! They have hundreds of different chopsticks on sale. Some are handmade by famous craftsmen. Some are made of wood and then lacquered, some from bamboo. Some are even made of silver and gold. I see one gold set that sells for over $1000 dollars!

I think I'll stick with the handmade lacquered wooden sticks for today, thank you. Within two seconds of standing there, looking at chopsticks, a saleslady asks us if we need help. We tell her the purpose of the chopsticks and she asks a few questions, then recommends several different sets.

We finally choose a beautiful set that includes the name of the happy couple to be engraved on each of the chopsticks. Even though they probably will never use these chopsticks, they are nice enough to show off in a display case in their house as a memento of their wedding day.

My wife pays for them and the saleslady quadruple checks to make sure we have the spelling for the name engraving correct, and then we head out of the department store. The chopsticks—due to the hand engraving—will be ready in a week. They will deliver them, or we can pick them up. Either way, when they are ready the department store will call us.

The whole thing sets us back a little more than a hundred and ninety dollars. Pretty cheap for a decent wedding present, pretty darned expensive for two pairs of little sticks! But as this present is more of a "decoration" and wishes for a happy marriage than it is for its practicality, I'm happy with it.

But as we are walking into the elevator, I say to my wife, "Wait a minute! Two sets of chopsticks, that means four chopsticks! Four is an unlucky number."

"No, it's not four," she replies.

"Yes, it is. One set of chopsticks is two chopsticks. Two sets is four."

"No. This is one set of chopsticks as they come in a very nice lacquered wood, single box. So it's not four; it's one." She scowls at me and gives me that "You dumb foreigner! Didn't you learn anything in school?" look!

Do not question the ways of my people! I think, and I start whistling as we head towards the entrance of the entire department store complex.

All that shopping, as well as food tasting, has made me hungry for something light to eat, so we head for one of the top bagel shops in Tokyo: Bagel People. This place has New York-style bagels as good as any I've ever had in America. Every time I go shopping, we just have to stop there for a bagel!

I just wish they'd do something about that sign.

A Photographic Trip to the Grocery Store

Well, the department store was fun, wasn't it? But even more than the department store, I like going to the grocery store. Why? It's closer and there's definitely *always* something new to see.

The little woman has given me a very short list of things she wants me to buy at the grocery store. We don't have anything else to do, so I thought you might like to take a walk with me and check it out. I have three things I must buy: *Osembei*, cooking sake, and *Mirin*.

The *Osembei* are rice crackers. My wife loves those.

The cooking sake is for cooking. Well, duh! You might think that statement is a bit ridiculous, but trust me—I know what I'm talking about here. I remember when I was a university student, and a friend and I were desperate to get high, er, I mean, we were desperate for a drink. We had zero money, so we decided to walk five miles to his mom's house and raid the liquor cabinet. Bad idea! She was a follower of Islam and didn't drink. Doh! You'd think her dumb son might know that! So my pal and I downed an entire bottle of cooking sake we found in the kitchen. After about 15 minutes, I knew I felt a different man; I had a headache and was sick. So don't drink cooking sake. In fact, I think that all Japanese sake should be avoided at all times. Drinking that stuff makes me go crazy, but cooking sake is especially dangerous. Take my advice and stick to beer.

Next on the list is *Mirin*. Don't even ask me what *Mirin* is. I have no idea what it's made of. It's something that's used in Japanese food like *Teriyaki*. And my wife told me to buy it. End of story.

Right. We have our shopping list. Let's go.

There are two big grocery stores near where I live. Incredibly, one is called, "Fuji Super" and the other is called, "OK Store."

Fuji is super. OK is just okay.

Fuji Super is for the highbrow crowd. They have all sorts of international food and cheese—stuff like that. OK Store is more local type of food: Seaweed and tentacles. And OK Store is a few yen (cents) cheaper for basic foodstuffs. While Fuji Super is really nice and sparkling clean and all—and they give you free vinyl grocery bags—I usually shop at OK Store because I know where everything is. OK Store charges 6 yen per grocery bag, but since I always use a backpack, I don't need a grocery bag. My excuse is that I'm Eco-friendly. The fact of the matter is that I'm a cheapskate and I don't wanna cough up 6 cents for a bag.

Because, as responsible adults, it is our duty to shop and price compare and save money anyway we can. Either way, Fuji Super and OK Store are right next to each other, so we'll stop at Fuji Super first.

Neither store has a parking lot—well, not like they do in America; they have a parking lot to park bicycles. That's it. They even have a valet guy there to help old folks bash their bikes into other folk's bikes when they park. Fuji Super has lots of space and is not nearly as crowded as OK Store. If I'm ever in a rush—which is hardly ever—I shop at Fuji Super.

The service counter

As I mentioned in the previous chapter, stores in Japan pride themselves on service. Well, that's true for even grocery stores. Fuji Super has a service counter that always has five or six people standing around, just ready to pounce on anyone who looks like they are even thinking about asking a question. Since we are here, I price compare cooking sake. I ask a girl where the sake is. She looks at me weird. Oh! She doesn't work here. Never mind. I ask the girl at the service counter where the cooking sake is. Mistake. Now I have three people wanting to help me, and one girl wanting to walk me to the sake section.

"No, thank you," I reply in a snooty manner. "Just window shopping."

Forget that. I'm not going to pay a few extra yen just for a nice store, good service and a free vinyl bag! We head on out to OK Store.

From what I hear, OK Store will move a few blocks away and into a brand new building early next year. They've been in the same old building now since I can remember. The current building looks a bit trodden upon, but I like that earthy feel. OK Store is a bit cheaper and old; the aisles are narrow. This place gets like a zoo past 4:00, so we can't dilly-dally, and we have got to get out of here as soon as possible. Since I'm an "OK regular," I know where everything is already, except the *Mirin*. Since I don't know exactly what *Mirin* is, I don't know where it is. Is it near the sake or the cooking oil? Well, I'm at the grocery store, so you know I'm warm. We'll look around and find it. While we're here, we'd better compare prices.

Stuff (clockwise from top left): About $1.60 for a head of cabbage, $1.60 for 3 carrots, $1.80 for a head of lettuce—a dollar cheaper than last year, tentacles, $6.50 for a steak that's about 6 ½" across and less than 3/8" wide—we don't eat steak, $4.30 for a pack of frozen blueberries—5 bucks for frozen strawberries, sounds about right. Don't forget that this is the cheap place.

More stuff (clockwise from top left): $1.30 for one white radish (that's cheap), $2.00 for three dinky red peppers, three little fishies, $6.30 for pre-sliced raw fish, $15.00 for a cooked chicken, fish-world, $5.00 for 12 fresh strawberries (not bad)...

Interesting, eh? Well, now that we have our stuff, let's head for the cash register...

My God! Look at the line! I told you not to dilly-dally. It's not like you've never seen a vegetable before, right? What are you doing? Get with the program, willya? Now half of the town is standing in line at the checkout counter. I can't take you anywhere. I don't know about you, but I'm not too interested in standing in line for 20 minutes to buy three things, one of which I don't even know exactly what it is.

So it's back to Fuji Super. We're in luck! They have everything we wanted, and we get a free vinyl grocery bag! After paying, we try not to look suspicious as we pack the booty into our back pack and we're off!

But don't look now—Fuji Super is handing out free booze! Isn't this place great? We stop by and drink several cups of red and white wine (this helps to defray the higher costs of shopping at Fuji Super). The cute girl keeps giving us samples as you act like you might want to buy some, but I don't drink wine; it makes me crazy. Of course, I'm a beer drinker, but when the booze is on the house, why not? We chat with the nice girl and wish her a merry whatever-day-it-is-today and head out the door.

In Japan, they hand out free cigarettes and free booze all the time.

And so a successful ten-minute trip down to the grocery store takes two-and-a-half hours, and we return home with alcohol on our breath. The wife doesn't look too happy, but she can't complain. I explain that it's your fault that I'm late, and after all, we did price compare.

Later on we'll go for a beer run together. That will be easier; the liquor store ain't a 30-second walk from my apartment. And I already know where everything is!

Haru Urara (I've Got a Horse Right Here)

Americans like to say that they always root for the underdog. Well, some people do. Some people don't. But when it comes to cheering for the underdog, today's Americans don't hold a candle to the average modern-day Japanese.

Sometimes when I watch, say, the Olympics, I am astounded that the Japanese mass media will focus entirely on some Japanese athlete that finished 27th or worse in some event.

In America, if you are not #1, it seems like no one cares. Hell, Americans are so used to winning that if you want to be a star in today's United States you have to win several gold medals! While the Japanese will root and cheer on their athletes to the very end, they don't even *expect* to win. Why? I think it has a lot to do with losing World War II and having your cities bombed into rubble, not to mention having two Atomic bombs dropped on you. I suppose that might do a lot to your national psyche. I've never seen folks who will root for the underdog like the modern-day Japanese do. Sometimes it gets to the point of near insanity. *Haru Urara* is an excellent case-in-point.

It was a cold, rainy Tuesday morning. I got up early and was just about finished with my usual second pot of coffee when the phone rang. It was Murakami from the news network that I used to work for.

Murakami-san asked me if I was available for a "pinch-hit reporter" role that day for one of the biggest sports spectacles in Japanese sports history: the eighth race at *Kochi horse race track* in *Shikoku*, Japan, later that same day.

Of course, I jumped at the chance—let's say, "galloped" at the chance—to cover this once-in-a-lifetime event.

Now, usually, an eighth race at *Shikoku* is nothing special. In fact, *Kochi racetrack* had been a miserable money-loser for these last few years. Last year alone the track lost something in the neighborhood of $60 million. There had even been talk of the track "going down."

The bankruptcy of a racetrack of the "Sport of Kings"? Never! At least not in Japan!

That day's eighth race was going to be history in the making. Arguably, the most famous racehorse in the history of Japanese horseracing, *Haru Urara*, was running that day with the Japanese version of Laffit Pincay. The "Willie Shoemaker of the Japanese derby-world," *Take Yutaka* (Ta-kay Yu-ta-ka), was finally hooking up with *Haru Urara* and was going to ride that proud steed in the eighth race.

And I was going to be there as sports history was going to be made.

Of course, Take Yutaka riding *Haru Urara* was a dream come true for all Japanese horse racing fans. I was quite qualified as a reporter for the horse races here, as not only do I drink heavily, but I also smoke, and my folks used to take us kids down to Santa Anita, Hollywood Park, Del Mar, and Caliente racetracks way back when.

I had personally seen them all. I had witnessed with my very own eyes the super horses of American horse races: Secretariat, Affirmed, Seattle Slew. I've even seen that really famous horse—ummm, what was his name—Chock Full O'Drugs, or something like that?

My folks had told me they had seen some of horse racing's legends in their time: Kelso, John Henry, Northern Dancer, and Sea Biscuit.

Of course I saw many great jockeys riding the big names in my day.

Horses have always held a special place in the hearts of men from all societies throughout the history of mankind! From ancient Egypt to today, what other animal holds that special place in lore and legend like horses do?

Who could forget Charleton Heston riding a horse-drawn chariot in that movie *Ben Hur* from Roman times? Or how about that *Robin Hood* guy that was played by that famous Flynn dude from a long time ago (you know, he had the little pinstripe mustache)? Or even *National Velvet* with Mickey Rooney? (In fact, I used to see Mickey Rooney at the satellite-track betting lounge in Ventura, California in the early 1980s! My dad used to talk to him sometimes!) Or even that classic horse movie, *American Beauty*! Wait a minute! Was there a horse in that movie?

Anyhow, I think you get the idea that horses have always played an important part of our lives and held an important spot in the hearts of all people everywhere!

Not only do horses hold a special place in the hearts of the Japanese, they hold a special place in the stomachs of the Japanese too! Yeah, you read correctly; many Japanese people *eat* horsemeat. It is a delicacy in Japan, and it's usually eaten raw!

Yep, if you like sushi, then you haven't lived until you've eaten raw horsemeat sashimi! Ummm, makes my mouth water just thinking about it! Lots of bars and drinking establishments here in Japan serve horsemeat sashimi. I'm not making this up! My regular watering hole, *Sakura* (Cherry Blossom), has it fresh just about every night.

I haven't worked up the courage to try any yet, but you can be sure that when I do, I'll be writing about it—probably after they pump my stomach.

There's even a city in the Tokyo Metropolitan area called *Bakuro-cho*. Now, let me translate this for you. *Ba* is "horse," *kuro* is "eat," and *cho* is "town." Now that I have translated it, can you fit these words together to figure out the meaning? Great. Now I'll wait until you return from getting sick in order to continue this fun book.

The "mama" and "master" of Sakura holding a scrumptious plate of "Trigger" (horse-meat sashimi).

Anyhow, I arrived at Kochi racetrack and I had already missed the first few races. But it's no problem. I drank heavily on the plane on the way over, so I was at about the fifth-race level of alcohol when I got there.

What a zoo of people! The track announcer pronounced it the largest crowd ever in the history of Kochi racetrack!

I made my way over to the "clubhouse" so I could drink with the other professional gamblers instead of having to stand around near the track with the regular "riff-raff."

The clubhouse was full, but I used my quick thinking and whipped out my press pass and acted like I couldn't speak a word of the language. It worked! (Actually, it works every time!) I was in!

I crawled up to the bar and ordered some cheap crappy "Old Grand-dad" (or was it "White-Horse?") rot gut whiskey for ten dollars a shot. It was okay though; I was going to make the news network reimburse me.

Nothing like mixing beer and whiskey to get you in the mood for the races, And in the right frame of mind to make a logical wager! (If there is such a thing as a "logical wager.")

There were some old timers sitting next to me and I asked them what race we were on. They didn't know either. They didn't care. Everyone who was anyone was only there for one reason: To see *Haru Urara* and Take Yutaka make Japanese horse racing history. Nay, *world* sports history!

I decided that I had better go make a bet on the race. That way, I figured, I'd be interested enough not to pass out before the race from drinking too much.

I raced out to the betting windows. There were very few people betting on the next race. Like I said, no one cared about anything but *Haru Urara* and the eighth race.

I walked up to the betting window and slurred out, "$100 to win on number 5 in the eighth race."

The bookie said nothing and just pointed to his left.

"Sign language, eh? I can do that!" I said as I teetered back and looked over to where he pointed.

My God! There had to be three hundred people at that line! The track had opened a special window exclusively for people to place bets on *Haru Urara*!

I stumbled over and got in line.

There has got to be a better way! I thought.

I must have stood in that line for 15 minutes, but it seemed like an hour and a half!

I have to have another drink immediately! I thought. *But first I have to get rid of the first five.*

I stood in line, crossed my legs, put my hands in both front pockets, and swayed from side to side. I thought I was going to drown!

When I finally got to the window I decided that after all that waiting, I was going to place a bet that was worth the wait. So instead of $100 to win, I told the guy:"$300 dollars on *Haru Urara* to win…And make it snappy!"

I grabbed my ticket and made extra sure I put it in my wallet; I have a bad habit of forgetting where I put things when I'm drunk. Funny that. After I double-checked the ticket, I ran back to the clubhouse. Have you ever seen that *Austin Powers* movie where he is brought back to life after being frozen in suspended animation? Yeah? Well, then you know how I felt when I hit the clubhouse gentlemen's room.

After finishing my duties, I found another seat at the bar and ordered more paint-stripper, masquerading as Bourbon.

I looked up to the big screen TV monitor and was shocked to see how the odds for *Haru Urara* to win had changed so drastically. Everyone at the track and their mother was betting on that horse!

I made sure I still had my winning ticket. Yeah, it was there! I looked at the TV screen. The odds had changed again! I couldn't believe it!

I thought about the situation. I hadn't planned on coming to the track that day (or any day for that matter). I had flown a plane an hour and a half just to get to the track. It was a historic day—the most famous horse, the most famous jockey—and I only had a measly $300 bet.

The stars were lined up correctly for me today, I figured. I looked at my ticket again.

I knew right then and there what I had to do. I downed my drink like a pro. I had to 'hedge' my bet. I ran back down to the ticket window and bet another $400 on *Haru Urara* to win. I knew that if I didn't, she'd lose for sure and my wife would kill me for blowing so much money at the track.

Nope. Not me. I'd been there before. Not again.

By the time I got through the long line, bought the ticket, and got back to the clubhouse, the flag for the eighth race was up.

I ordered a double shot of whatever it was I was drilling holes through my stomach with and said a silent prayer.

The race started, and the horses shot from the starting gate. *Haru Urara* was yellow number five and the jockey was wearing pink. I tried to focus my eyes on the big screen, but I couldn't see it too well.

Was it my eyes? Or was it because the big screen kept pixelating every 15 seconds or so? I couldn't tell, but I was beginning to feel sick.

The race was over a mile and a quarter, which was good, because *Haru Urara* was last out of the gate. That was okay though. Take Yutaka's nickname is "The Genius Jockey"; he's a master at positioning his horse to win. In fact, one of the other drunk "pros" at the clubhouse told me that:

"*Haru Urara* is a 'stretch runner' and if Yutaka's riding, it's a 'sure-fire' winner." He showed me his cheap-o $20 bet. I chuckled to myself.

Loser! I thought.

The horses came around the clubhouse turn. Like I said, I couldn't see well, and it looked to me like *Haru Urara* was running in the middle of the pack. People were screaming and shouting. I couldn't even hear what the track announcer was saying.

They came into the stretch, and *Haru Urara* was coming on strong! I started screaming and yelling, too! I think my blood pressure was probably something like 240 over 170!

I couldn't believe it! I could see *Haru Urara's* pink just rocketing past horses on the outside. The crowd was at a fever pitch! I ordered another celebratory drink!

"Yeah! Yeah! Go! Go!" I shouted and pumped my hand in the air as I had worked myself into a frenzy!

Five horses crossed the finish line at the same time. It was a photo finish!

"Yes! Yes! Oh thank you, God!" I thought…

All those times at the track in America that I had lost a bundle, all those times I kicked myself for changing my mind at the last moment and changing my bet, they were all coming back to me. I was going to be redeemed today!

"I was going to win—and win 'big time!'"

It was weird, though! The entire clubhouse fell eerily silent. I thought to myself, "Uh, oh! This is not a good sign! Maybe the other guys watching the race saw something that I didn't?"

My heart sank. The old guy sitting next to me looked at me and said, *Dame da!* ("It's no good!") And he laughed.

"What are you laughing about, dude?" I thought. "This was no laughing matter!"

The numbers flashed on the screen: 4, 12, 2, 6.

What? I thought. *What happened to Haru Urara?* They then showed a replay of the race again. I stumbled over to the other side of the bar and watched the finish on a different TV.

Sure enough, the horse with the pink-shirted jockey was just nipped at the finish line.

"But wait a minute!" I thought. I kept watching the screen.

All the horses were packed up in groups. Finally, the horse that finished last crossed the line.

The horse that finished fourth, number six, was also in pink.

The horse that I had bet $700 to win on had actually finished 27 lengths behind, in dead last.

The horse that was going to make history that day, the most famous jockey in the history of Japanese horse racing who was going to make history that day…did!

For that day's 50,000 to 1 shot, *Haru Urara* had made history for finishing *dead last* for the 106th race in a row!

Notes on Haru Urara: Incredibly, fans of *Haru Urara* in Japan keep their losing bets and tickets and often laminate them and hang them in their automobiles. Why? It's a kind of belief in luck: *Haru Urara* never wins—she never "hits" as in "hit the jack-pot." That means, for the superstitious, a *Haru Urara* bet—a forever "miss"—hung from your car's rear-view mirror will protect your car from ever getting hit…Well, I guess a little extra insurance couldn't hurt.

Japanese Hostages Wanted, No Experience Necessary

The Japanese public, as the American public, is often at odds with official government foreign policy, but some Japanese have a very independent way of showing it. This is the story of three of the five Japanese who were kidnapped in Iraq in 2004.

A total of five Japanese were kidnapped by the desperados in Iraq and subsequently freed, but the story doesn't end there. Oh no. It's just getting started.

The word on the streets is that the Japanese government paid ransom money for the release of the initial three hostages.

Since people have such short attention spans (yes, the Japanese too) the government has not commented on that little tidbit of information, and so there is no more news about it. But there is other news about the suffering of these three people and the heroic efforts of the government to get them released.

The Japanese press, as cohorts with the government, has started spreading information about the plight of those poor (or stupid, depending on your point of view) Japanese hostages' mental state.

A Japanese psychiatrist who met the three when they returned to Japan (in order to pack some clean underwear and socks, I presume) claim that the Japanese are suffering from acute stress.

Acute stress? Creepin' Jiminy Christmas! How could that be?

You'd think that after being kidnapped, blindfolded, and having some guys hold Ginsu knives to their throats that the hostages would never want to step outside of their houses again. Not to mention, the kidnappers speak Arabic, so they had no idea what the kidnappers were saying. But no! That's not the problem!

The psychiatrist says the former hostages are suffering from acute stress due to—are you ready for this?—acute stress due to criticism from the Japanese government!

The girl—Ms. Takato in particular—claims that she has been emotionally unstable and is obsessed with the thought that she is at odds with society. So what? Big deal! Join the club.

Some people just can't stand prosperity. They go to Iraq (that right there would seriously stress me out), then they get kidnapped (yes, I would be somewhat upset, I suppose), threatened with death (been there, done that), then they get released and they are stressed out because people criticize them? Are you kidding me?

You should have seen me when I was a fourth grader! I was in the principal's office every day, and he wasn't complimenting me on my exemplary behavior, either.

No wonder I bit my nails when I was a little kid. I should sue my elementary school for the acute stress they caused me.

Not only do these people get criticized for going to Iraq and getting themselves kidnapped, they get criticized for bad acting while they were in Iraq. That's right.

According to the police here in Japan, the video that was taken of the hostages and aired on Al Jazeera was staged. Yeah, pretty cool, eh? I guess the militants asked the Japanese people to look and act more scared so they could make a more convincing video.

"Cut! Take two! Try it again you guys. This time with feeling!"

That just shows how confused those amateur cine-militants are. If you've ever seen any recent Japanese-made TV dramas or movies, you'd know that, generally speaking, Japanese are hack actors.

Now that this interesting item is a hot topic here in Japan, lots of people think that those three Japanese actually wanted to be kidnapped—and planned it with their Iraqi buddies. No joke.

"I was kidnapped in Iraq and all I got was this lousy scarf."

I reckon that the rationale for this is that in spite of what the Japanese government says, still 80 percent or 90 percent of the public is against the war in Iraq. The rumor is that those three planned their own kidnapping in order to force the government to withdraw the troops. No dice. Japan will never give in to the demands of the terrorists. And the Japanese government vehemently has no comment about paying any ransom.

In spite of this, the Senior Vice Foreign Minister Ichiro Aisawa announced that the government will indeed send a bill for compensation to the families of those who were held hostage. Aisawa told the Japanese parliament that he was going to bill these folks about $6500 to pay for the chartered flight from Baghdad to Dubai. No, that's not $6500 each; that's $6500 for all three for a chartered plane.

Some of you reading this might think that this price is far too cheap to charter a whole plane for just three people, and I can understand that. But you'd think that after the Japanese government shipped those 550 or so troops to Iraq, they could have used their zillions of accumulated frequent flyer miles and gotten the flight for free. But then again, knowing how the government does things, they probably did use their frequent flyer miles and got the flight for free, while still charging those families. I mean, after all, the government needs that $6,500 because that'll just about cover the tab for their "Congratulations Hostage Release" sushi party that they are probably going to hold.

—*Cabinet ministers and their secretaries by invitation only.*

The Keitai Conspiracy

In the year 2004, according to the Japanese National Police Agency, there were over 723 murders in Japan. Compare that with the UK, which reported 1,048 murders from March 2002 to March 2003, and US figures that show the FBI estimated about 20,000 murders in America per year.

Japan has about one-half the population of the United States, so this 723 may not seem so bad to folks in the West, but to the Japanese, this is an out-of-control crime explosion.

Also, in these last several years, another thing that has exploded on the scene are sales of cell-phones, called *Keitai* in Japan, with a sales estimate of well over 22 million units this year alone.

In late 2003, 4 girls, all aged between 12 and 13, were kidnapped here in Tokyo, resulting in an incident that left one person dead. This kidnapping caused a media sensation in Japan.

It seems that the girls were all looking for some extra spending cash and found an advertisement looking for part-time workers. Generally speaking, in Japan it is impossible for anyone who hasn't turned at least 16 to find any sort of employment. Even though you and I might think an employer that would agree to talk to 12- and 13-year olds must be up to no good, the girls, perhaps in their innocent youth, must have thought that they were just extremely lucky.

Even so, it might have entered the girls' minds that their parents would not approve of them taking a part-time job, so instead of calling from their homes, where their parents might over-hear, they used their cell-phones—their *keitai*—to contact the advertiser.

And here is where the "*Keitai Conspiracy*" begins.

When the girls answered the ad, they talked with the potential employer and were quickly set up for a meeting and an interview. The place of the meeting was a shopping district in Tokyo, called Shibuya. There an older gentleman picked up the four girls from the designated meeting place in the afternoon, in front of a famous department store, and drove them to a famous hotel in Akasaka in Tokyo.

Once the four girls arrived at the hotel for the interview, they probably all felt that something was very wrong with this situation. They were not taken to one of the many meeting places that all major hotels arrange for their clients. No, they were taken to a regular hotel room. There were no desks in the room for interviews, nor were there any other staff personnel to greet them upon their arrival.

When they began asking questions, the older gentleman, who had been a kind old man a few minutes before, began to angrily shout at them and ordered them to sit on the floor in the corner or he would kill them. I'm sure they all thought that they were going to be raped and killed. They must have feared for the worst, and they began crying.

After ordering the girls to get on their knees and telling them that if they didn't keep silent they would be killed, the old man picked up his cell-phone and called his contact, who was part of this kidnapping conspiracy.

But there was something wrong! Something must have gone very wrong with the kidnapping that these criminals had so meticulously planned, as the old man's contact was not answering his phone. There was a messaging service on which the old man left dozens upon dozens of messages, but no return phone call. What could have happened?

The old man kept trying to reach his partner-in-crime for several hours, but he could not. Finally, by the time it had grown dark and the old man was exhausted with a room full of four little girls sobbing for mercy, he made one last attempt to call his co-conspirator. This was the straw that broke the camel's back. Upon dialing this time, his partner's phone had had its power shut off.

The old man must have come to the realization that the power being shut off could have meant only one of two things: Either his partner had gotten "cold feet" and backed out, or the police had found out about their plans, his partner had been arrested, and now the police were coming for him and the girls.

What a criminal in the West would do in a case like this is anyone's guess., However, this old Japanese man took what he perceived as the only way out of this mess, the only way to avoid the shame of arrest and the shame that his arrest would bring upon his family and loved ones: he committed suicide, right there in the hotel room in front of the girls.

The girls, afraid to get up and leave the room (you must remember that we are talking about children here), grabbed their cell-phones—their *keitai*—and called their parents. The parents then called the police and rescued the girls.

The girls are now safe. The old man, once a seemingly nice old gentleman, was now dead. His partner? He is probably in jail now.

And that is how the "Kidnapping Conspiracy" ended.

When this story broke on the Japanese mass media and was reported to the public, all the TV and radio stations touted the same line, and that line was, "How fortunate we are in this day and age to have cell-phones so that those girls could call their parents when they were trapped in a room with a man who had kidnapped them and had just killed himself."

The implied message to all this was: "All kids need a cell phone for their personal safety. Don't your children deserve the same?"

But this article is not about a *kidnapping* conspiracy; it is about a *Keitai* Conspiracy. I call this a Keitai Conspiracy because that is how I perceived this real-life drama and I think it adds an even more bizarre, but real, twist to this story.

Consider this: Would this kidnapping have ever occurred in the first place had those 12- and 13-year-old girls not had their own personal cell-phones? Or, even if they had been kidnapped and held in a room with a man who had just killed himself, couldn't they have used the hotel room phone to call home and call for help? That they didn't actually need a cell-phone to call for help? In fact, isn't the cell phone what got them into trouble in the first place?

When you consider this and you understand that the mass media conveniently forgets to mention these critical points but will dwell over and over on the one point that the girls used their cell-phones to call for help, you realize just how bizarre all of this is and just how much "under the thumb" of sponsors our mass media really are.

How did I find out about this story? I saw it first on a news topic show—a news topic show that just happened to be sponsored by the biggest cell-phone maker in Japan!

How does the *ending* of the *Keitai Conspiracy* go? I don't know. But I do know that right now, due to the influence of the mass media, Japanese people feel we have a crime explosion in this country. And since we have a crime explosion, the mass media, sponsored by huge cell phone makers, is telling all Japanese parents that their children need their own personal cell-phone...*for their safety.*

And that's how the *Keitai Conspiracy* **goes.**

Kung Fu Master for Beginners

"Approach students. Close the circle at the feet of the master. You have come to me, asking that I be your guide along the path of Ti Kwan Leep. But be warned; to learn its ways, you must first learn the ways of your own soul. Let us meditate upon this wisdom now..."—*The Frantics*

It was 1985. I had been in Japan for just a few short months and I had somehow found myself a "regular" job on an early morning kids' show called *Ohayo Studio* (Good Morning Studio). I had a small part, but it was a regular part, with spoken lines nevertheless. I had fulfilled my dream of becoming a TV star.

Ohayo Studio was geared for little kids' viewing as they were eating cereal or whatever and preparing for school. The show started at 5 a.m. and ended at 6:30. This was sometimes a problem for me, as I was often extremely hung-over.

As well as taking part in skits, dressed up as a human tomato or turnip, I used to give the kids a "one-point English lesson"—useful stuff that they could go out and use immediately like, "I don't know," or "I can't understand," or "Say what? That's whack!"

The producers of the show would also send me out to do strictly "Japanese things" and give my dumb foreigner impression of it, which I was very good at because I couldn't understand half of what people were talking about.

I made Tofu, Japanese *Washi* traditional paper, Japanese dolls, and I learned how to become a Kung Fu master all in one day; I mean, not *all* of them in one day, of course; each task I spent a day learning.

It was an extremely cold February morning. The TV staff came and picked me up for that day's shooting somewhere near Shibuya (in Tokyo). We arrived at the Buddhist temple at about 3:30 a.m.

The priests in training were just getting ready to start their day. I wanted to know if there was someplace warm where I could sleep. But no! That was forbidden. How was I to learn the ways of the ancient masters if I were sleeping and warm in a comfy bed?

231

You know, these *Za-Zen Buddhist* monks are a peculiar lot. Some start out training to be priests and it takes an entire lifetime for some of them to reach enlightenment. Even at that, some never make it.

The really hardcore guys—and until today, it is said that there have only been 12 who survived the 1000-day ordeal towards enlightenment—actually run a 42 kilometer marathon every day for 300 days. Then they fast for a few weeks, drinking only tea. Then they run the 300 days again. More fasting. And they keep this up until they reach the 1000 days. Most of the priests who try this out, die.

Funny that.

Meditating or fossilized? You decide!

I'm not making this up, either. These guys are out of their minds. When they are fasting, they hide out in some cave at the top of some mountain and meditate. It is said that their senses become so acute that they can hear the sound of melted wax run down the side of a candle.

I tell you what, if I was starving and sitting in some scary mountain cave in the dark, I'd be hearing things, too. I probably wouldn't be able to sleep a wink, either.

Anyhow, we arrive at the temple, and the younger priests are all outside in a single, very thin, cotton "robe." The TV director makes me put one on too. It's freezing—probably about 5 degrees below freezing—and these fruitcakes are out there doing calisthenics, and I have to join them. I'm so cold I can barely move. I ask the director if I can wear my heavy jacket over my robe. The answer is, "No!"

I jump into the circle with the bald headed boys and start jumping around. We're doing all sorts of stretching exercises and such. The priests-in-training don't seem to be bothered by the coldness in the least. I guess, I could see how, if you were to keep this up for any period of time, you'd be brain dead.

But that was okay for me. Because while they were spending their entire lives learning the wisdom and ways of the Eastern masters—how to make the body and soul come together as one, as the flower sprouts from the vine—I was going to take it all in, like in what? An hour or so?

Since I was soon to be floating like a butterfly and stinging like a bee, I suppose I should pass on some wisdom to you, dear reader, about the origins of martial arts.

Japan is an ancient country that was established over 2,700 years ago. Beliefs and ways of life are handed down through many generations. Of course all things change over time. But even in today's Japan, not only handguns, but even *Katana* (Samurai swords) are illegal for the average person. It has always been this way in Japan.

At about the time of the death of Christ, all Asian countries were very class-segregated societies. There were the aristocrats, the farmers, the merchants, the warrior class, peasants, outcasts, etc.

Even in the old days of Western class society, during the European Monarchies, it was forbidden for classes to intermingle. This is where many ideas of fables of princes marrying commoners, like Cinderella, were born. In Asia, it was the same—except the girls had dark hair.

Those were the days of struggle for control of the land between various warlords. So in most of Asia, including Japan, only the warrior classes were allowed to have weapons.

For over a thousand years, wars were fought between the warrior classes for control of territory and for honor. These wars were first-generational warfare. The armies would decide when and where to meet, and they would fight it out at the appointed place. To be defeated would mean to bring disgrace upon one's name and family.

Those battles, as well as who won or lost, usually did not affect the people in the other classes. For the merchants and farmers, it didn't matter who was warlord at the time. They would be taxed. Of course there was no concept of democracy, or even the notion of the people rising up and fighting the warrior class. But if only warriors could have weapons, then how did the other classes of people defend themselves?

Here is where Martial arts like Kung Fu and Karate were born. Even though the exact history is unknown, it is generally believed that the origins of Martial arts in Japan can be traced back to around 2,000 years ago. Even further back, these methods of training and self-defense are said to come from a priest from India, named *Dharma*, almost 4,000 years ago.

Since the peasants and farmers were not allowed to own weapons, they learned how to use farm tools and sticks as lethal weapons for self-defense. The local warlords could not outlaw sticks or scythes from the farmers. The farmers needed these tools to care for their crops.

These tools, then, became the tools for Kung Fu and other ancient Eastern ways to fight. Karate, by the way, means "empty hand."

Since the warriors were all employed by the aristocrats, the warlords, in order to consolidate power, ordered all weapons to be taken away from the other classes. In Japan's case, *Toyotomi Hideyoshi* instituted this law, which was called the "Sword hunt" in 1585. The collected weapons were all melted down and the Great Buddha statues were built.

Okay, now since I knew when all this stuff happened, all I needed to know was how. After jumping around in the freezing cold at 4 in the morning, I was ready to go out and start trashing bozos.

After exercising, we had to go in and clean the temple. The place looked spotless to me, but I guess the youngster priests had to clean it every single day as part of their ritual training.

This particular temple was 700 years old, and it was huge! The other young-guy priests grabbed these tiny little pillow-shaped cloths and started running up and down the hallways of the domed temple. The cloths weren't 6 inches across. I said, "Don't you guys have a mop or something?" They ignored me and kept running. Funny, these Buddhist priests, they don't talk too much.

I opened a few doors that I thought were closets to see if I could find a vacuum cleaner, but there was none. The director and the camera crew came into the room and the director got mad at me for goofing off. He ordered me to get on my hands and knees and clean the temple like the other guys were doing.

Oh! What backbreaking work! It took four of us over an hour to clean that entire temple with those dinky cloths.

Haven't these people ever heard of electricity? I wondered.

After cleaning up, it was time for breakfast, and I was starving. All the priests gathered around a long table and the head dude sat at the end. Before we went into breakfast, the director told me, "Now Mike, in this particular Buddhist sect, you are not to make a single sound when eating. Not even the clanking of utensils. No noise whatsoever."

Kind of strange, sure, but I didn't care! I was ready for some waffles, bacon, grits, gravy and eggs. Well, the food came out and it consisted of a small bowl of rice, two pickled vegetables, and a bowl of fish-flavored steam.

What? Is this all we're going to get? I'm going to starve, I thought.

It was eerily quiet. It was weird; no one made a single sound, Except for one of the young assistant directors, a guy named Takahashi. He belched. I started to snicker. Then the director couldn't control himself and he started to laugh too. You know how it is when you are trying to be quiet, but you can't stop laughing? Well, that's what happened to us. We were all laughing. Rice was coming out of my nose.

Then at the end of the table, the head priest slowly looked up to us and scowled. This guy was scary, and we shut up immediately. You know that even though he was at least 85, he could wipe the floor with all of us at the flick of a wrist. You don't mess around with these big-shot priest dudes.

After we screwed up the solemn atmosphere of a ritualistic breakfast, I had to go back to the temple and chant and pray for enlightenment.

What? No cigarette break?

The younger priests-in-training and I all sat down in the temple, facing the walls. We were to chant some lines 100,000 times each day. No kidding! I couldn't remember the words so I wrote them down on a piece of paper.

Everyone began chanting. From where you were sitting, you couldn't see the head priest dude; for all I know he was having an Egg McMuffin and laughing at us behind our backs.

This chanting business went on for a long time and every once in a while I could hear this "whack!" sound.

What the hell is that sound? I thought. I kept chanting. I was soon to find out what that sound was as just as I began to think, *Man, this is bogus. How long is this enlightenment stuff going to take? All day?*

The head dude-priest walked up behind me and whacked me hard with this big stick he was carrying around. I guess he hit me for thinking bad thoughts. I was shocked! How did he know what I was thinking? And I was thinking in English, too!

Well that was it for me. I was outta there, man! I got up and ran outta the temple and back to the TV crew van.

"Let's go!" I said, "I'm enlightened...never want to do that again!"

In a few hours I was back at home and in my warm bed—a little bit wiser and a better person for it.

But I did learn something about Buddhism and martial arts that I would like to pass on to you young grasshoppers. Zen Buddhists say *Mu* is happiness. "Mu" translated into English means "nothing." You see? "Nothing is everything. So everything is nothing." The true key to happiness is nothing.

And I learned it well. For what took many people a lifetime to achieve, I had achieved in just a few hours. It's called *Satori* in Japanese. *Satori* means "enlightenment." So I enlightened my cigarette, turned on the TV, and I stayed in my warm bed for the rest of that day, doing absolutely nothing.

I had achieved heaven.

Mike's Easy Earthquake Survival Guide

Recently, we have been having a lot of earthquakes in Japan. Or more exactly I should say, Recently we have been having a lot of earthquakes in Japan that you folks in the West have been hearing about.

There are several plausible reasons for this: the first being that the earth is always moving, and huge tectonic fault lines that lie deep under the earth's surface shift and cause these earthquakes. Considering the fact that Japan has earthquakes every day, this possibility can be discarded.

The real reason for Japan having earthquakes that you folks in the West hear about is due to what is generally referred to as a "slow" news day. Up until the late 20th century, this would have probably been the main reason for an earthquake in Japan to be reported on western news. But since George W. Bush became president, a new factor in reporting "Japanese earthquakes" has come into play; that factor is the "Bush administration screwed up something big-time *again*, so we've got to try to hide it somehow!"

Japan is always good for news that is used to cover the numerous errors the Bush administration—and, quite frankly speaking, George W. Bush himself—is constantly making. Why? Because no one over there can speak Japanese, so it is impossible to verify any of these outrageous stories.

Let me give you some good recent examples. In the news a while back, it was reported that George W. Bush lost 370 tons of high explosives in Iraq. We all know that's not true. George may lose his car keys or forget where he is or what he is doing at any given moment, but he didn't lose 370 tons of bombs and stuff. I mean, really, where could he have possibly put that stuff? Not in the trunk of his car! Have you ever tried to put a few tons of explosives in your car trunk? Well, it ain't easy, and let me tell you that it is nearly impossible without at least a little help.

So how does a reputable news service, like say Fox News, cover George's absent-minded butt? Well, the answer is Japan, of course.

Here were the possible news stories from Japan on that day that the explosives went missing:

Japanese businessmen drink too much.

Japanese in Tokyo enjoy sushi.

Earthquake in Japan shakes some buildings and scares some people and stuff.

Of course the "head-honchos" at both Fox and CNN went with the earthquake stories. Why? It's easy to show buildings shaking and stuff; just shake the camera!

Anyhow, I got lots of e-mail from my readers, asking me if my family and I were okay. Well, don't worry; we are all okay. In fact, I didn't even know we had an earthquake until I read the e-mail and then confirmed it with my wife. Now, some of you folks may think I'm being *facetious* here (gratuitous use of a big word), but I'm not. I'm serious here. I didn't even know we had an earthquake. Or maybe I did. I don't know. We have them all the time. I think they come with the contract. What's the big deal?

Heavily earthquake prone areas of Japan are shown here in various shades: Striped areas are striped (some areas are different kinds of stripes—I'm not so good with Paintshop yet); Checkered areas represented by checkered boxes; there are some other areas that look kinda whitish; and dots…. are those dots? Looks like dots to me.

Since it seems that so many people are concerned with earthquakes, I thought I'd better write an article telling you what to do, how to survive, and what to say during an earthquake.

First off, from reading the above, I think you can pretty well guess that earthquakes, like winning the Lottery, are things that happen to someone else. If you keep this in mind, then you will realize that your continuing to read this will just be one huge waste of time. Hopefully you'll get a few chuckles.

Case in point: Have you ever met anyone who won the Lottery? No? Have you ever met anyone who died in an earthquake? No? "Proof's in the pudding," as they say.

Anyhow, when dealing with earthquakes, it's important to remember to be prepared: Always have food and drink available at your home. A well stocked home is important. Well, duh! Who wants to run out to the Liquor Barn every time you need a cold one?

Also, I just love those little cans of sardines when you put them on Saltine crackers. You know, the "King of Norway Sardines" that have the little key-thingy that rolls open the cans. Those rock!

Also, a bottle of very strong alcohol could come in handy as a disinfectant and a cleaner for injuries and for taking huge swigs out of during games of Poker or Cribbage when there's nothing better to do. So do not buy this "alcohol" from a "pharmacist"; buy it from a reputable adult beverage dealer. Hey! Aren't you and your family worth a few cents more?

In the event of an earthquake: Do not—I repeat, do not tune in to your local government sponsored radio or TV broadcast. It's all a waste of time. You know what they'll tell you? "Yeah, we had a big earthquake, located somewhere."

Don't you just hate that? I do. I get a sore throat, so I go to the doctor's office. I sit there for an hour. Then, when I finally get in to see the doc, he looks in my throat and says, "Looks red." Then they charge you up the ass for some aspirin and tell you to come back in a week! Yeah, right! And I was born yesterday.

Anyhow, where was I? Oh, yeah. In the event of an earthquake, avoid all government-sponsored broadcasting and evacuation areas like the plague. If you turn on the TV news, they'll show a bunch of stupid people who will say things like:

"Yes. The ground started shaking. I was frightened."

"I was standing, over there, and the ground started shaking. I was frightened."

And, "I was doing something and the ground started shaking. I was not only frightened, but I was surprised also."

I cannot stress this point enough: If there is a huge earthquake in your area, go immediately to the fridge and open the door (it may get jammed shut during an earthquake). Grab a beer and tune the TV to "Cartoon Network." Cartoon Network is the best in any sort of emergency. Hell, it could be the coming of the Four Horsemen of the Apocalypse, and Cartoon Network will still be showing old Roadrunner cartoons (that Yosemite Sam still cracks me up!). So have a brew. Hopefully, the earthquake will be big enough so that your boss will not even question your calling in sick to work that day, or even for the rest of the week.

Avoid all government-run evacuation areas.

"Oh, yeah, right. We just had a 7.2 earthquake and thousands of people have died and you clowns want me and my family to go to the local high school with 10,000 other people and sleep on the floor? And the high school only has one men's and one ladies' room. And no shower? Get real!"

Oh, yeah, that's what they want you to do. And once you get inside of the school gymnasium, they'll never let you leave! Don't do it! For God's sake! Don't do it! Turn back! It's a trap!

Also, during an earthquake try not to dive under furniture or moving vehicles. I don't care what the government tells you in this case; they are wrong.

Other "dos" and "don'ts" during earthquakes are:

* Never eat soup while wearing a necktie.

* If drinking Martinis, make sure you gulp your drink before putting it down.

* Do hold your head with both hands, running in circles and yelling, "The world is coming to an end! The world is coming to an end!" This is especially effective if you are in your pajamas or in a bathrobe. Ladies, don't forget to wrap a towel around your head!

* Jump into your car and speed down to the convenience store to load up on drinking water. Make sure that you do not take the time to stop at any red lights. Hell, we just had an earthquake; for all you know, that red light may not be working properly!

* If you see any TV news cameras reporting on the disaster, always walk behind the reporter and start yelling, "Repent! Repent! For the end is near!" And start charging towards the camera—tackling a reporter, if possible! (This is useful for any type of disaster, not just earthquakes.) I, like anyone else, enjoy good TV, so anytime I see a reporter "reporting" on some "disaster," I'd love it if some people would run up behind the reporter and screw up their report. Now wouldn't that make for some great "disaster reporting" on TV?

I'd love to see that, even just once. I am so sick of these Roadrunner re-runs.

My Fear of Flying

I'm just about getting fed up with people bashing George W. Bush all the time. I'm sick and tired of it.

Many years ago, before I came to Japan, I worked as a salesman for a very famous insurance company in America. I was hot stuff—the "Top Gun." I was the young Tom Cruise-type guy—a high-flyer who got all the chicks.

I was working on a sale to a prospective client named Tim Dawson. Tim was rich. Tim worked doing something or other for Hollywood movies and stuff. He had a huge house, a beautiful wife, and handsome children.

I had met Mr. and Mrs. Dawson several times and proposed some very good investment plans. Mr. Dawson was considered a high-risk client because he had his own airplane, so it was difficult to find a company that would insure him. My company would, though—for a very hefty price.

Many times I thought I had the sale locked up, only to be rejected by Tim telling me, "Let me think about it."

But I was not about to give up so easily. I remember there was a used car salesman named Cal Worthington on TV all the time back in those days. Cal wore an old-time "vaudevillian" straw hat and he had a dog named Spot, which was actually a Siberian tiger. Old Cal would often say on his TV commercials, "I'll stand on my head, I'll do a back flip, I'll get on my hands and knees; I'll even eat my hat. I'll do whatever I have to do to get you to buy a car!"

Cal was impressive. I took pointers from him.

The next time I went to see Tim, I decided to play the "Cal Worthington Gambit." I told Tim, "Mr. Dawson, I will do anything to get you to buy this plan. I'll wash your car, mow your lawn, anything!"

Tim leaned back in his chair, grinned and said, "Anything? I don't buy anything from anybody unless they'll fly in my plane."

"Fly in an airplane? Why, that's not a problem in the world, Tim. I'd be proud to fly in your plane with you." I mean, what's the problem in getting a free airplane ride, right? Sounds like fun.

"All right. You fly in my plane, then we'll come back and I'll sign the contracts."

Oh, stay my beating heart! I thought. I tried to act cool, as those delicious commission dollar signs were floating about my head.

Tim and I hopped into his truck and we drove to the diminutive Camarillo Airport, not 30 minutes away.

When we got to the airport, we just drove in the gate. Tim parked the truck, and next thing I knew, we were in his little airplane.

I think those kinds of tiny one-propeller jobs are called "Cessna," but I'm not too sure about that. I sat right behind Tim, and as we taxied down the runway, he shouted over the engine noise to me, "Mike, you've flown in planes before, right?"

"Yeah. 747's. My dad was a Marine, so I have also flown in helicopters a few times. Even been on an aircraft carrier a few times."

"You ever get sick flying?"

"Nope!"

"All right then, see that wing?" He pointed to the left side. "See those struts underneath there?"

"Uh-huh. Yeah," I shouted back.

"Well, those are not ordinary struts! Those are special struts designed to withstand enormous stress and pressure! You see, Mike, this is no ordinary plane."

"Uh-huh. Yeah."

"You know that I work in Hollywood movies, right?"

"Uh-huh. Yeah."

"Well, I'm a professional stunt-pilot."

Now, right here, most people might just shit their pants. But not me! I was totally into it. Not only was I going to make a big sale, but I was going to get to ride in an actual stunt plane, write about it years later, and really cash in on the story.

Well, three out of four ain't too bad.

Tim started us off easy. First we did some light climbing and slow diving. No problem. Then we did some wide "barrel rolls"; yes, my blood pressure began to go up a bit. Then we did some faster and tighter barrel rolls. I didn't really like that too much, but I thought, *Be tough, Mike. Suck it up.*

"You okay back there?" Tim shouted.

"No problem, Tim! This is great!" Sweat was pouring down my brow by then, but I couldn't be a wimp! Good thing Tim couldn't see my face from the pilot's seat; I was probably whiter than a ghost!

Well, the honeymoon was over right then and there. Tim took us into some other stunts that really began to freak me out. The stunts got more and more hairy as we went along. For the first time since I was born, and I'm serious here, I feared for my life. And believe me, folks, I've done some pretty wild stuff in the past and lived to tell the story, but this time I wasn't so sure. I thought I was going to die. Tim was maniacally laughing the entire time. Had I gotten into an airplane with a cracked madman who had a death wish?

The final straw that broke the camel's back for me was when Tim took the aeroplane on a straight up climb, and then stalled the engine. The noise stopped. All I could hear was the sound of wind rushing by the plane. We were pointed straight up towards the sun, and the engine was off. The plane was not moving. I looked to my side, and I could see the tops of mountains hundreds of yards below us.

The plane slowly started dropping, tail first. Then it turned around and started hurtling towards the earth. Oh sure, I wanted down—but not that way. We sped towards certain death for what seemed like minutes. I was screaming,

"Turn the engine on! Turn the engine on!"

Tim was just laughing, and a few seconds later the engine kicked back on and the plane started flying level again, but that didn't matter to me I was already in a state of panic and in a full-blown hysterical breakdown. I would have started choking him to death, but he was piloting the plane.

"Don't do that again! Don't do that again! Land the plane! For the love of God, man! Land the plane!"

Tim's space madness grew worse, the more I shouted. His frenzied laughter only served to confirm my worst fears: I had indeed gotten into an airplane piloted by a raving, uncontrollable lunatic. I was flying with Satan himself.

Tim said nothing; he only continued his insane laughter. Suddenly, without warning, the plane began a steep ascent again.

"No! Tim! Noooooooooooo!"

We climbed high into the sun. Tim was Icarus. I was "Dead"-alus. The engine stopped again. The wind rushed by. I saw the mountains. Deja-vu. I held onto my seat as hard as I could. I was surely a goner this time…I searched for a parachute. There was none. The plane sank back towards certain death. I saw a Lear jet fly by us at a lower altitude than we were at!

But once again, through some miracle, the plane's engine started up. I was in a near delirium. By this moment, I didn't care if I died. I wanted to die. I never wanted to do that again.

"Please, Tim! Land the plane! Please!"

I wasn't getting through to him. I kept hearing the words, "Mayday! Mayday! Mayday!" running through my mind.

Tim was now silent, his transformation complete; he had become the Grim Reaper.

And then the unthinkable happened; the plane began once again its nocuous, straight-up climb into the heavens.

I shouted to the alien creature that was now piloting the plane, "Stop! Please stop! I'm going to be sick! I'm going to throw up!" But by this time things were getting blurry. I was probably mumbling the words so that only I could hear them. I slumped over.

"I'm going to throw up...I'm going to throw...."

I was done for. I began to pray to God.

"Please God. If you get me down from here alive, I promise to be a good person. I promise to go to church each and every Sunday. Please, God! Please! Help me! I'm going to be sick. I don't want to die! Please, God, I'll be a good person!"

Suddenly, Tim interrupted my prayer. He shouted, "Don't get sick! Don't throw up in my plane, man! Please don't throw up in my plane! We're going down right now!"

I continued my prayer to God, and said, "Thanks God, but never mind...I'm okay now."

We landed the plane and I have never been so happy to be back on solid ground in my life. Later, Tim and I signed the contracts and I had made the sale.

It was a success.

But let me tell you one thing: I will never, ever, for the rest of my life, get into one of those little airplanes that can do high speed climbs, dives, barrel rolls, stop in mid-air, or any other kind of stunt. No way! I think anyone who would do so willingly has to be either completely crazy or totally drunk.

So that's why I don't want to hear anymore of this nonsense about George W. Bush being too afraid to fly or being too drunk to fly. Why, hell, yes! Anyone with a lick of sense would be the same way!

There's a big difference between being brave and being stupid.

A Parable on Little-League Umpiring

When I was about 24 or so, one of my best friends from high school ran the Ventura County Youth Recreational Center.

My high school friend would sometimes ask me to help out whenever there weren't enough dads to coach a kids' team, due to the fact that over 60 percent of the kids came from broken homes and many of these little kids had never learned how to throw a baseball, kick a soccer-ball, shoot a basket, or even how to make any friends.

Sadly, most of these kids were so clueless that they couldn't spot ugly at a Mick Jagger-Imelda Marcos mud-wrestling match.

My "pal" would call me up every once in a while and ask me to even be a head coach of a kids' basketball or soccer team—Which I would do, and always later regretted.

I coached a kids soccer team called "The Green Machine" that was so bad we lost every single game over two seasons. Not only that, we were so inept that we didn't even score a single goal during those two years!

In Europe it's called, "Football." In America, it's "Soccer." The team I coached played a sort of hybrid. We often lost by scores of 11-0, or 16-0. Call it what you want, sounds like a football score to me.

One day my "pal" asked me if I could stand in as an umpire for a little league baseball game. "Sure!" I said. Unlike soccer, to which I didn't even really know the rules, I had played baseball as a tyke. I had even won some pitching trophies.

It was a wonderful day for the game. In order to protect my vital "family jewels," I actually went out and bought some "protection"—don't want to start singing like Smokey Robinson or Michael Jackson after the game, you know.

Being an umpire is a thankless job, especially umpiring for some spoiled brats. But umpire I was. And, as umpire, I was the king of all I surveyed. I was the ultimate master of the "field of dreams." And I intended to, and was doing, a damned good job...Well, up until about the third inning, anyway.

I can't remember the details exactly, but it seems to me that there were two runners on base. The batter hit the ball on a hot grounder that forced the short-stop to make a diving stop.

Wow! What a play! I thought. The short stop got up to his feet and threw the ball to the baseman covering second. The runner was most probably safe by a step, but I was so impressed with the shortstop's effort that I shouted, "He's outta there!"

Oh Lordy! What a mistake that was. The kids in the red uniforms all poured off the bench and started verbally attacking me. It was like a swarm of killer bees.

"Are you blind? What a stupid umpire! What a jerk!" They were yelling and shouting at me. Oh! The treasures from the mouths of babes! Even their coach, Mr. Myers—who I knew because when I was 10 years old or so, I was his news-paper-delivery boy—even he began to berate me.

But the die was cast. I was the umpire, wasn't I? How could I, the "king of all that is good and fair" (that's me), change my mind? What would my subjects think of me if I weren't the resolute, cold, hard, nerves-of-steel leader that is required of all world conquerors and little league umpires?

"I said he's out, so he's out!" But my determined answer did little to quell the hearts of the angry natives. Thank God that I was at least 16 years older than their oldest player! I began calculating my chances of survival. My body weight versus a bunch of 8-year-old children; there were about 11 of them...I definitely would have a reach advantage...

I was beginning to fear that I would have to wipe home plate with the lot of them...But then again, they had baseball bats...I kept my facemask on just to be on the safe side.

Then Mr. Myers came to my rescue and ordered the little savages back to their cage. I tried to look like I knew what I was doing, but before Mr. Myers walked back to the bench, he gave me a short, but nasty, look. Was he mad about my call? Or did he figure out finally that I had mistakenly charged him twice for his newspaper delivery so many years ago? Or had he known that I had overcharged him all along?

I tried to forget about the entire episode. Double charging Mr. Myers...was that Mrs. Johnston? Had he known all along, but never said anything? And what about that call at second base? Come to think of it, that kid was probably safe by at least two steps. I wondered if I gave Mr. Myers two receipts for the same month?

Come on, Mike! Shake it off. Snap out of it! I thought. I had to be professional. I had to concentrate on the game at hand. But what the hell, even if I did over-charge him, it was only a dollar or two.

The game progressed and it was a close one. Actually, it probably wouldn't have been a close one if I hadn't blown that call at second base.

The kids on Mr. Myers' team were batting. It was the bottom of the sixth; two men on, or was it bases loaded? Mr. Myers' team was down by a couple of runs.

This big kid came up to bat and on the first pitch he just pummeled a line drive that bounced off the left field fence. One kid ran in and scored easily. But that kid in left field, did he have an arm, or what? He fired a perfect one-bounce strike to the catcher, who was guarding home plate, as this next kid came storming in from third base.

This was going to be close. I steeled myself to make the right call!

The runner began sliding into home. The ball bounced towards the catcher's glove. Suddenly, the entire world went into slow motion.

People were screaming. My life flashed before my eyes. I saw Mr. Myers, not standing at the dugout, but the time he smiled at me at his front door when I think I overcharged him. I looked to the left; all the dads and moms were clutching the chain-linked fence to get a closer view. They were in a frenzy. I couldn't hear well. Everything was like a low-pitched drone.

I looked back at the play about to happen at home. I tried to stare at only the runner's foot, the catcher's glove, and home plate—difficult to do when you only have two eyes. *Concentrate, Mike! Concentrate!*

Damn! If only I didn't make that bad call at second! I thought.

Reality returned. Things sped back up to normal. I threw off my umpire's mask. I heard a "pop" sound as the ball hit the catcher's glove. The runner slid into home. The catcher swung a bit and tagged the runner. Was he safe? Or was he out?

Everyone stopped for a split second and looked at me. I paused, and then I stuttered, "…S…S…Safe!"

The catcher threw off his mask and threw his glove at me. The entire team of kids in the yellow tee-shirts ran full speed towards home and began screaming. Once again, I was surrounded and being stung like I had walked into a hive of wasps. The parents were booing and shouting.

"God! What a crappy umpire! Blind as a bat! You're the worst umpire in the world!" Of course these little, innocent, bright-eyed bastards all had other, more colorful things to say about me, but those cute little phrases cannot be printed here.

Amongst the cacophony, my mind again drifted away. I wished I were somewhere else that moment; a famous poem popped into my head.

> *Oh, somewhere in this favored land the sun is shining bright.*
> *The band is playing somewhere, and somewhere hearts are light.*
> *And, somewhere men are laughing, and little children shout,*
> *But there is no joy in Ventura—because even though I said, 'safe.'*
> *That kid was clearly, 'out.'*

In my thinking, I thought I had redeemed myself. I mean, come on, that was a bad call at second in the third inning. I had to make up for it. When I looked over to Mr. Myers and the kids on his bench, I expected to see the smiling faces of children after a hard-fought battle. But no, they weren't smiling; they were laughing. Laughing at me! I could read their lips and they were saying things like, "What a moron! That's the worst ump I've ever seen." Mr. Myer's cracked a half smile and nodded at me, but I could read his mind, he was thinking, *Hopeless! This boy should have stuck to delivering newspapers. At least I could still be getting my subscription for free half the time.*

What a disaster that was! Never again!

And now, I have laid out my heart and my shameful past to you, the public and my dear readers. If you were a player in that disastrous little league game, I am sorry. Forgive me.

For you other folks, you be the judge. Am I such a bad guy? Was I wrong to try to make up for my errors in the past? Wouldn't you have done the same thing?

I can sincerely say that I now try to learn from my mistakes and to never repeat them. That is why I, Mike Rogers, promise you this: I will never umpire any sports game again.

If I can hold to this promise, and I will, I can honestly say that I will not be responsible for subjecting you or your kids to the mental anguish that goes along with my making a bad call.

I don't know about you, but I refuse to make the same mistake twice.

Bonenkai

Oh no! Here it comes again: *Bonenkai* season in Japan!

You've heard wild, unsubstantiated stories that people in Japan like to drink? Rumors that many Japanese get drunk daily? You've also heard sordid tales of drunk Japanese businessmen terrorizing the streets of Tokyo at night? *Tondemonai!* (poppycock!), I say I deny that completely. I haven't had a drink for at least several hours now.

Bonenkai literally translates into "forget the year party." The Japanese love *Bonenkai*. It's a time to eat and drink until you want to explode. It is somewhat like Thanksgiving in America.

With the year-end party season to get underway soon, a very popular magazine in Japan called *Nikkan Gendai* issued this warning the other day: *Women who become obnoxious while in their cups are on the increase.*

Yes, you may want to re-read that sentence again. Got it? Well, learn it, know it, live it—because it's completely true.

I think what they are really trying to say is "Very drunk women can be obnoxious."

But I'm not sure. I didn't translate this, and I haven't seen the original text, so I'm only guessing here.

"Very drunk women can be obnoxious?" Look who's talking!

At *Bonenkai*, the people all get together with their work associates and have a huge year-end bash and eat and drink. Some of us have a "drinking problem" and we drink a wee bit too much; when we have one, well then we have to have two, then three, four, seven, twelve, sixteen—who knows? I always lose count.

I'm sitting in a roomful of strangers. I shuffle my feet and look at the floor and mumble, "Hi! My name is Mike, and I'm an alcoholic."

"Hello, Mike. Welcome!" They all say in unison.

The big problem with *Bonenkai* is that part about drinking with "work associates." That is where this entire *Bonenkai* business gets just a tad bit out of hand. When the Japanese say "work associates," that doesn't mean just the people you work with in your office. Oh no! That means *all* work associates.

Let's say you are a salesman. Great! You have a job; you get to go to *Bonenkai* with the co-workers from your own office. And you also get invited to *Bonenkai* to several of your clients' company parties too. If you are a typical employee of some company, you may get invited to anywhere between 3 and 10 (maybe even more!) *Bonenkai* parties, starting about December 10th until December 28th or so. That's a lot of drinking!

Too much drinking, if you ask me.

Drinking can be an interesting experience anywhere you go in the world, but in Japan it can be especially interesting as there are all sorts of rules of etiquette that must be followed in order to make the drinking experience a good one for you and your guests. Unless, of course, you are like me, and you wind up being one of the first people "on the floor," sliding under the table like melting Jello. In this case, the Japanese are kind. They will always "let you slide" on your manners and behavior if you are so drunk you have no ability to control any of your sensory or motor functions.

If you are a guest (*the drinker*) or the host (*the drinkee*), you must follow a strict set of rules. In Japan, it is considered polite to always do these things while drinking: First, you must absolutely never pour your own drink first. You must always pour your guests' drinks first. And there is a proper way to pour drinks. You must never "backhand pour" a drink; this is considered extremely rude. The palm of your hand has to be towards the guest for whom you are pouring, and your other hand must be held flat on the bottom of the bottle you are pouring. Never pour a drink using just one hand.

The receiver of the drink must hold their glass up in an honorable "receiving of the booze" ritual. To not hold your glass up is rude; people will think that you consider yourself a snotty-nosed king or queen or something.

This part often can lead to heated (but friendly) discussions on who pours the other person's drink first. The drinkee (host) wants to pour for the drinker (guests), as the drinkee feels it is his or her obligation under Japanese ancient moral codes (*Bushido-Edo Law* section 209.1.0). The drinker must at least feign a desire to want to pour the host's drink first as an appreciation of being invited to the party (*Zenigata Heiji Law* section 112.0098). The drinkee and drinker will battle it out in a test of etiquette will until one of the two gives in to the demands of the other and allows their drink to be poured. In this case, and especially if it is the first drink of the evening, the host (drinkee) will usually win out as a matter of custom (you wouldn't want the host losing face and committing *Hari-Kiri* at the start of the party, thereby putting a bit of a damper on the evening's festivities).

This life-and-death struggle for who gets to pour the drinks and save their family's honor will continue for the entire evening, until either the drinker or drinkee becomes too drunk to care anymore.

Second, your guests' drinking glasses must never be empty. This is a huge faux pas in Japan and a sign that you are manner-less, barbarian, savage—or an American (like me).

It took me years to figure this part out; that's why I always drank too much. It wasn't my fault.

You see, the Japanese never say "No!" Nor do they ever say "Yes!"

I remember years ago, when I was living in the United States and I was unfamiliar with this peculiar Japanese way of thinking. I had a Japanese guest, named Mr. Yamada, staying at my home. Mr. Yamada could speak a little bit of English, but I couldn't speak Japanese at all at the time, and I did not know the ways of the Japanese.

Well, every morning for about three days I would get up and make breakfast. Mr. Yamada would be sitting in the living room, wearing a suit and necktie. I would stagger into the kitchen in a tee shirt and shorts, looking my usual disheveled self.

"Would you like breakfast, Mr. Yamada?" I'd ask in my surly "just-woke-up-so-don't-bother-me" tone of voice.

"No, thank you," Mr. Yamada would bow, smile, and politely reply.

"All right then, suit yourself."

No wonder these Japanese guys are so skinny, I thought *They never eat.*

A few days later my mother got mad at me and asked me why I wasn't giving Mr. Yamada anything to eat while he was at my house. She told me that he had politely brought it up to her that he was always starving at my home.

"What? But mom!" I protested. "He always says he doesn't want to eat! What am I, a mind reader?"

My mom just told me to make food for him and put it on the table. If he doesn't want to eat it, he doesn't have to. If he is hungry, he'll eat it. So I did what my mom ordered me to do. Man! Did that Yamada guy eat like a horse or what?

Anyhow, the point of this little vignette is to point out to you folks in the West how to stop drinking in Japan. You see, the Japanese think that if you say "No thanks. I've had enough to drink," you are actually being polite and showing manners and reserve. They like that. So that's why, like I said, it wasn't my fault that I drank too much at a Bonenkai party. It was the fault of the drinkee; she or he kept filling my glass when I wasn't looking.

I said, "Okay. That's it. This is my last drink," and I downed my beer. Then I looked away for just a second to talk to somebody, and when I looked back, my glass was full again.

"What? Hey! Didn't I just drink that?" I asked my Japanese friends who were sitting next to me. They acted like they didn't hear me and I was be so drunk by then that I wondered if I did or didn't drink that last one, so I drank it again.

Now, in this case, I was the guest: the drinker. It was the moral duty of the modern day Japanese, who all descended from the ancient Samurai (well, not actually, but it sounds cooler that way), to make sure I had a good time, so they just kept filling my glass.

"Now look here, I'm serious you guys. Don't pour me another drink! Really." And I downed the next one and made small talk with someone else. I looked back a second later, and my glass was full again! Like I said, Japanese people don't say "No!" or "Yes!" They thought I was being polite when I said, "No more," when in all actuality, I didn't have a clue as to table mannerisms in Japan.

This may sound strange to you in the West, but if you are in Japan and you don't want to drink any more, then don't. It's kind of a Zen Buddhist type of thinking: When your glass is full, and remains that way, that is a sign that you are full. Get it? When you think you've had enough, just leave your full glass on the table and don't touch it. The Japanese will make a few efforts to get you to drink at least one or two more. Okay, maybe. But after that, don't fall into the trap. Leave the glass full.

In this way, and in only this way, can you stay relatively sober and make it through the Bonenkai season and the other New Years celebrations without having a stroke or a heart attack, or needing kidney dialysis.

Then you can start out the new year fresh and invigorated: A healthy new you!

That is, until the *Shinenkai* ("welcome the New Year" parties) with all your work associates begin on about January 10th and continue through January 24 or so.

So, "Happy New Year!"

By the way, we do have a "Happy New Year" expression in Japan, but it is reserved for after the new year starts. The Japanese say, *Akemashite omedetou gozaimasu*! In my case, I think I better say it to all you folks now. Why? I have to go to at least 10 Bonenkai parties every year; I may not make it to New Years!

So, *Akemashite omedetou gozaimasu*!

Photographs and Memories Never Die

An ancient Zen Buddhist story goes like this:

> A very wealthy family in China bought a large farm and built a beautiful palace upon it. They wished for good luck, health, and fortune, so they decided to ask a famous Zen Buddhist priest to write a scroll for them to hang in their den. The priest accepted the job and went back to his temple to pray for enlightenment.
>
> After a few days the priest returned with the finished scroll, and the entire family gathered around in great anticipation to see the words that the priest had written for them. The priest said a short prayer and opened the scroll and hung it on the wall. The scroll said:
>
> > *Grandfather dies.*
> > *Father dies.*
> > *Son dies.*
> > *Grandson dies.*

The entire family was furious at the priest. They shouted and demanded that he go back to the temple and rewrite the scroll for them. The priest sighed and said, "I will rewrite the order of names on the scroll in any way you wish, but I think there can be no other sequence. If all die in this order, I think that is true prosperity."

My own mother died in a freak car accident in 1994. Of course, I was crushed. I was in Japan and she was in America. After the car accident, she was taken by ambulance to the hospital. I understand that she floated in and out of consciousness before she died. Since I was so far away, I had no way of seeing her, holding her hand, and saying, "I love you, Mom. Thank you for everything."

At least I can be thankful that my father was there to do so when she went away. Many people who die are not fortunate enough to have a loved one with them—to hold their hand, to whisper in their ear "I love you. We all love you...Please rest. You may go now."

With words like these, my mother "let go" and passed away. I will always regret that I couldn't be there with my mother in her time of need. I thank God that my father could be.

There are too many people in this world who die alone. Could there be a more woeful way to die, than when loved ones cannot be there by your side to say their last "Good-bye"?

After my mother died, though, I was angry. I was angry at the world and I was angry at God. For months after my mother's death, I had recurring nightmares and the most bizarre dreams. Many of the dreams involved times when I was a boy. I would be playing in a playground and I would see my mother on the other side of a chain-link fence. I would cry out, "Mom! You're back!" And I would begin to sob uncontrollably.

My mother would grow angry at me and she'd start to leave. I'd cry out again, "Mom! Come back!" As she walked away, she would turn around, look at me, and always say the same thing, "I cannot come to visit you if you are going to cry every time I see you." And with that, she'd disappear into a field of tall grass. I would always promise not to cry the next time, but I couldn't keep my promise. I think I saw this same dream just about every night for at least six months. Then one night I had the most bizarre dream of all. My mother, as usual, walked away because I was crying. I was on my knees. I had my head in my hands, trying to hold back the tears, and then suddenly I found myself in a huge chamber. It was like a colossal courtroom. I looked up and there was an old man sitting in a chair, looking quite irritated at me. He was brushing his beard. I knew exactly who he was, yet I was not afraid of him; I was furious. I shouted, "It's not fair! It's not fair that my mother died in an accident. My mother was still young and healthy. She should still be alive, you bastard!"

The old man just stared at me. I continued to shout at him, and I began to cry. Then he calmly said, "So you think it is unfair that your mother has died?"

"Of course it's unfair!"

The old man sighed and said, "Very well, then, I shall allow you to be reborn and I will give you a different mother and that mother will still be alive today. Would you find this acceptable?"

"A different mother?" I said. "No. No, thank you."

I suddenly awoke from my dream. My pillow was wet with tears.

I pondered this strange dream for many weeks after that. Then it dawned on me. Instead of being angry that my mother died in an accident, I should be thankful for all of the wonderful times we spent together—all the hugs and bed-time stories, all the laughs and the great dinners, all the special times that my mother made me feel special, and all the other times she cheered me up when others did not. I should thank God for all the wonderful memories I received from having been the son of this loving woman. She was always there for me when I needed her.

Now, whenever I see her in my dreams I do not cry. In fact, the dream I often have with her now is one where I am on her side of the fence and we are sitting in the field and having a picnic and smiling together. I haven't seen her in a while, but I look forward to the next time I do.

I told this story to a priest who has become my friend. He asked me to show him a photograph of my mother. I did. He said, "Your mother was a very beautiful woman. Always keep this image of her in your heart. You are most fortunate that it is you, and not her, who has but memories and a snapshot."

How profound! I thought. And I have always kept his words of wisdom in my heart. I share these words with my friends whose parents or loved ones have passed away.

Dying at home due to sickness or accident is something that, in many cases, cannot be helped, for everyone dies someday. I guess it's when people needlessly die that we get most upset.

I have wondered about people from long ago, before the age of photographs. How did they remember how their loved ones looked? Of course, royalty and the very wealthy could always hire a famous artist to paint portraits. But what about the regular people—the people like you and me? What did they do?

And what of the wretched youth who died in needless wars in the past and present? What about their mothers and fathers? How did those folks remember or worship the children they had lost? Who held their children's hands when they passed away? A stranger? No one?

All the surviving members of the poor souls of the past—they should be very much pitied, for they only have memories in their hearts. The parents must have had so much rage and regret, for when it comes to war, the young ones usually die first. What a deplorable situation!

But thank God for "progress," because in today's day and age, even though we stupid humans seem to have learned nothing in thousands of years of senseless war, we now have the technology so that lucky parents can take those treasured photos of their children. Photographic memories will last a lifetime to share and to hold.

Thanks to America now running its own war of aggression and its own empire in some far-off lands, American parents can share the Technicolor memories of their children who will *never* return.

How much joy those photos of their dead children must bring! Those handsome young men and beautiful young women will always have youth; they won't age and have their bodies grow old and miserable, like yours or mine. Even if the parents were not there in that far away, lonely land, to hold their child's hand and whisper in their ear as their life slipped away; they can always have the photos to have, to hold, to hug, and to cry to. Aren't photographs of young people who heroically died in foreign war just great? I wouldn't trade those photos for anything in the world. Would you?

Otoshi-dama

What is Christmas in Japan like? Well, compared to the United States or other western countries, I'd have to say that Christmas is not really celebrated all that much in this country—somewhat like Saint Patrick's Day in the United States. Sure, everyone knows that it is Christmas, but in Japan, practicality trumps all other considerations in how the season is celebrated.

Of course there are Christmas decorations around town; there's a large Christmas tree with lights at most of the big train stations and window dressings at some shops and department stores, but at most people's homes and apartments, Christmas decorations are usually confined to a wreath at the door.

The only time I have ever seen a Christmas tree at someone's home was at my house. Japanese homes and apartments (especially in Tokyo) are very small, so it is not practical to have a six- or seven-foot-tall Christmas tree inside the house. When people do have trees displayed, they are usually 1-foot-tall artificial trees (or smaller) that are folded away after the 25th and kept in use for several years in a row.

Christians in Japan, of course, celebrate Christmas with much more fervor than do most Japanese, but I still suspect that the celebrations are generally confined to the church. In fact, Christmas is not a work holiday here; for most, it is a typical workday like any other.

Of course Japan is changing and the younger people seem to enjoy the day more then their elders, but the biggest celebration of Christmas is usually a Christmas dinner for two at a restaurant or father bringing a Christmas cake home from work. Besides young couples giving jewelry to each other, presents are seldom given on Christmas.

Instead of Christmas presents, most children receive from their parents and grandparents a gift of money in an envelope on New Year's, which is called, *Otoshi-dama*. *Otoshi-dama* is given to children from age zero until 20 years old. The gift is usually in smaller amounts from parents, up to hundreds of dollars at a time from the grandparents, and the amount of money goes up every year as the child grows older.

Generally speaking, the money received from the grandparents will go into a savings account for the children, and the money from the parents, the kids can spend on toys that they want. This custom allows for children to save into the thousands of dollars—sometimes tens of thousands of dollars—by the time they reach adulthood, which is considered 20 years old in Japan.

As I have mentioned before, in Japan, practicality trumps all other considerations when it comes to holiday gift—giving, and saving money is always a priority for Japanese people. It is also taken into consideration that teaching the children the benefit and wisdom of saving from a young age is of utmost importance. Perhaps this custom came about due to Japan being such a poor country for so long.

For myself, Christmas in Japan always confused me. I know that gift giving this day wasn't such a common practice, but being from the United States, I was unfamiliar with the custom of *Otoshi-dama*. Now that I think about it, though, *Otoshi-dama* makes such good common sense: It seems to me that kids these days have so many toys that they don't know what to do with them. Giving them money—and saving it for them—teaches the children the value of saving and the responsibility that goes with it.

Everyone wants to save for their children's future, but it is hard to do with bills to pay. We all want to "start sometime," but many never do. So how to do it? Simple. Take something that you buy every month that you don't really need, for example the daily newspaper. I came to the conclusion three years ago that I didn't need the daily paper being delivered to me for two reasons. First, probably like many of you who are you reading this, I get my news from the Internet. If so, then great! Why pay money for news that I already knew about or news that's late? And second, why pay for news that is slanted or biased? It's kind of foolish, when you stop to think about it.

Now that I haven't received a daily newspaper in all this time, I don't miss it for a second. I think subscribing to a newspaper is a sort of out-dated habit that we all were handed down from our parents. This is, after all, the age of electronic communications, so why pay for old news from a newspaper when you can get it up-to-the-minute for free on the Internet? Isn't subscribing to a newspaper just a sort of (bad) habit for most of us?

I have read surveys that said most people don't trust reporters. Well, I suppose that a newspaper could only be as good as its reporters, so why should I pay them to feed me lies and nonsense? I shouldn't, should I? And why should you? We should vote with our wallets. If the newspapers are not going to be dedicated to the truth in reporting, then I'll take my business elsewhere.

Until the start of the second Iraq war, I was getting and reading three different newspapers a day. This was costing me about $75 dollars a month—not a lot of money. Still, when you figure that amount over a year, at $900 dollars, that makes for one heck of a nice little deposit in the kid's saving account. And I'm still more "up" on the news than most people.

Let's face it; the Japanese have a very good lesson to teach us here. We need to start teaching our children the habit and value of saving, and we need to start teaching them now, not tomorrow.

If you want to do this, there are lots of things that would work as well as the easy one of canceling your newspaper. Perhaps this could be just one more incentive to stop smoking? Or maybe to quit eating out one day a week, or even to stop having a drink one night a week? Anything will do.

So cancel that newspaper or that pay-TV subscription; you don't need them. Take the money you saved and put it in a piggy bank every month. Accumulate the money, and at the end of the year open up an *Otoshi-dama* savings account for your child. If you have a newborn, or if you are the grandparents of a newborn, you could save at least $5000 for that child by the time they are ready for college just by canceling your newspaper subscription alone!

Now really, think about it, especially you folks who have a computer sitting at home. Do you really need that newspaper subscription? Or does that child really need that extra toy? Which will be more important to them in ten years time? Knowing the value of saving, and the savings that go with that; toys that they will play with for just a short time; or wasting money on the habit of buying newspapers or other subscriptions?

Seems to me like *Otoshi-dama* is a word we need in the American-English vocabulary, starting today.

Seijin no Hi—Pomp and Circumstance

January 10 of every year in Japan is *Seijin no Hi*. *Seijin no Hi* translates into "Coming of Age Day." It is the day that all 20-year-olds in Japan become adults. At 20 years old, all Japanese young people have the right to vote, drink, and smoke cigarettes.

Seijin no Hi is one of the few days of the year that you can see many beautiful girls, dressed in kimonos, walking around any city or town in Japan. It was trendy for young men to wear Western-style clothing on this day until the last few years, but recently, traditional dress has also come back into vogue for fashionable young Japanese men.

Besides *Seijin no Hi*, the only other time that you can see many kimonos is at college or university graduation time, at a wedding, or New Years. In the summer, during *Hanabi Taikai* (fireworks celebrations), you can see men and women in summer kimonos, but those are called *Yukata*; they are lighter and much more casual than the traditional dress.

My oldest daughter just celebrated her Coming of Age Day, and even though I am a foreigner, I still must recognize the rules and customs of my new country and home and pay for the pomp and circumstance that this day involves.

Almost all 20-year-olds must, on this day, go to a proper hair stylist and fashion stylist to have their hair and kimono set by a professional. This usually will set back the parents of such a ceremony *at least* $500 to $1,000. Add to that a professional photography session and the ceremony that is held at the local government ward office at another $500 dollars or so. After these ceremonies are held, the parents will usually take the son or daughter to lunch or dinner at the finest restaurant in the area. This is held exclusively for immediate family only.

After these duties are performed, the new adult must make the rounds to *all* the people who helped them all their lives: Grandma and Grandpa, people who helped at work, and people who did special favors for the debutante. Also, many teachers and principals from as far back as elementary school will be visited in some cases.

The Japanese hold these ceremonial occasions in utmost respect, and these events are not to be taken lightly. The new adult must show up in person and solemnly bow and speak especially polite honorific Japanese and say "Thank you for all you have done for me. I'm sorry to have been such a burden" in front of every person who helped them through their first 20 years of life. They must also take a gift of thanks and appreciation for the help they received for all these years. The gift will usually be traditional Japanese cookies or cakes, costing anywhere from $20 to $200 a box. *Seki han* (red rice with beans) is also a favorite. Flowers are *not* given on this occasion.

Of course the people who receive the young adults are kind and extremely happy, to the point of tears, to receive this visit and to know that their little child or grandchild, or child that they supported, has finally become an adult. This also instills a sense of responsibility in the new young adult that they must succeed in life as to make their *Seiwa ni nata kata* (people who took care of them) proud of them and to give those elders pride that they succeeded in making those young ones that they cared for into responsible, useful adults.

After *Seijin no Hi*, the former children no longer expect to receive *Otoshidama* at New Years. From this day on they are adults, and it will be they who are the ones who will be expected to carry on the teaching of social responsibility to the young ones of the future.

Making it through *Seijin no Hi* is a very troublesome and tiring experience for all involved. It is extremely expensive, and for modern Japan a relic left over from hundreds, perhaps thousands of years gone by.

But Japan is a country that respects tradition and culture. It is also a reason that young people feel a social bond and a social responsibility, and I believe, just another reason that crime—compared to the West—is still unheard of in this ancient country. It is also another reason why young people respect their elders and their neighbors and even people they don't even know.

Seijin no Hi no minna-san, omedetou gozaimasu. Kore kara mo shikari shite, gambatte kudasai. (Congratulations to all 20-year-olds. From now on, be strong and persevere.)

A Present I'll Never Forget

Every year, for as long as I can remember, it seems to me that the mass media has reported that retailers had poor numbers for the Christmas shopping season. The claim is that people don't have much money due to the poor economy, rising living expense and high gasoline prices. I heard a reporter on TV say that because parents don't have much money, perhaps this Christmas won't be so merry for many children.

That's a pretty sorry statement, actually. I think that not having the money to buy presents is not necessarily a bad thing.

I really think that lots of us have "lost our way" when it comes to giving gifts, and I'm not just talking about Christmas either. It doesn't matter if it's a birthday, Valentines Day, an anniversary, or other occasion. I think many people have confused spending money with gift-giving.

If you are a parent who is wishing right now that you could have afforded a certain present for your child or you are worried that your children will be disappointed this Christmas, I want to tell you about the best present I ever received. It was a present from my mom.

I didn't realize it at the time, but when I was a young boy, my family was poor. My father was a sergeant in the Marines, so you know he didn't make much money. My mother raised three sons and kept home, all the while picking up sewing jobs whenever she could. She didn't come from a wealthy family, and even if she had, it wouldn't have mattered. Her family in Japan disowned her for marrying an American. They couldn't believe that she would marry someone from a country that had so mercilessly bombed their homes. Some of my mother's relatives didn't speak to my mom again for almost 35 years.

Even so, those were the happiest days of my life. My mother taught us many ways to make do without money. I remember that on Valentines Day, we didn't have the money to buy Valentines cards like the other kids at school; we had to make our own. We didn't even have the money to buy white glue to construct the cards. What did we use instead of glue? Cooked rice. One grain of cooked rice makes a great paste that sticks when it hardens. Of course we didn't waste paper and always made do with used paper. At the time, I wasn't too happy about

263

it, but those were the best times—making things with my mom. She taught me much about creativity and "making do."

My mother—Takako "June" Rogers

Even though my folks were not wealthy, my mother worked out the household budget so they were able to buy three homes by the time I was 13 years old. I don't know how she did it, but she did. I guess some people are just talented with money.

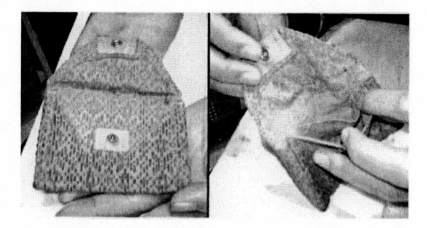

But back to the best present I ever got. It was a corduroy wallet my mother handmade for me. At first I wasn't happy with it. I wanted a toy from the store, but when I looked into my mother's eyes, I saw all the love she had for me. I saw all the love she put into making that wallet. You could tell by the design and fine workmanship just how much of her heart had gone into making it. I will never forget that look in her eyes. She had so hoped that I would approve of the present she made. And I did. I still do.

I loved that wallet so much that I have kept it for probably 45 years now.

I learned an important lesson in life from that day and from the wallet I received. Now, whenever it is a gift-giving occasion, I tell my children that I want nothing from the store. If they are going to give me something, I would love for them to make something by hand or to cook for me.

Make something for me and let's spend time together; a hug and an "I love you" will make the best present—the best memory—anyone could ever hope for.

We all should never forget that. I never will. And I'll bet your children wouldn't either.

It is never too late to give a truly unforgettable present.

Afterword

As I mentioned somewhere in this book, I know that I could live in Japan for a hundred years and still not understand everything. That's okay, I have come to accept that which cannot be changed. I have never met a Japanese person who claimed to know everything about Japan either. It just cannot be done. The country and its society are constantly changing, as are all countries and their people, and as it changes, so do my perceptions of the Japanese, as well as my perceptions of my own country, The United States of America.

I suppose, like anything else in this world, one person's experiences will differ from the next. Even those who witness the very same car accident or watch a movie together will come out of that experience with different feeling and emotions that often relate directly to how they were raised and the environment they were brought up in.

Understanding another country—and in turn growing to understand one's own country better—is a life-long struggle. It is a struggle for truth, and dedicating one's life to truth, as well as living right by others, it's a very high mountain to climb. Those who do wish to find truth will spend the rest of their lives climbing that mountain and will probably never ever reach the top.

But, that being said, isn't the search for truth—the road that ultimately leads us to happiness and contentment—the only road to follow? And, although there are many detours and obstacles along the way, what other choice do we really have on our short time on this planet?

Keep an open mind and try to understand others. They have had different experiences than you or I. They must have some motivation for what they wish or do. Our attempt to understand this cross-cultural divide is the only way we can reach happiness and a world of peace for our children.

And for that, I believe the Japanese have much to teach us about living with ourselves, each other, and at harmony with nature.

I thank my mother and father for bringing me into this world, and looking back, I can see where many things were predictable. I suppose that if the reader, were very alert, the reader too, could catch these signs in their daily lives also. Live by doing what's right by yourself and by others and by attempting to understand what others think and why they do the things they do. In this way, you can look at life in a more adventurous vein and with much more humor in your heart.

Lastly, never forget a saying that I have developed to help me to cope with the daily stress and strain of everyday life. It matters not whether you live in Japan or America, or wherever, keep in mind that "Every day is an adventure." Every day can teach you something if you only keep an open mind. Every experience, every person you meet, all have something to teach you. One person might be able to teach you how to be liked by everyone, another might be able to teach you how to not get along with others, and another may teach you how to live at peace with yourself and how to enjoy life.

I hope, after reading this book, that you may be able to find a person to help you do just that. This country has helped me to do so, and I hope this book helps you, if even just a little bit, to have a better understanding of yourself, your world, and Japan.

Index

Williams, Sir George 88
Wills, Garry 66
Wilson 161, 162
Winbush, Mr. Nelson 48
wining and dining 163
winning contests 119
wisdom 107, 111, 162, 231, 233, 255, 258
Wolfgang Puck's 29
words of wisdom 255
World xvii, xxi, 6, 10, 12, 13, 16, 23, 26,
  27, 28, 30, 31, 32, 33, 35, 36, 37, 40, 42,
  43, 44, 46, 47, 50, 51, 52, 53, 55, 57, 58,
  60, 61, 65, 69, 70, 71, 73, 79, 82, 83, 85,
  87, 88, 89, 91, 92, 95, 96, 97, 100, 101,
  102, 106, 107, 110, 113, 114, 116, 144,
  149, 151, 153, 156, 160, 162, 164, 165,
  166, 168, 182, 183, 187, 190, 193, 194,
  195, 197, 200, 203, 207, 214, 217, 218,
  220, 240, 241, 246, 247, 250, 254, 256,
  267, 268
  Cup 17, 54, 60, 61
  Heavyweight title match 113
  news xviii, 9, 19, 36, 42, 46, 51, 58, 61,
    66, 73, 77, 89, 90, 102, 103, 141, 164,
    166, 167, 194, 199, 217, 220, 224,
    230, 237, 238, 239, 240, 258, 259
  resources 53
  Series 100, 113, 114

Trade Organization (WTO) 165
  War I xxi, 23, 26, 44, 54, 58, 65, 67, 73,
    74, 75, 76, 83, 88, 91, 92, 96, 144,
    164, 217, 226
Worthington, Cal 241
Wray ix, 128
Wright Brothers 42
  Wyoming 49
WWF 113
www.Lewrockwell.com 31, 76, 96, 106

Y

Yakuza 26
Yamada, Mr. 251
Yen 119, 120, 121, 123, 125, 126, 127,
  175, 183, 184, 189, 204, 211, 212
Yin and Yang 70, 71
Yokohama 160, 189, 190
Yokosuka 47
Yomiuri (Tokyo) Giants 100
Yosemite Sam 240
Young, Cy 99
Yuan 165
Yuka ix, 204

Z

Za-Zen Buddhist 232
Zen Buddhist 190, 232, 236, 252, 253
zero emissions 187

978-0-595-34662-2
0-595-34662-6

Printed in the United States
38895LVS00014B/45